HOMEWORKING WOMEN

Homework; work that is categorised as informal employment, performed in the home, mainly for subcontractors and mostly undertaken by women. The inequities and injustices inherent in homework conditions maintain women's weak bargaining position, preventing them from making any improvements to their lives via their work. The best way to tackle these issues is not to abolish, but to bring equality and justice to homework.

This book contributes a gender justice framework to analyse and confront the issues and problems of homework. The authors propose four justice dimensions – recognition, representation, rights and redistribution – to examine and analyse homework. This framework also takes into account the structures and processes of capitalism and the patriarchy, and the relations of domination that are widely held to be the major factors that determine homework injustice. The authors discuss strategies and approaches that have worked for homeworkers, highlighting why they worked and the features that were beneficial for them.

Homeworking Women will be of interest to individuals and organisations working with or for the collective benefit of homeworkers, academics and students interested in feminism, labour regulation, informal work, supply chains and social and political justice.

Annie Delaney is Senior Lecturer, School of Management, College of Business, RMIT University Melbourne, Australia.

Rosaria Burchielli is Associate Professor (Honorary), Department of Management, La Trobe University, Australia.

Shelley Marshall is Vice Chancellor's Senior Research Fellow, RMIT University, Australia.

Jane Tate worked as Coordinator of Homeworkers Worldwide, Leeds, UK, until September 2018.

HOMEWORKING WOMEN

A Gender Justice Perspective

Annie Delaney, Rosaria Burchielli,
Shelley Marshall and Jane Tate

Routledge
Taylor & Francis Group

LONDON AND NEW YORK

First published 2019
by Routledge
2 Park Square, Milton Park, Abingdon, Oxon OX14 4RN

and by Routledge
711 Third Avenue, New York, NY 10017

Routledge is an imprint of the Taylor & Francis Group, an informa business

British Library Cataloguing-in-Publication Data
A catalogue record for this book is available from the British Library

Library of Congress Cataloging-in-Publication Data
Names: Delaney, Annie, author.
Title: Homeworking women : a gender justice perspective / Annie Delaney
[and three others].
Description: Abingdon, Oxon ; New York, NY : Routledge, 2018. |
Includes index.
Identifiers: LCCN 2018029447| ISBN 9781783533626 (hbk) |
ISBN 9781783535323 (pbk)
Subjects: LCSH: Home labor. | Home labor--Labor unions--Organizing. |
Employee rights. | Sex discrimination in employment.
Classification: LCC HD2333 .D45 2018 | DDC 331.4--dc23
LC record available at https://lccn.loc.gov/2018029447

ISBN: 978-1-783-53362-6 (hbk)
ISBN: 978-1-783-53532-3 (pbk)
ISBN: 978-0-429-43012-1 (ebk)

Typeset in Bembo
by Taylor & Francis Books

This book is dedicated to Jane Tate (1945–2018) who has worked tirelessly to support homeworker recognition, organising and to support and sustain homeworker networks. Jane will be missed by many, she was a good friend and colleague. We also dedicate this book to the many homeworkers who face hardship and disadvantage but show amazing courage to find collective solutions to their problems.

CONTENTS

ILLUSTRATIONS

Figures

Boxes

CONTRIBUTORS

Dr Annie Delaney is a senior lecturer in the School of Management at RMIT University Melbourne, Australia. Prior to commencing an academic career, she worked for the Textile, Clothing and Footwear Union of Australia (TCFUA) (1994–2004) and developed expertise on homework, international garment and supply chain issues. Annie led national initiatives to improve garment home-workers' working conditions and recognition in the fashion industry and by Australian federal and state governments. The successful implementation of a suite of regulatory mechanisms to protect homeworkers including the homeworkers code of practice, homeworker specific state legislation, and deeming provisions of homework in national labour regulation are key outcomes of her work at the TCFUA.

Annie's knowledge and industry experience has informed her research career, in which she has focused on high quality research outputs and a commitment to social impacts. Annie's research interests of gender, homework, informal economy, corporate accountability and supply chains have led her to collaborate and consult with a wide range of organisations. She has published extensively on homework, is the recipient of several grants to conduct homework related research including non-judicial mechanisms and redress and corporate denial techniques in global garment supply chains.

Rosaria Burchielli migrated with her parents to Australia from Italy in the 1960s, at a time when immigrants predominated in Australian manufacturing industries, and where her parents found work. Her early experiences as a migrant shaped her interest in socio-political participation and after completing university studies, she worked in education, human rights and for the trade union movement in Melbourne, Australia. In the mid-1990s she undertook a PhD in union effectiveness and began an academic career. Her research and publications are in the areas of gender, work and human rights, and labour unions. Following a research project based on homework organising, in 2005, with Annie Delaney, she developed a particular interest in informal and home-based work. She subsequently supervised two doctoral theses on homework and has since then collaborated closely with Annie Delaney on numerous research and related projects on homework. She is currently Associate Professor (Honorary), Department of Management, La Trobe University.

Dr Shelly Marshall is an expert in the regulation of informal work and labour law and in poor and middle income countries. She has undertaken empirical studies of home-workers and other informal workers in a diverse range of countries, including Bulgaria, India, Indonesia, Australia and Cambodia, and has published widely based on her findings. She has been awarded a number of large multi-country competitive grants to conduct these studies. Shelley has advised various governments about the implementation of laws to protect home-based workers. In 2017, she was appointed the Vice Chancellor's Senior Research Fellow at RMIT University, Melbourne, a position that gives her four years to pursue independent research.

Jane Tate worked tirelessly on homework related issues from the 1980s to 2018, including at HomeNet International (HNI) and Homeworker Worldwide (HWW). Her involvement in and coordination of the mapping program at HomeNet and HWW, as well as being a foundation member of the Federation of Homeworkers Worldwide, gave her a comprehensive knowledge and understanding of the issues affecting homeworkers. Jane died in September 2018; she leaves a legacy as a feminist activist dedicated to improving homeworkers recognition, rights and collective organising.

INTRODUCTION

Homework and gender justice

This is a book about homework, work that is categorised as informal employment, performed in the home, and mostly undertaken by women. We take a feminist, political-economy approach and utilise a historical and contemporary perspective to analyse and present the major knowledge we have developed over time, and through our research and activism about homework in different countries around the world. Homework is a form of work performed in the home for subcontractors, also referred to as industrial homework, 'by own account' or self-employed. Involving millions of women around the world, homework is distinguished from unpaid domestic work performed at home. Throughout this book, we shall argue that a variety of interdependent factors render homework as both highly invisible and highly precarious. Characterised by sub-minimum pay-rates and poor working conditions, the supply of work to homeworkers is irregular and insecure; the labour and economic contributions of homeworkers are unacknowledged; their working conditions are uncertain, unregulated and largely unorganised, and their social positions and futures are unprotected. In contrast, through homework, suppliers to national and multinational corporations increase their profits by reducing their costs and risks, transferring the price and time pressures imposed by lead firms onto the most vulnerable workers at the bottom of supply chains. Homework is thus a form of work characterised by inequalities and injustices. Despite the problems besetting homework, we do not advocate for the abolition of homework, which is frequently the only available source of income for homeworkers; rather we advocate for bringing equality and justice to homework.

We start by introducing ourselves, the authors, to position our ideological perspective. We are four women who have had a long association with homework and with each other, as researchers and activists. **Jane Tate** has been a tireless advocate, researcher and activist for poor women and homeworkers for over 30 years and is considered a foremost expert in homework in the European Union. She was a founding member and coordinator of key homework advocacy groups such as HomeNet International and Homeworkers Worldwide and the Federation of Homeworkers Worldwide. An early advocate for the ILO Convention on Home Work, she was also the recipient of a British and European Union grant to investigate international homework. She has produced numerous reports for such organisations as the ILO and the European Union and has been at the helm of initiatives to improve the conditions of homework – developing and coordinating the mapping program across 14 countries, for example. **Annie Delaney** is an academic activist with over 20 years' experience in homework and is regarded a key expert in homework in Australia with a growing international profile. As the Textile Clothing and Footwear Union of Australia (TCFUA) homework coordinator she investigated, documented and organised garment homework in Australia. She established a collaborative partnership with Tate and was able to collate critical knowledge, subsequently used in government and industry enquiries. The knowledge and experience gained in this role later informed her PhD and academic publications, examining issues in homework and garment supply chains. **Rosaria Burchielli** has been an academic activist in homework for over a decade. This began with her supervision of Annie Delaney's doctorate and later developed through a collaborative partnership with Delaney and Tate. She initiated a project of research into the scarcely documented area of Argentinian garment homework, and she has led or collaborated in numerous academic publications on homework. **Shelley Marshall** began her involvement with homework as a university student collaborating with Delaney in the FairWear Campaign in Australia. She practiced as a public interest lawyer in the late 1990s, advising the TCFUA regarding the enforcement of labour laws for homeworkers. Bringing degrees in political science, development studies and regulatory studies to bear on the topic, her research over the last 15 years on multicountry projects has informed various governments and social initiatives including the International Labour Organisation. Our research interests and experiences with women homeworkers have clearly shaped our views and perspectives.

Many excellent books have already been written about homework. The earliest, written by feminist scholars, documented homework in specific locations, such as the UK, US and Mexico. These established the historical roots of homework within the cottage industries of pre-industrialisation or within agricultural economies, which were easily exploited by capitalism and patriarchal relations to supplement factory production. As the home was separated from the locus of production, it became the place where women performed domestic and care work which was unvalued and unpaid. By extension, women's paid work at home was affected by their unvalued reproductive work, and productive work remunerated using the piece-rate system, at rates below those paid to factory workers. Being unacknowledged as workers and undervalued in their social and economic contributions due to patriarchal social relations, women working from their homes provided capital with a ready source of extremely cheap and flexible labour (see Allen and Wolkowitz, 1987; Beneria and Roldan, 1987; Boris and Daniels, 1989). These early works clearly linked homework to capitalism, patriarchy and class.

Subsequent books confirmed and expanded on the earliest writings by providing new case examples in different country locations and industry contexts (see Boris, 1994; Martens and Mitter, 1994; and Mitter, 1994;Fernandez-Kelly and Shefner, 2006; Toffanin, 2016). These texts also shone a light on the role of class alongside gender in understanding homework (see Phizacklea and Wolkowitz, 1995; Prügl, 1999) and explained the ongoing use of homework under evolving forms of capitalist labour processes, such as globalisation, outsourcing and the use of homeworkers in global South economies, as a development strategy which encouraged the growth of homework (see Dangler, 1994; Gringeri, 1994; Boris and Prügl, 1996; Mezzadri, 2016). Importantly, these works documented the persistence and spread of homework under evolving forms of capitalism. An important contribution of these works was documenting and analysing social and institutional responses to homework, such as attempts to ban and to regulate homework, legislation to protect homework and key mechanisms to influence and monitor firm behaviour, such as codes of practice and other multi-stakeholder mechanisms (Delaney, Burchielli and Connor, 2015). Although the vast majority of these responses failed to bring about any positive change to homework, a small number of more fruitful responses were documented, such as attempts to organise homeworkers and establish international advocacy organisations like Homeworkers Worldwide, with the express purposes of increasing homeworker participation in political debates (see Tate, 1994a; 1994b; 1996a; 1996b; Boris and Prügl, 1996; Rowbotham, 1999).

Other bodies of literature have made important contributions to knowledge about homework. The ongoing analysis of gender in the context of work, within feminist approaches, has been integral to understanding the predominance of women in homework, including the valuing of production and reproduction (Allen, 1987; Boris and Daniels, 1989; Prugl, 1999; Delaney, et al., 2015; Burchielli and Delaney, 2016; Toffanin, 2016). Feminist, development, economics and politics scholars have contributed critical knowledge about informal and precarious forms of work, similar to homework, under existing capitalism (Bair, 2010; Mezzadri, 2016). Under neoliberalism, many emerging forms of work have begun to resemble the worst features of homework. The past 20 years has seen the growth of precarious and devalorised work, that has pushed many workers into a blurred middle ground towards a type of work which is unpaid or not paid correctly; is neither professional nor manual; is not properly protected; is not considered to be work, and where workers have little or no power or collective identity (Krinsky, 2007; 2012).

Thus, studies on the changes to work more broadly also help to clarify issues affecting homeworkers. They have renewed our interest in understanding the processes explaining these trends from feminist, economics and political perspectives, and to examine the possibilities for resistance. Key themes include global supply chains and subcontracting and their role in marginalising women engaged in informal work; corporate and institutional responses, such as corporate social responsibility (CSR) and development strategies/policy. (See Barrientos and Kabeer, 2004; Pearson, 2004; 2014; Barrientos et al., 2011; Barrientos and Evers,

2014; Benería, Berik and Floro, 2016; Mezzadri, 2016) This literature is related to homework insofar as it brings a deeper understanding to issues that bring to bear on homework, such as development issues, supply chains and CSR (Jenkins, Pearson and Seyfang, 2002). Critically, the current processes of labour remind us that the study of homework, and subsequent insights, can no longer be relegated to a marginal interest category; rather it contributes valuable knowledge to broader labour issues and studies.

Specific messages are consistently conveyed in homework related literature from the 1980s to the present day: homework represents one of the worst examples of labour rights violations; homework exemplifies both class and gender exploitation; and, it is a form of work that, contrary to expectations, has persisted and spread, practically unchanged, over the past two centuries. Homeworkers themselves have commonly expressed similar sentiments about their work.

A New York homeworker who made artificial flowers in 1910 commented on her work:

> "We all must work if we want to earn anything... You can't count homework by the day, for a day really is two days sometimes, because people often work half the night."
>
> *(Flower maker homeworker cited in Daniels (1989:17)*

A homeworker in India describes the multiple tasks she undertakes and the lack of recognition for her work:

> We are like second class citizens here. Even now, people want us women to be like Sita[1] (Hindu goddess). But most of us cannot read or write. Atrocities against us women are common, for example, dowry torture and death, female infanticide and domestic violence. I have to work hard, I work from the early morning to late at night. I do all the housework, I sew for piece rates, I do the agricultural work; I take care of animals, children and old people. But I have no recognition for any of this work, either in my family or in the community.
>
> *(Homeworker, India 2008)*

That homework started off, pre-industrialisation, as subsistence-level work does not justify it remaining so after all the social, political, and technological change that has influenced changes in employment in the last 200 years. The homework specific and related literatures suggest two key processes of capitalism and patriarchy and their related structures, herein the social relations of domination, to explain the continuities in homework in terms of its persistence and characteristic inequalities. We therefore argue through the social relations of domination, capitalist and patriarchal processes and hierarchies create the multiple inequalities and injustices in homework. In addition, we argue that the social relations of domination are manifested in all the labour rights violations and exploitation based on divisions of labour, class, race, ethnicity, and gender.

The unchanged, persistent nature of homework, its invisibility and the many characteristic injustices for women employed within it are key factors motivating this book. We believe that understanding homework requires an awareness of intersectionality, accounting for the various interdependent factors that have and continue to shape homework and the documented inequalities and injustices that accompany it. On this basis, we propose a gender justice perspective for re-analysing what we know about homework. Various themes in gender justice are discussed in both feminist and development literatures (see Fraser, 2005; 2008; Utting, 2007; , Sudarshan and Milward, 2013;) as critical issue-related areas for understanding justice and injustice in relation to gender. The themes include *recognition, representation, rights*, and *redistribution*.

We understand these in the following ways in relation to homework. *Recognition* refers to issues related to social acknowledging, valuing and making visible. *Representation* is about self- and collective advocacy; activism and resistance. *Rights* refers to basic labour and human rights. *Redistribution* is about challenging and correcting institutional and structural inequalities and injustices. The themes are clearly related. For example, recognition and representation could be used practically interchangeably to discuss the relationship between homeworkers and a (hypothetical) union covering them. Similarly, a specific legislation, that defines homework and establishes the relationships and conditions of work, may touch upon all four areas. Notwithstanding any overlapping meanings, acknowledged in the course of our analysis, we re-interpret these as distinct dimensions of gender justice.

We view justice as a social, economic and political construct, with links to power. On this basis, we propose the four justice dimensions be understood from this standpoint too: as social, economic and political constructs, similarly linked to power. In this book, we are mainly concerned with the materiality or realities of homework. Thus, we define the four dimensions in relation to social, economic and political acts and behaviours with real world consequences for homeworkers in specific areas. In so doing, we can separately examine and understand specific types of injustice in homework. We summarise the dimensions in Figure 0.1.

We propose to use these dimensions in a gender justice framework as areas within which to re-analyse the key conditions of homework, thus contributing a new perspective to our analysis. The dimensions of gender justice are one part of the framework. The other part refers to the principle determinants of injustice in relation to homework, as identified in the homework and broader literature. Capitalist and patriarchal processes and structures are manifested via the social relations of domination, briefly discussed earlier. We theorise that current forms of capitalism and the patriarchy, and the social relations of domination, create injustice outcomes for homeworkers in each of the four dimensions of gender justice. Our gender justice framework is represented in Figure 0.1.

The relations of domination capture the combined and multiple facets of ideological and socio-political constructs that contribute to the exploitation and

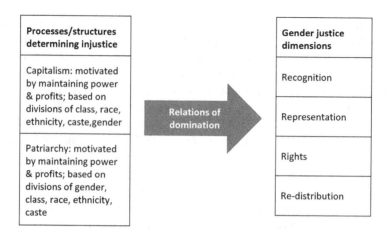

FIGURE 0.1 A gender justice framework for homework

oppression experienced by homeworkers. The structures of capitalism and patri-archy include dominant institutions such as corporations and governments, as well as their devices, such as supply chains and exclusionary laws. The processes and structures of capitalism and patriarchy, include: the normalisation of unpaid women's socially reproductive work (such as child rearing, caring for the family, unpaid housework, unpaid community work) as less valuable and is linked to the struggle for social power, recognition of economic contribution and normal-isation of exploitation; invisibilisation via devaluation of women's work and social reproductive contribution, discourses and acts of violence against women that is supported by socio-political factors replicated in the workplace and else-where; neoliberal patterns of work such as feminisation, informalisation, and neoliberal regulation regimes that contribute to workers being redefined as entrepreneurs, self-employed and non-workers (Peterson, 2002; Federici, 2012; Mies, 2014). In addition, global trade and uneven development, the features of supply chain capitalism, are some of the manifestations of the relations of dom-ination that affect homeworkers and other workers (see; Fraser, 1996; 2005; 2008; 2017; Tsing, 2009; Tsing, 2014; Burchielli and Delaney, 2016; Bhatta-charya, 2017). The current forms of capitalism and the relations of domination are explored in more detailed meanings as the subject of our discussion in the various chapters of the book.

This framework enables us to discuss the interconnections between gender, class, race, ethnicity and caste and how they contribute to what we see as a sys-temic oppression surrounding homework. In this book, we use this framework in three ways. *Firstly*, to focus our analysis on the intersectional processes identified as determinants of homework conditions and injustice, arguing that these pro-cesses result in injustice outcomes in the four dimensions of gender justice. The influence of the determinant processes in the various areas of gender justice is represented by the arrow in Figure 0.1. *Secondly*, we use the framework to organise our discussion of strategies and avenues for positive change in home-work, where we argue that initiatives based on the gender justice dimensions, particularly those that focus on two or more dimensions, can have a mediating effect on the intersectional processes that have thus far determined homework and its conditions. For example, an initiative to increase the recognition of homeworkers, through improved representation and increased rights may mediate capital/labour relations. This enables us to present a more detailed gender justice framework in the final chapters of this book. *Thirdly*, we use the framework to shape and organise the structure of our book, where the dimensions of gender justice provide unifying themes to the distinct chapters, while the processes determining homework provide the basis of analysis throughout the book.

We see our proposal and use of the gender justice framework as one of the contributions of this book. The gender justice framework has an integrative effect, enabling us to bring together and link the different lines of research in the field of homework, which is characterized by a range of perspectives that, although related, have not been fully brought together: gender; employment modes; agency, activism and organising; global supply chains; public and private regulation; homework, advocacy and resistance.

As researchers, we further contribute our use of unique empirical data and cases, with which we have been personally involved, such as HomeNet International, Homeworkers Worldwide and the Federation of Homeworkers Worldwide, and the international homework mapping project (IHMP, 2000–2005). Other projects documenting Australian, Indian, Argentinian and other instances of homework (2000–2018), are also described in various chapters throughout this book. The voices of homeworkers captured from interviews, exchanges and documentation are woven into chapters to represent their lived experience, and perspectives. Finally, we contribute our perspective as activists that clarifies our motives and intentions for this book. Due to the continuities of injustice in homework, it is important for us to continue to find ways to highlight its presence; to continue to discuss the unacknowledged and undervalued labour of women homeworkers. It is equally important to continue to underscore the crucial contribution of homework to our world economies and resist the systems that ignore, misrepresent and devalorise this labour. Acknowledging both the failures and successes of past attempts to address the problems of homework it is important for us to continue to imagine, to press for and to expect positive change.

We have structured the book as follows. Chapters 1 and 2 are linked by the common theme of *the gender justice dimension of recognition*. In the context of homework, applying a gender justice approach means first *recognising* the characteristics and conditions of homework, so that the injustices and inequalities in homework become obvious. The aim of Chapter 1 is to begin to *recognise* homework, to define and discuss its particular characteristics and conditions, and to foreground related labour issues, such as protections, regulation and rights. In this chapter we answer fundamental questions about homework: examining what homework is and where it occurs, who does it and why, and the critical notions and global dynamics that sustain it. We analyse homework from an intersectional perspective, viewing it as an economic activity and a form of labour and production predominantly carried out by women, which leads us to examine the links between women, home and work, to understand the gender divisions of labour, and other social constructions that facilitate the existence of homework. Our analysis includes understanding the location of homework both in the informal economy and in global value supply chains, thus we draw out the connections between capitalism, patriarchy and development to achieve the surplus value to capital that comes through exploiting women's paid work at home. This chapter establishes that capitalism and patriarchy are the principal factors (determinants) that shape the unjust nature of homework, enabling us to foreground related labour issues, such as protections, regulation, rights and bringing positive change to homework, that are the subjects of subsequent chapters.

In Chapter 2, we extend our discussion of the lack of recognition of homework. In the first part of the chapter, we examine homework invisibility and its implications for equality and justice for homeworkers. Drawing on feminist debates, we propose that work invisibility is socially and politically constructed, through the social relations ideologically consistent with capitalism and the patriarchy, using mechanisms of gender and class divisions of labour (Allen and Wolkowitz, 1987; Boris and Daniels, 1989; Thornton, 1991). We also utilise a concept of 'invisibilisation' (Krinskyand Simonet, 2012) to discuss the attainment of invisibility via social processes, arrangements and actors that contribute to recasting work as non-work, 'invisibilising' both work and workers. We apply the concept of invisibilisation to homework, arguing that it has been rendered invisible through such tactics as renaming, trivialising, normalising, ignoring, denying and justifying homework, by governments, political parties and their legal instruments, such as employment contracts, to diminish and devalue homework, in order to reduce labour power and lower labour and governance costs, in line with a neoliberal agenda. We demonstrate that for individual women homeworkers, this has resulted in a range of inequalities, including an almost total lack of recognition and rights (Burchielli, Buttigieg and Delaney, 2008; Burchielli and Delaney, 2016).

The second part of the chapter discusses the role of research as a means for supporting other visibilisation strategies. We discuss large and small-scale research about homework and the types of evidence that each have provided. We argue that there are a range of valid empirical approaches, quantitative and qualitative, large and small-scale, that can deepen our knowledge about homework and homeworkers. These approaches can provide the evidence to inform policy development and implementation, and support homework advocacy and organising to advance a justice agenda for homeworkers. Using relevant research approaches to understand homework and understanding the tactics, processes and players that construct invisibility helps to identify alternatives, which may be used to reverse invisibility and bring about the recognition and rights that come with visibility.

Chapter 3 describes the different ways that labour laws have regulated homework since the late 1800s, focusing on two aspects of the gender justice approach:

recognition and *rights*. It highlights the considerable achievement of homeworker organisations in achieving the regulation of homework in many countries around the world after the passing of ILO Convention 177, based on the extension of the contract of employment. Yet in the same period that homeworker laws have been implemented, income inequality has increased markedly around the world. Though this inequality has numerous causes, one set of causes relates to the undermining of worker organisations and the decline of the standard employment contract as the cornerstone of labour protections for working people due to the success of the neo-liberal project and the vertical disintegration of work. In light of this erosion of labour power, the chapter proposes a range of regulatory forms that might lead to stronger forms of gender justice for homeworkers. We propose that it is time for a new legislative program that assigns responsibility for homeworker rights throughout supply chains.

Chapter 4 extends the discussion of the *gender justice dimension of representation*, delivering a critique of corporate social responsibility (CSR), a corporate-centric, voluntary approach that has become the default response to the current regulatory gap. We argue that the vast majority of existing CSR initiatives tend to replicate philanthropic approaches, aiming to do some limited and general 'good works', without actually addressing the harms produced by corporate activities. We further posit that CSR projects rarely address labour rights, let alone homework. Examples discussed in Chapter 4 demonstrate the more common approach by brands is to ban homework to avoid any perceived risks to the corporate reputation. CSR approaches frequently fail for this reason to recognise homework. The chapter describes CSR approaches to homework that compartmentalise responsibility and shield corporations from taking responsibility for the realities of homeworkers' work conditions, thus enabling the corporation to continue business-as-usual, prioritising profit over people with little thought for consequence. Given the voluntary and corporate centred approach of CSR, we argue that CSR approaches do not contribute to improve representation of homeworkers, since they are failing to address the fundamental rights' issue associated with representation – freedom of association in the rights and representation dimensions of the gender justice framework.

In Chapter 5 the focus is on *the gender justice dimension of rights*, which we define as advocacy on behalf of homeworkers, freedom of association and collective bargaining. So as to understand the lack of representation of homework, this chapter analyses the supply chain as a major instrument of capital. It examines the surge of homework in the 20th century through business strategies such as outsourcing and the creation of transnational supply chains. For this reason, then, the focus of the chapter is the structure and activities of the supply chain. It argues that homework is embedded in supply chains that make use of historical and geographic inequalities based on gendered constructs of social reproductive labour, class, race, and colonisation. The social relations of production through supply chains maintain cheap and flexible production, locking homeworkers, fearful of losing their work, into irregular work on low piece rates, whilst limiting their opportunities to collectively organise. At the same time, the invisibility of homeworkers at the margins of long supply chains poses limitations for the proper representation of homeworkers by unions and constrains their ability to demand their rights. In conjunction with pre-existing gender inequalities – homeworkers' location in the private sphere of the home and the devalorisation of women's reproductive work in particular – this further entrenches inequalities and constraints to justice. The chapter argues that corporations take advantage of location-based and gender inequalities to maximise their profits without concerns for the most exploited workers. Chapter 5 thus focuses on the lack of rights for homeworkers, brought about by a range of social, political and economic structural forces that increase their invisibility and enable corporations to ignore their rights.

Chapter 6 discusses various transnational, grassroots and labour initiatives that directly facilitate the organising of homeworkers; it seeks to understand what has made some strategies more successful than others. We find that successful collective organising depends on taking into account the specific needs of women in designing organisational structures and representation strategies. The gendered nature of homework has implications for how collective organising occurs, what form it takes, and how homeworkers are able to navigate their way from the private to the public sphere – the space outside the home. We describe the importance of network functions in helping to achieve institutional change and create opportunities for resistance as discussed in the examples of homeworker organising. We build on the industrial relations literature by drawing on the transnational organising and network theories, using these frameworks then to analyse how the international homeworkers network (IHN) at the transnational level has functioned to support homeworker advocacy and organising around the globe, exploring the importance of the IHN in developing new homeworker informal associations and unions and homework representation at the local and transnational level. The evidence that we present in this chapter shows that homeworkers need a collective organisation to gain visibility, and to be heard and recognised by governments, unions and corporations. Their position as workers is linked in many different ways to their identities and situations as women in the family or society at large, or as members of particular communities, such as indigenous women or minorities. Our discussion concentrates on the needs of homeworkers to develop collective strategies underpinned by the notion of rights. The concept of 'rights' in the gender justice framework is linked to fundamental rights of freedom of association and collective bargaining. We argue that organising impacts across all four dimensions of the gender justice framework outlined in the introduction to this book; recognition, representation, rights and redistribution.

In Chapter 7 we revisit the purpose of this book, to contribute a gender justice approach as a new perspective to analyse and confront the issues and problems of homework. The inequities and injustices inherent in homework conditions constitute a common thread throughout the body of literature on homework as they invisibilise homeworkers, predominantly women, and maintain their weak bargaining position, preventing them from making any improvements to their lives via their work. We discuss activist strategies and approaches that have worked for homeworkers, highlighting why they worked and the features that were beneficial for them. In this final chapter, we revisit our analysis of the relations and circumstances that have failed homeworkers, in relation to the four gender justice dimensions. We also review the initiatives that have supported homeworkers along the lines of the gender justice dimensions, discussing these important and positive initiatives as examples of what works to create avenues of countervailing forces of resistance for and by homeworkers. We then suggest that whereas the dominant paradigms of capitalism and patriarchy have acted to achieve injustice impacts across the four dimensions, the structures and processes to achieve justice impacts via resistance are necessary as a countervailing force for good. We end by revisiting the gender justice framework to explore the relationship between the dominant paradigms, the four dimensions and the relations of resistance.

We hope the book will be used by individuals and organisations working with or for the benefit of homeworkers, academics and students interested in feminism, informal work and the future of work, labour regulation and those with an interest in social and political justice.

Note

1 Sita: a Hindu goddess held as the model of spousal and feminine virtues for all women, the perfect Hindu wife.

References

Allen, S. and Wolkowitz, C. (1987) *Homeworking: Myths and Realities*. London: Macmillan.

Bair, J. (2010) On Difference and Capital: Gender and the Globalization of Production. *Signs: Journal of Women in Culture and Society*, 36: 203–226.

Barrientos, S., Mayer, F., Pickles, J. and Posthuma, A. (2011) Decent Work in Global Production Networks: Framing the Policy Debate. *International Labour Review* 150: 299–317.

Barrientos, S. and Kabeer, N. (2004) Enhancing Female Employment in Global Production: Policy Implications. *Global Social Policy* 4: 153–169.

Barrientos, S. and Evers, B. (2014) Gendered Production Networks: Push and Pull on Corporate Responsibility? In S.M. Rai and G. Waylen (eds) *New Frontiers in Feminist Political Economy* (pp. 43–61). London and New York: Routledge.

Beneria, L. and Roldan, M. (1987) *The Crossroads of Class and Gender: Industrial Homework, Subcontracting, and Household Dynamics in Mexico City*. Chicago, London: University of Chicago Press.

Benería, L., Berik, G. and Floro, M. (2016) *Gender, Development and Globalization: Economics as if People Mattered*. New York: Routledge.

Bhattacharya, T. (2017) *Social Reproduction Theory: Remapping Class, Recentering Oppression*. London: Pluto Press.

Boris, E. and Daniels, C. (1989) *Homework: Historical and Contemporary Perspectives on Paid Labor at Home*. Urbana and Chicago: University of Illinois Press.

Boris, E. (1994) *Home to Work: Motherhood and the Politics of Industrial Homework in the United States*. New York: Cambridge University Press.

Boris, E. and Prügl, E. (eds). (1996) *Homeworkers in Global Perspective: Invisible No More*. New York: Routledge.

Burchielli, R., Buttigieg, D. and Delaney, A. (2008) Organizing Homeworkers: The Use of Mapping as an Organizing Tool. *Work, Employment and Society*, 22: 167–180.

Burchielli, R. and Delaney, A. (2016) The Invisibilization and Denial of Work in Argentinian Garment Homework. *Relations Industrielles/Industrial Relations*, 71: 468–493.

Dangler, J.F. (1994) *Hidden in the Home: The Role of Waged Homework in the Modern World Economy*. Albany: State University of New York Press.

Daniels, C. (1989) Between Home and Factory: Homeworkers and the State. In E. Boris and C. Daniels (eds) *HomeWork* (pp. 13–31). Urbana: University of Illinois Press.

Delaney, A., Burchielli, R. and Connor, T. (2015) Positioning Women Homeworkers in a Global Footwear Production Network: How Can Homeworkers Improve Agency, Influence and Claim Rights? *Journal of Industrial Relations* 57: 641–659.

Jenkins, R., Pearson, R. and Seyfang, G. (eds) (2002) *Corporate Responsibility and Labour Rights*. London: Earthscan.

Federici, S. (2012) *Revolution at Point Zero: Housework, Reproduction and Feminist Struggle*. Brooklyn: PM Press.

Fernandez-Kelly, P. and Shefner, J. (2006) *Out of the Shadows: Political Action and the Informal Economy in Latin America*. University Park: The Pennsylvania State University Press.

Fraser, N. (1996) Social Justice in the Age of Identity Politics: Redistribution, Recognition, and Participation. *The Tanner Lectures of Human Values*. Stanford University.

Fraser, N. (2005) Reframing Justice in a Globalizing World. *New Left Review* 36: 1–19.

Fraser, N. (2008) Mapping the Feminist Imagination: From Redistribution to Recognition and Representation. *Scales of Justice: Reimagining Political Space in a Globalizing World*. New York: Columbia University Press.

Fraser, N. (2017) Crisis of Care? On the Social-Reproductive Contradictions of Contemporary Capitalism. In T. Bhattachaya (ed.) *Social Reproduction Theory: Remapping Class, Recentering Oppression*. London: Pluto Press.

Gringeri, C. (1994) *Homeworkers and Rural Economic Development*. Lawrence: University of Kansas Press.

Kabeer, N., Sudarshan, R. and Milward, K. (2013) *Organising Women Workers in the Informal Economy: Beyond the Weapons of the Weak*. London: Zed Books.

Krinsky, J. (2007) Constructing Workers: Working-Class Formation under Neoliberalism. *Qualitative Sociology* 30: 343–360.

Krinsky, J. (2012) La Servitude et le volontaire : les usages politiques du travail invisible dans les parcs de la ville de New York. *Sociétés contemporaines* 87: 49–74.

Krinsky, J. and Simonet, M. (2012) Déni de travail: l'invisibilisation du travail aujourd'hui. Introduction. *Sociétés contemporaines* 87: 1–5.

Martens, M. and Mitter, S. (eds) (1994) *Women in Trade Unions: Organising the Unorganised*. Geneva: International Labour Organization.

Mezzadri, A. (2016) Class, Gender and the Sweatshop: On the Nexus Between Labour Commodification and Exploitation. *Third World Quarterly* 37: 1877–1900.

Mies, M. (2014) *Patriarchy and Accumulation on a World Scale: Women in the International Division of Labour*. London: Zed Books. Pearson, R. (2004) Organizing Home-Based Workers in the Global Economy: An Action Research Approach. *Development in Action* 14: 136–148.

Pearson, R. (2014) Gender, Globalization and the Reproduction of Labour: Bringing the State Back. In S. Rai and G. Waylen (eds) *New Frontiers in Feminist Political Economy* (pp. 19–42). London and New York: Routledge.

Peterson, V.S. (2002) Rewriting (Global) Political Economy as Reproductive, Productive, and Virtual (Foucauldian) Economies. *International Feminist Journal of Politics* 4: 1–30.

Phizacklea, A. and Wolkowitz, C. (1995) *Homeworking Women: Gender, Racism and Class at Work*. London: Sage.

Prügl, E. (1999) *The Global Construction of Gender: Home-Based Work in the Political Economy of the 20th Century*. New York: olumbia University Press.

Rowbotham, S. (1999). *New Ways of Organising in the Informal Sector: Four Case Studies of Trade Union Activity*. Leeds: HomeNet.

Rowbotham, S. and Mitter, S. (1994) *Dignity and Daily Bread: New Forms of Economic Organising Among Poor Women in the Third World and the First*. London: Routledge.

Tate, J. (1994a) Homework in West Yorkshire. In S. Rowbotham and S. Mitter (eds), *Dignity and Daily Bread* (pp. 193–217). London: Routledge.

Tate, J. (1994b) Organising Homeworkers in the Informal Sector: Introduction to Part III. In M.H. Martens and S. Mitter (eds.), *Women in Trade Unions: Organising the Unorganised* (pp. 61–93). Geneva: International Labour Office.

Tate, J. (1996a) *Every Pair Tells a Story, Report on a Survey of Homeworking and Subcontracting Chains in Six Countries of the European Union*. Leeds: European Homeworking Group.

Tate, J. (1996b) Making Links: The Growth of Homeworker Networks. In E. Boris and E. Prügl (eds), *Homeworkers in Global Perspective: Invisible No More* (pp. 273–290). New York: Routledge.

Thornton, M. (1991) The Public/Private Dichotomy: Gendered and Discriminatory. *Journal of Law and Society*, 18: 448–463.

Toffanin, T. (2016) *Fabbriche Invisibili: Storie di Donne, Lavoranti a Domicilio*. Verona, Italy: Ombre Corte.

Tsing, A. (2009) Supply Chains and the Human Condition. *Rethinking Marxism* 21: 148–176.

Utting, P. (2007) CSR and Equality. *Third World Quarterly* 28: 697–712.

1

UNDERSTANDING HOMEWORK AND HOMEWORKERS

Introduction

Homework, involving millions of women around the world, is widely understood to be a highly precarious form of work, with sub-minimum pay-rates and working conditions. The labour and economic contributions of homeworkers are unacknowledged; their working conditions are uncertain, unregulated and largely unorganised, and their social positions and futures are unprotected and insecure (HWW, 2003; 2004; Burchielli, Buttigieg, and Delaney, 2008). Through the use of homework in urban and rural locations, suppliers to national and multinational corporations reduce their overheads and economic risks by transferring the pressures of prices and tight deadlines imposed by lead firms onto the most vulnerable workers at the bottom of supply chains (Mezzadri, 2016). In this way, homework represents one of the worst examples of labour rights violations and gender exploitation through a form of work that has persisted, practically unchanged, over the past two centuries (Allen and Wolkowitz, 1987; Barrientos, 2013; Delaney, Burchielli and Connor, 2015; Toffanin, 2016).

A prior condition for gender justice, and for any achievements in equality and equity, relates to an understanding about specific instances of gender *injustice*, and the idiosyncratic inequalities that shape it. Thus, a gender justice proposal must first uncover, describe and ultimately *recognise* the nature and scope of a particular injustice. The aim of this chapter is to begin to *recognise* homework, to define and discuss its particular characteristics and conditions, and to foreground related labour issues, such as protections, regulation, and rights. In this chapter, we answer fundamental questions about homework: examining what homework is and where it occurs, who does it and why, and the critical notions and global dynamics that sustain it. Understanding homework requires an awareness of intersectionality, accounting for the various interrelated factors that have and continue to shape homework. We see homework as an economic activity and as a form of labour and production performed predominantly by women. This leads us to examine the links between women, home and work, to understand the gender divisions of labour, and other social constructions, such as notions of home and work, that facilitate the existence of homework. This analysis explains why women undertake homework and why it is undervalued and unprotected/unregulated but does not explain the positioning of homework in global supply chains. A more complete analysis is rendered by looking at homework from a broader perspective: understanding its location in the informal economy and how homework is used by capitalism, thus drawing out the links between capitalism and the surplus value created by paid work at home.

In simple terms, homework is paid work performed at home, largely undertaken by women. As homework occurs in all parts of the world, in global north and south economies, there are many jobs performed as homework, across all industries: from electronics to embroidery, footballs to food, clothing to cigarettes, giving the impression of varieties of homework. This, however, is a fallacy. We shall argue in this chapter, and throughout this book, that there are key common features that characterise homework: the gender of homeworkers, the home as workplace; the work and employment conditions of homework; its invisibility and its use by capitalism. In fact, as others have argued, in order to make sense of homework, it is useful to focus on these common features and to draw out the relationships between them (Allen and Wolkowitz, 1987; Rowbotham, 1998).

Beginning with homework and homeworkers, we paint a picture of the various defining characteristics of this work and the women who do it. Our data sources include primary data collected by the researchers and activists who are the authors of this book. Other data was collected by the homeworker NGO, Homeworkers Worldwide (HWW), with which the authors have had a longstanding collaboration. We also report on secondary data published by the International Labour Organization (ILO) and from international literature within various disciplines.

In the first half of the chapter, we focus on homework as women's work, discussing the over-representation of women in homework alongside the range of work done as homework in different parts of the world. We analyse work and employment conditions based on the home as workplace, including precarious supply of work, extended working hours, low pay-rates, occupational health and safety concerns and lack of protection and rights. We examine why women work at home and establish that the gender of homeworkers and the home as workplace are key features of homework, subsequently arguing that societal constructions of gender and the home underpin and help to explain homeworkers' invisibility as workers. In relation to homework, the term invisibility refers to the non-recognition of the 'work' in homework, with grave implications for the rights of homeworkers, and is reflected in their poor working conditions, such as irregular work and low incomes, lack of adequate representation (through viable unions) and lack of labour rights.

Later in the chapter, we discuss homework in the context of informal work and employment, to further explain the lack of employment standards and protections inherent in homework. Informal work is often manual and labour intensive, while informal employment is neither registered nor regulated by the powers of the state. We analyse homework in relation to capital, discussing the integration of homework as a method of capitalist production systems. We argue that since industrialisation, homework has created surplus value for capital in different historical contexts and that the benefits to capital far outweigh the sub-minimum incomes that barely compensate homeworkers. Finally, we look at formal definitions of homework, in the context of institutional recognition of homework including the ILO's Convention 177 on homework. Within this discussion, we engage with the complex question of own-account homeworkers – a category that is often misinterpreted and yet is pivotal to policy-making.

While this chapter aims to focus strictly on recognition, to understand the current non-recognition of homework as defined in our gender justice framework, our analysis suggests that recognition is linked to the dimensions of representation and rights. We conclude that repositioning homework, so that it is accurately and properly recognised, as per our justice framework, requires combining recognition strategies with representation and rights, and will require an enormous struggle from civil society in general. Homework has, for centuries, been a key method within capitalist production systems and continues to be highly profitable under neoliberalism, thus capital will not easily relinquish this source of great profit.

Homeworkers: who and where?

According to the International Labour Organization (ILO), homework is paid work performed at home, and women constitute the 'vast majority' in homework around the world (ILO, 2013: 46). As an example, the International Homeworker Mapping Program (IHMP), conducted by Homeworkers Worldwide, found women doing homework in Asia, Europe and Latin America, in a variety of different jobs (HWW, 2004). These data suggest that homeworkers are women between the ages of 14–80 years, the majority aged between 30–40 years, and mostly married with children. Education levels are generally low with many women having low literacy rates (HWW, 2004).

Homework is found in widely different parts of the world and its specific characteristics are linked to the nature of the local economy. Around the world, homeworkers carry out different types of work, with significant numbers working within manufacturing and trade (ILO, 2013). The international homeworkers mapping project found that in Chile, women living in the capital were hand-sewing parts of expensive shoes destined for local and international markets. In the state of Rio de Janeiro, Brazil, the town of Nova Friburgo was full of small, home-based workshops, many of which put out work to women homeworkers, sewing underwear for national sale. In China, women in small villages sewed tablecloths with Christmas designs, for export to the USA; others strung together pearls, a valuable export commodity. In Bulgaria, Turkey, the UK and Australia, women were sewing fashion garments for national and international markets. In Thailand, women assembled garments and artificial flowers in rural and urban areas (HWW, 2004). Other studies have found women stitching leather footballs in Pakistan (PILER, 2009) and assembling electronic circuitry in the UK (HWW, 2004). Most work these women undertake is similar to factory work, except that their workplaces are their homes. Also known as dependent or subcontracted homeworkers (ILO, 2013), some of the characteristics of this type of work are piece-rate payments determined by an employer, with no worker control over deadlines, designs, products, and raw materials. Moreover, income is generally far below minimum wages, or average earnings for equivalent work.

Other homeworkers sew, knit, crochet, assemble, cook, paint, embroider, and weave for local markets, selling to neighbours and friends. They design their own products, buy raw materials and find markets wherever they can. In some places, this work is traditional handcraft work that women have learned from their mothers and grandmothers. In Bulgaria, women do traditional embroidery. In Chile and Bolivia, women raise alpaca and llamas, then spin and weave the wool into shawls and scarves. In Thailand, many village women weave silk and cotton. In other, rural areas, women collect natural products from the mountains, countryside and coast, which they then process at home. In Jharkhand, formerly South Bihar, women make leaf-plates, used all over India, from leaves they collect from the forest. In remote rural areas of Ghana, women collect Shea nuts and make Shea butter for sale at local markets, from where it is often exported to the USA and Europe for use in the cosmetics industry (HWW, 2003). Some of the characteristics of this type of work are: limited access to raw materials; limited or no access to markets and credit; inadequate and precarious incomes. While these workers are often differentiated as self-employed or independent, they are mostly living and working at subsistence level, especially if they live in rural areas, under various types of dependencies. We discuss the dependent/own-account distinctions and related issues later in this chapter.

Homeworkers are not a homogenous group: they perform many different jobs from vastly different locations. However, the gender of homeworkers, seen in the predominance of women in homework, and the home as the workplace, are principal features that characterise this work. Homeworkers also share similar working conditions and employment standards as discussed later in this chapter.

Work and employment conditions

For homeworkers, a supply of work is not guaranteed. For women who are dependent on a subcontractor, the supply of work is subject to the variables affecting the subcontractor, such as loss of supply contracts and price changes. For dependent homeworkers, work may be seasonal and could suddenly disappear. Own-account workers have similar challenges as demand for their products is subject to the many fluctuations that affect demand. Some have not enough work while others have so much that they are affected by tight deadlines leading to long hours of work. In all cases, precarious work leads to insecure incomes.

The spread of working hours extends throughout the day. For some, the average working day is ten hours, but it is not unusual for homeworkers to work longer hours, at times around the clock, without sleep to complete orders, as reported in the garment industry in Argentina (Burchielli et al., 2014; Burchielli and Delaney, 2016), and other industries around the world. In any case, it is common for the paid work and the unpaid domestic work to occur in tandem, so that women are constantly working, paid or unpaid, for up to 16 hours per day.

> I get up at 5'clock in the morning, clean the house, even the outside of the house too. There is a water problem in our area, we won't get water every day, so we have to go walk and get 10 pots every day. Then I clean, make breakfast and lunch for the children, then send them off to school. I do the rest of the housework, then send off my husband. Then I sit for this work. Between lunch hour and sitting together with other women workers, by 4 o'clock the children will come and then I will do some snacks and things for the children. Then my husband comes, I cook the dinner, then do more stitching work. I will sleep at 11 to 11.30 at night.
>
> *(Homeworker Chennai, India 2012)*

> At home you are never paid enough. With the excuse that I was at home, I always worked in bits and pieces and so I would be up until midnight in order to get the job done. I would get up at seven in the morning. At 8 o'clock my children would go to school. I worked two hours in the morning and then in the afternoon from two until six, then I would make dinner and after dinner, I would work from nine until midnight or 1 o'clock. The interruptions were many and varied.
>
> *(Italian footwear Homeworker: 1990s, cited in Toffanin, 2016: 187)*

Homeworkers earn very low rates for their work. For example, homeworkers in the footwear industry in Tamil Nadu, India, reported earning 4–6 INR per shoe (approximately 4–6 cents, $US), with daily earnings in the order of 50 INR ($US 0.75), or approximately one-third of the minimum wage in that industry (Delaney et al., 2015). Systematic underpayment, compared with industry standards, is typical in homework and has been widely reported (Allen and Wolkowitz, 1987; HWW, 2004; Delaney et al., 2015). Even in the case of self-employed (own-account) homeworkers, who may sell their work directly, earnings are so irregular that the income barely meets costs of production let alone basic needs. Income patching (finding different, additional sources of income via different jobs) is commonplace especially in rural areas, where seasonal work needs to be supplemented and is subsidised at other times. Earnings are often as little as one-fifth to one-third of minimum wages in each country and homeworkers often report not being able to make ends meet.

In terms of occupational health and safety (OHS), most homeworkers report some type of health condition as a result of their work (HWW, 2004). Common problems include backache, headaches, asthma, poor eyesight, toxic effects of chemicals, pesticides and dyes, and general lethargy or poor health. In some extreme cases, there are reports of loss of limbs, miscarriages, deafness, electrocution, poisoning and respiratory problems. Where homeworkers have done the same work over an extended time period, there are examples of repetitive strain injuries (from sewing for long hours) or skin problems (prolonged exposure to raw materials treated with chemicals). As homework is informal, illness linked to occupation is unlikely to be acknowledged compared to other workers. While in some countries, such as the UK or Argentina, free health provision exists, in others either it does not exist, or else services are inadequate, as in most parts of India.

Other, work-related problems include having to supply their own materials at their own cost (HWW, 2004; Burchielli et al., 2008), social isolation brought about by working alone at home (Burchielli et al. 2014) and bullying from intermediaries, including sexual harassment (Delaney et al., 2015); see Example 1.1 below. As homeworkers often have no access to labour benefits or social support mechanisms such as sickness benefits, medical costs associated with work injuries are likely to fall on the homeworker, where they might be ignored, or bring related hardship such as debt. Although sometimes assisted by other family members, women are disadvantaged by homework as they are underpaid, frequently working long hours, often providing their own materials, in unsafe workplaces (Delaney et al., 2015).

Homeworkers are unprotected by institutional mechanisms such as labour unions or labour regulation, which perpetuates poor working conditions relating to working hours and pay rates (Çagatay, 2003) – more about this in Chapters 5 and 6. In addition to the various types of work-related disadvantages, women homeworkers are also socially disadvantaged by homework, which keeps them isolated in their homes. Moreover, the nature of production in the home is conducive to child labour (Delaney, Burchielli and Tate, 2017). Poor working conditions, low income or earnings, irregular work and poverty often lead to children's occasional or full-time involvement in homework. Dependent, low paid, piece-work coupled with tight deadlines often requires family members to help with the work. Lack of income and work opportunities for rural and own-account work can contribute to children 'helping' the family generate cash income. One consequence of women working for long hours is that young girls end up shouldering the childcare and other responsibilities while the mother works. This perpetuates a gendered cycle of disadvantage for female family members.

Despite the fact that homeworkers are not all the same, by and large, they are women, who work from home, and who share similar working conditions. Irregular work, long working hours, underpayment, working in unsafe conditions, and lack of protections and rights are the norm for homeworkers. Some of these working conditions are present in other non-standard, precarious jobs that are increasingly the norm due to neoliberal globalisation. In homework, however, these features generally occur together, and have always been present as the combined characteristics of homework.

As we shall argue in subsequent sections, the two most common characteristics of homeworkers – the gender of homeworkers and the home as the place of work – are the two single, critical features that underpin and help to explain homeworkers' common working conditions discussed above, such as irregular work and low incomes. However, we shall also see that gender and the home location can explain *other, common* features of homework: homeworkers' responsibilities for unpaid household work and their position in the family and society; the absence of social protection, security or worker rights for homeworkers; and, the value they create for business and capital.

We propose that the two key common features of homework, gender and the home as workplace, have a determining effect on the other common features of homework, such as sub-standard working conditions, degraded employment standards and the invisibility of homework. To understand the varieties of homework around the world, it is useful to focus on these two characteristics and the other common features of homework together. We argue that these two characteristics help to explain why homework is one of the more extreme examples of labour inequality and gender injustice and why it is simultaneously one of the cheapest forms of labour and production. Given the dire working conditions and standards in homework, we begin by looking at why women do homework.

Why women work at home

The question of why women work from home does not have a sole or simple answer and is dependent on existing conditions in local economies. Homework is linked to women's social reproductive role, since women often find themselves at home in their role as mothers (Allen, 1989; Boris and Daniels 1989). Women homeworkers endure numerous disadvantages through having primary responsibility for raising children, caring for family members and earning income for the family survival. Since women are often homeworking to survive, they take whatever work is available to them, under whatever conditions on offer, combining it with their child-care and other family and household responsibilities (Dunaway, 2014). Where men have migrated in search of work, women often have responsibility for subsistence agricultural work such as in the North of Portugal and Hunan, China (Dunaway, 2014).

Even though a number of women homeworkers choose this mode of work while they have young families, as a means of achieving work and family balance while meeting their income requirements, the overwhelming majority of women homeworkers have no other work choice (ILO, 2013; HWW, 2004). They may be forced to engage in homework because they are heads of households, with no other possible income. Particularly in developing countries, women often lack life opportunities, such as literacy, numeracy and a basic education precluding them from finding other work (HWW, 2004; National Sample Survey Organisation, 2007). Women's jobs may have been lost due to industry restructure and they are forced to do homework in order to ensure their own and their children's survival

(CEM, 2003; TCFUA, 1995). Women may live in rural areas, where the only possible livelihood is eked from various combinations of informal work (HWW, 2004).

In developed countries, women face real obstacles in entering the formal labour market particularly the lack of affordable childcare or social services for the care of the elderly. For those with young children, homework may be the only alternative while their children are very young, and they take up other part-time work as soon as this can be fitted around school hours. For minority women in developed countries, however, a further obstacle is racism in the labour market, which restricts opportunities for work outside. Research from the UK has shown that minority women spend more years doing lower paid homework than white, British women.

In developed countries, a high proportion of homeworkers are found to be among migrant or ethnic minority communities, for example, in the UK, Canada, Australia and Argentina. In this case, language or other barriers may preclude some women from other kinds of work except homework. In underdeveloped countries, women from indigenous communities do homework, for example in Bolivia where women process the wool of alpaca and llama, or in Jharkhand, India, where Adivasi women depend on forest products and make leaf plates (HWW, 2004); in these cases, lack of travel, or skills training may narrow the work options for women. In many urban areas, women have caring responsibilities for either young children or elderly or sick relatives, with no outside care support and have no work option other than homework.

In many rural areas, women have an increased need for a cash income (HWW, 2004). Using modern farming methods, there is a need for cash inputs (fertilisers, insecticides, seeds) usually leading to debt, and migration, particularly by men. Women are often left behind but need an income, and so do whatever work they can to earn cash. Women in rural areas such as Jharkhand, India, do subsistence agriculture; they migrate to West Bengal for waged work on rice cultivation, and do home based work – all in one year, depending on seasonal and other factors. In Bulgaria, many of the women homeworkers also do some agricultural work, such as growing tobacco, tomatoes or raising sheep. This is also the case in the mountains in the North of Portugal. Many women do agricultural work to maintain family links to land or risk losing it; their ties to the land is another reason why women do homework.

Work to yield cash earnings may involve traditional skills, such as silk weaving in Thailand, or embroidery in India and China, or newly introduced hand-skills such as basketry, in Thailand and the Philippines; or industrial piecework, often encouraged by government in order to create employment in rural areas and discourage migration. Women from the poorest communities often have no alternative to homework. As shown in a BBC documentary film broadcast in 2008, subcontractors for a factory producing clothes for a major UK brand were putting out work in over 100 refugee camps in Tamil Nadu, in South India. In all cases, women generally carry family financial responsibilities and often bear sole responsibility as heads of households or when men have migrated in search of work elsewhere.

In general, homework is the only choice for the poorest women in both urban and rural communities. The major reason that women undertake homework is economic, and their incomes from homework are crucial to support their families. The 'need to earn a livelihood' is highlighted universally as the motivation for women doing homework, as captured by international research over time (Allen and Wolkowitz, 1987: 71; Delaney et al., 2015; Toffanin, 2016). Alongside the need to work for a living, there is a host of other intervening social factors that shape and limit women's work participation. These can include: their other caring or family roles; skills; the (un)availability of other jobs; lack of transport, as in the case of women living in rural areas where few alternative job opportunities may be available; and, importantly, societal attitudes about work and gender, as we discuss later.

With respect to labour force participation, homeworkers experience similar types of predicaments as other working women, whose work choices and constraints are shaped by such social structuring factors as class and gender and the opportunities and/or limitations linked to those, such as access to education and other social benefits and/or resources, including gender divisions of labour. For homeworkers, these predicaments are more pronounced, with fewer choices and greater constraints, due in part to the invisibility of homework, and to the fact that homework is a type of informal work.

Thus far, we have examined homework by looking closely at homeworkers, the types of work they do, the conditions in which they work and why they do homework, which enabled the identification of key common characteristics that define and shape homework. However, a more complete understanding of homework requires examining broader social, economic and political issues with an influence on homework. The invisibility of homework is an important characteristic that explains the work and employment conditions from a social and gender relations perspective.

Homework invisibility

A key characteristic of homework is its 'invisibility' (Allen and Wolkowitz, 1987; Boris and Daniels, 1989; Burchielli and Delaney, 2016; Toffanin, 2016). In relation to homework, the term invisibility refers to the non-recognition of the 'work' in homework, with grave implications for the rights of homeworkers. In this sense, invisibility is a critical concept, to which we return in various chapters in this book.

Homework contributes to the global economy but is invisible in public domains. It is invisible to labour market regulators, such as unions and legislators (see Chapters 3 and 6), and homework is not adequately represented, protected or properly legislated (see Chapters 3 and 4); it is mostly invisible to economists, sociologists, political scientists and historians, who by and large, have failed to take account of this type of work (Allen and Wolkowitz, 1987; Toffanin, 2016; see also Chapter 2); it is invisible to business firms and brands, that frequently ignore or deny its existence and the contribution of homework to their value-chains (Burchielli and Delaney, 2016; see also Chapter 5); it is largely invisible to consumers who are unable to associate homework with the production of consumer goods. Furthermore, homework may be invisible to homeworkers themselves, in the sense that they may not identify as workers and have no voice (Hill, 2005; see also Chapter 6).

The invisibility of homework is related to gender and to its location inside the home. Beginning with industrialisation, the home was constructed as distinct from the workplace through the polarised notions of public and private spheres. Prior to industrialisation, the home had always been a place of work. However, the rise of factories and the need to determine the nature of the economic and labour relations within them, resulted in an artificial separation of work and home. The public/private artifice was then used to construct gender roles and to determine frameworks and boundaries of various legal responsibilities. Importantly it underpinned key concepts in labour regulation (employment relationships, skill, wage-levels, productivity) that to this day explain the gender wage gap in general (Allen and Wolkowitz, 1987) and the extremely low pay rates of homeworkers in particular. The home thus became the private realm of women's reproduction: the location of women's unpaid caring work and a location 'beyond regulation'. It followed from there that any production work undertaken in the home was not remunerated or regulated in the same ways as work undertaken outside the home. Feminist texts understand the public/private dichotomy as legitimising inequalities, devaluing women's work and, importantly, avoiding state intervention (Thornton, 1991).

The term 'work invisibility' initially suggests work that is not seen as work. In not being seen as work, it is not recognised as productive activity either, which is taken to explain and justify the lack of work benefits and protections that accompany 'invisible' work activity, such as homework. Used in relation to work, *invisibility* has therefore come to mean more than 'not seen'. In fact, the term has become synonymous with precarious and devalorised work; it refers to work that is lacking any social and economic recognition and acknowledgement, and to workers who have little or no power, voice or collective identity as workers (Burchielli and Delaney, 2016) or voice. Homework is not only invisible, but also silent and silenced (Toffanin, 2016).

The nature of homework is that it is invisible work performed in the home, largely by women (Beneria and Floro, 2004 Burchielli et al., 2008). Homework is spatially invisible, in terms of its 'private' location in the home; it is economically invisible, since it is inadequately remunerated as a work activity, and it is sociopolitically invisible, in the sense that few homeworkers are members of a trade union, self-help group or organisation (Burchielli and Delaney, 2016). As such, they lack a voice in terms of social participation and capacity to improve their own social position. Homeworker invisibility, linked to gender and the home, is an insidious product of dominant gender and labour relations within capitalism that places women workers in an individual and collective state of isolation, inconspicuousness and neglect, and a relatively powerless social and political condition (Burchielli et al., 2016). From this position, it is difficult to develop any associational power to access any existing rights and protections (Wright, 2000).

The invisibility and isolation of homework affects women's identities; it affects their knowledge about choices and in terms of social participation; it perpetuates their poverty since homework offers no opportunities for personal and skills training and silences their voice. Homeworker invisibility impacts negatively on attempts to measure, understand and organise homeworkers, as we shall see in subsequent chapters. Understanding that homework invisibility is socially constructed enables us to highlight the notions and assumptions that originally marginalised homework and that continue to create inequality and injustice in this form of work. Analysing homework invisibility broadens our understanding of the social factors involved in making homework what it is today and points to what needs to be questioned and changed to recognise homework appropriately. Similarly, it is instructive to contextualise homework as informal work.

Homework as informal work and employment

In popular representations of homework, such as media coverage of sweatshops, child or slave labour, homework is frequently associated only with developing economies. In fact, homework occurs in both developed and developing nations, across all countries within their informal economies (ILO, 2013). What differs between developing and developed nations is the relative size of informal employment in their national economies – that is, the number of workers engaged in informal work. As an example, the highest proportions of informal employment are currently reported in the developing regions of South East Asia, Africa, Latin America and Eastern Europe: 84% in India, 93% in Pakistan, 82% in Mali, and 76% in Tanzania; 75% in Bolivia, and 58% in Honduras; 59% in Kyrgyzstan, and 20% in Armenia (ILO, 2013).

According to the International Labour Organization (ILO), informal employment includes casual, seasonal and sub-contracted work across all industry sectors, in jobs such as hotel and restaurant work, cleaning, labouring, piecework and homework, such as in the garment and footwear industries, and most agricultural work, although statistics are not kept in the agriculture sector. In general, informal work is manual and labour intensive. The ILO has identified four broad categories within informal employment: domestic workers, homeworkers, street vendors and waste pickers (ILO, 2013).

Informal work goes under many names such as 'cash-in-hand' and 'unregistered' work. The ILO defines informal employment as 'all employment that lacks legal or social protection' (ILO, 2013: 1) and distinguishes it from 'formal employment'. 'Formal employment' refers to employment regulated by minimum standards and defines the persons and conditions in an employment relationship. The current definition of informal employment reflects the considerable debate and changed thinking about the meaning of the informal economy. Originally conceived as family or unregistered enterprises providing work in developing economies, it was previously argued that as economies modernised and with increased wealth, informal enterprises would formalise, and informality would disappear. However, post-globalisation evidence challenged this conception.

Over time, it was gradually understood that the informal economy consisted of many different activities, and included workers in many different employment relationships, specifically those who were disguised waged workers, as opposed to micro-entrepreneurs, owners of small enterprises or self-employed business people. Another dimension was the understanding that many of those working informally were producing goods and services linked to formal workplaces or production and distribution chains or global production networks. Since globalisation, there has been increasing evidence of a web of linkages between formal and informal employment.

Formal enterprises both large and small use other formal and informal enterprises in their supply chains or production networks via outsourcing, and purchase products directly or indirectly from informal workers, such as homeworkers. Moreover, workers move between formal and informal work on a needs basis, according to availability of work and their survival needs. For example, in Argentina and other Latin-American countries, where local jobs were lost to restructuring trends or globalisation, workers increasingly turned to informal employment to maintain an income (Burchielli et al., 2014).

Similarly, within formal employment, there is evidence of the growth of non-standard forms of work, including casual, part-time, and seasonal work, and it is acknowledged that the lowest level jobs within the formal economy share key characteristics with informal work (in terms of poor pay, low protection and a high degree of precariousness see ILO 2013). Workers and enterprises considered to be informal are currently recognised to extend across economic sectors and categories (Trebilcock, 2006); for example, informal workers, such as garment homeworkers, are employed (alongside formal, factory workers) within the garment manufacturing sector of specific countries, e.g. Italy, Argentina, Bulgaria. In recognition of this more nuanced understanding of informal employment, the ILO recognises that informal employment occurs in a range of employment relationships across enterprises and economic and work activities from formal to informal, whether in 'formal enterprises, informal enterprises or households' (ILO, 2013: 3).

Acknowledging the size and significant contribution of informal employment to the global economy was integral to a changed understanding. For example, the ILO now acknowledges 'the links between informality and [economic] growth, on the one hand, and informality, poverty and inequality on the other' (ILO, 2013: 1). The debates around homework contributed to the understanding that the informal sector was not a separate sector of the economy but that there were links between formal and informal. This changed understanding includes recognising that it was not only a question of supporting enterprise development but importantly, recognising the rights of informal workers.

International research suggests that informal employment is growing (Jütting and de Laiglesia, 2009; Meagher, 2013). The ILO acknowledges both the growth of the informal economy and the lack of rights of informal workers in its reports on global informality (ILO 2002; 2013) and in its Decent Work Agenda (Trebilcock, 2005). The gendered nature of informal work is well documented (Fudge and

Owens, 2006; Vosko, 2010). Women's participation in the labour market has increased, and their ongoing responsibility for social reproduction has contributed to stereotypical notions of women as more compliant, nimble-fingered or less reliant on ongoing employment, resulting in their over-representation in industries with high levels of precarious, informal work such as production of garments, footwear, textiles and electronics, and the provision of care and domestic work (Bair, 2010).

The rise in precarious and informal work is commonly attributed to broader social and economic forces such as neoliberalism and globalization that have given ascendancy to the market-driven urges of capitalism for increased privatisation, greater flexibility, reduced regulation and a decline in worker protection (Kalleberg, 2009). Countries worldwide have adopted neo-liberal philosophies and practice, especially the over-reliance on markets to provide regulating functions (Burchielli et al., 2014; Barrientos, 2013; HWW, 2004). Globalisation has provided firms with opportunities to access new product and labour markets: business has eagerly adopted the movement of production to countries with cheaper labour costs, and management practices associated with flexibility, outsourcing and subcontracting are widespread (Delaney et al., 2015). These trends have stimulated the demand for labour in developing countries which has been met, in part, by informal employment.

Capitalism, neo-liberalism, globalisation and business demand for increasing flexibility have created greater vulnerabilities for workers. Key characteristics of informal employment are lack of secure contracts, no worker benefits and no social protection (ILO, 2013). Non-standard and precarious work within formal employment is also growing and shares many of the features of informal work. In general, precarious work may be seen as a broad category of work, sharing such characteristics as deterioration in occupational health and safety conditions, limited access to labour laws and standards, lack of recognition as a worker and lack of decent work (Kalleberg and Hewison, 2013). Precarious work exists across formal and informal employment (Vosko, 2010) although it is a continuous characteristic of informal work.

Situating homework within informal employment, which is by nature precarious, unregulated and unprotected, offers a further perspective on the characteristics and conditions of homework. Homework is the most invisible category of informal employment in which women make up a majority of those working in the worst conditions. In developed countries, this takes the form of precarious work, so that employment is outside most forms of regulation, with few rights (agency work; zero-hour contracts) and homework. In developing countries, the majority of workers have always worked outside formal protection but are now being incorporated into global supply chains and production systems (Mezzadri, 2016).

Homework as a capitalist method of production: historical and contemporary specificities

Historically, informal work and homework have always existed. Working from home was the form of production underpinning the cottage industries that preceded industrialisation. Industrialisation was responsible for taking *some* work out of

the home, into factories. The formalisation or systematising of production syst.
and labour relations as we currently know them came out of the struggle between
capital and organised labour. Production from homes continued and there began a
steady separation of the notions of home and work, and the segregation of labour
by gender, as described above, in the section about homework invisibility.

Despite the existence of factories in early industrialisation, historical evidence suggests that homework was integrated within capitalist production systems. Marx
(1990) describes the army of workers in domestic industries, commanded by capital
as an extension of factory production. By the late 19th and early 20th century,
homework, or 'outwork' as it was then known, was associated with the 'sweated
trades' in countries such as Britain, the USA and Australia. Homework was found in
numerous trades, mainly associated with the fashion industry, but not restricted to
this sector. It was widely assumed, however, that homework would die out as an
outmoded form of employment. This was the case until the 1970s, when feminist
activists, trade unionists and researchers highlighted the continued existence and
growth of this form of employment in both developed and developing countries.

By the start of the 21st century, a number of different trends are apparent. On
the one hand, while there are still homeworkers working for national markets (e.g.,
rolling *bidis* cigarettes, India) and for local communities (foodstuffs, Chile), the
globalisation of production means that others are working for global supply chains
in the production of shoes (Tamil Nadu, India, Bulgaria), garments and household
textiles (India, China) and assembly of parts in engineering and electronics (Brazil,
UK). What we are seeing here is the trend of informalisation of production,
whereby production processes are 'devolved out of large firms into the home'
(Allen and Wolkowitz, 1987: 20).

At the same time as some of these disguised waged workers have been incorporated into global production patterns, in other areas formerly independent own-
account workers are drawn into dependency on global supply or marketing chains.
Embroidery or weaving previously done for household use is now a source of cash
income for women in rural areas of Thailand or India and is often exported. The
collection and processing of natural products such as seaweed (Chile) or forest
products (Serbia) is done by women for export to transnational companies. This
illustrates another trend in capitalism, of incorporating what was already informal
(e.g. embroidery, weaving) into a cash economy, either local, national or global.
Both trends come together in homework.

To grasp the importance of homework to capitalism, it is worth analysing the
reasons for its use and the range of benefits that homework provides to production
processes. Homework is used for those parts of production that are labour intensive
or require manual or specialised skills (Prügl and Tinker, 1997). Despite technological advancement, labour intensive, and specialised manual activities add value to
products across supply chain processes in different industries, from procurement, to
manufacturing and after sales service. Homeworkers' skills are used in the identification and collection of specific natural raw materials, such as seaweed for cosmetics manufacture; in the hand-stitching that is integral to the manufacture of

various clothing items; and in packaging, packing and various types of maintenance that illustrate different parts of the supply chain.

The use of homework improves financial performance via the absence of fixed costs and management costs and low labour costs. Fixed capital and running costs including workspace, heating, lighting and costs of machinery are often removed to the homeworker (HWW, 2004). Labour costs are kept low where production is outsourced via competition between subcontractors and competition between homeworkers. There are no costs involved in management functions: no recruitment, training or employee development costs. Moreover, the piece-rate payment system used to remunerate homeworkers only pays for output. Subcontracting and use of intermediaries is a way of hiding and breaking the direct employment relationship; it invisibilises the workforce further down the chain of production in order to pay lower wages and reduce other employer responsibilities (Burchielli and Delaney, 2016). In the case of dependent workers, once the product of the homeworkers' labour and the final user or retailer are identified, it becomes clear that the homeworkers are waged workers.

Homework provides a large and cheap labour force that offers extreme flexibility to capital. Homeworkers can be deployed in the specific production processes described above when there are spikes in demand, such as in the fashion industries. As there are no contracts, when demand is low, workers are not laid off, nor compensated in any way; they are left to wait until they are required again.

Firms frequently argue that by operating in low wage economies, and using homeworkers, they are providing a social benefit to people living in poverty and offering the opportunity for development. These arguments attempt to disguise and justify the enormous profit homework represents to capital. Low-cost homework adds great value to capitalist production. The benefits to capital far outweigh the sub-minimum incomes that barely compensate homeworkers. The value homework creates for capital illustrates the profit reason for homework's incorporation into capitalist methods of production and is key to understanding homework and its persistence. It is also crucial to understanding the forces against recognising and making improvements to homework.

The recognition of homework has been approached via different perspectives: theoretical and political. An important approach has been the attempt by the ILO to define homeworkers as workers and to introduce an international standard governing homework.

Definitions of homework: the ILO Convention on Home Work

The International Labour Organization (ILO) Convention on Home Work, No. 177 is the internationally accepted labour standard governing homework (ILO, 1996a). Adopted over 20 years ago by the ILO, it came into force in 2000. The Convention 177, comprises a preamble and 17 articles, as well as a separate set of specific recommendations, known as Home Work Recommendation, 1996, number 184 (ILO, 1996b). Together, Convention 177 (C177) and Recommendation 184 define homework and the homeworker and make recommendations in respect of homework to the various nations that comprise the ILO membership.

C177 acknowledges that 'homework' comprises an absence of basic labour conditions that warrant the application of labour conventions, and that homeworkers constitute a distinct category of worker, whose employment status may not be recognised. The convention 177 differentiates between 'homeworkers' and other 'employees' who may occasionally work from home, such as teleworkers, or other white-collar workers. According to C177, homeworkers are distinguished from other workers on two key dimensions: employment status and sub-standard working conditions, including remuneration.

The ultimate intention of Convention 177 is expressed in the key clause, to 'improve the situation of homeworkers' and to 'promote...equality of treatment between homeworkers and other wage earners' (ILO, 1996a: Article 3). This was important as an international standard to give visibility and recognition to homeworkers as part of the workforce entitled to the same rights as others. However, its implementation was dependent on ratification by member states who had to introduce new laws and a national policy in consultation with workers and employers (Prügl, 1999).

C177 formally defines homework as 'work carried out by a person, to be referred to as a homeworker, in his or her home or in other premises of his or her choice, other than the workplace of the employer; for remuneration' (ILO, 1996a: Article 1). This first part of the definition clearly identifies the homeworker as a *dependent* worker, who works from home in exchange for payment. The definition further states that homework 'results in a product or service as specified by the employer, irrespective of who provides the equipment, materials or other inputs used, unless this person has the degree of autonomy and of economic independence necessary to be considered an independent worker under national laws, regulations or court decision' (ILO, 1996a: Article 1). This part of the definition alludes to the possibility of including own account homeworkers within the ambit of the convention. It was positive that the ILO included the clause on economic dependence, i.e. not needing a direct employment relationship, but its effectiveness was limited by the qualification that it depended on national standards, which usually allow own-account homeworkers to be classed as independent.

Many countries still consider homeworkers as independent. In India, traders giving out work to women who roll *bidis* (Indian cigarettes) deny that they are workers and classify their relationship as 'commercial'. They argue that women come to buy materials in the morning and return the finished product for sale at the end of the day. Organisers from the Self-Employed Women's Association (SEWA) have fought long battles for recognition of these women as workers. In the UK, homeworking groups found that homeworkers were classified by employers as self-employed, in order to avoid giving them rights as employees (HWW, 2004). Where women are doing work assembling products for an end-user or retailer, such as the hand stitching of leather shoes in India or Bulgaria, they are similar to factory workers, except that their workplace is the home.

By defining homeworkers as workers, C177 'significantly expanded the meaning of worker' and recognised that homeworkers should have similar rights as other workers. This was a significant achievement of the convention, since it challenges discourses casting homeworkers as non-workers and excluding them from labour laws, that has enabled their systematic marginalisation. However, there are still major obstacles to homeworker recognition, even in terms of C177. It remains the case that only ten countries have ratified the convention. Furthermore, convention ratification does not necessarily result in the policy development contemplated by the convention (Burchielli, et al., 2014; Burchielli and Delaney, 2016). Moreover, some of the distinctions made between homeworkers – dependent and own account – may prevent their full recognition.

Definitions of homework: dependent and own-account

A range of terminology is used to discuss homework. For example, the ILO and some researchers differentiate between homework and *home-based work*, to distinguish between dependent and own-account homework (ILO, 2013). Dependent homework refers to the production of goods for an intermediary, agent or employer, whereas own-account homework, also known as self-employed, refers to the production of goods marketed by the worker. In this section we discuss the distinctions made between dependent and own-account homework; we examine how they are used, and question whether this distinction serves the recognition of homework.

First, it is important to examine the issue of dependency, since it is the basis for determining and recognising homeworkers and excluding others deemed not to be homeworkers. 'Dependent' homework refers to the homeworkers' dependence on an intermediary and ultimately on a firm or brand supplying the work. Despite the hidden nature of the employment relationship, the homeworker is dependent on this relationship for work and income. However, we argue that there is evidence of various types of dependence in homework. In addition to dependence on an employment relationship, there is dependence on traders/suppliers and economic dependence on a range of others.

Own-account workers comprise some of the poorest and economically dependent of homeworkers. These women may make things not knowing whether there is a market. They literally take their products to local markets, hoping to sell them there or in their local community. Some work for intermediaries and/or traders who may share many common features with employers. No employment contract exists, but the homeworker may nevertheless be totally dependent on the trader, often for raw materials, for credit, or equipment. With a traditional product, such as a *kilim* carpet (Turkey) or silk scarves (Thailand), the homeworker usually has control over all the production process and has traditional skills. As these workers are drawn into modern commercial networks, however, the work becomes more and more dependent, and often less and less skilled. The prices also fall.

The question of any differences between dependent and own-account homework was a central issue in the international debate on 'informal employment'.

Advocates for informal workers argued for the recognition of the *similarities* between the majority of women workers who work outside formal workplaces and have no identifiable employer (Bhatt, 1989; HomeNet, 1997; HWW, 2002). The key similarity between dependent and own account homeworkers is the level of economic dependency (Prügl and Tinker, 1997). For a homeworker, this is mostly at subsistence level, well below any relevant poverty line or calculation of minimum earnings. This shared economic dependence is recognised in the ILO Convention on Home Work, which defines a homeworker by excluding only those who 'have a degree of autonomy and of economic independence' (ILO, 1996, pp. Article 1-iii), and who may thus be considered genuinely self-employed. The level of economic dependency should also be the critical distinction between the micro-entrepreneur and homeworker. Own-account homeworkers who are living at or below subsistence level and who in many situations are in the majority (HWW 2004), should be seen as employees rather than micro-entrepreneurs.

Own-account homework demonstrates various levels of dependency. For example, in the North of Bulgaria there were women knitting woollen socks and making lace/crochet. They would make their products and then go and show them to traders who would give them orders for export to Greece. At other times, they sold to friends or anywhere else they could. Women making leaf-plates in Jharkhand, or processing shea butter in Ghana, sell their products to traders who come to their villages. Their only alternative is to sell at local markets where they can get better prices, but they have to spend more time travelling. Similarly, many traditional craft workers are not independent as their products have become commercialised. Women in villages making the famous Kutch embroidery, in India, had little alternative to selling to traders who buy at low prices. In Turkey, women weaving traditional *kilim* carpets, have no other alternative – due to lack of markets – than to work for traders who dictate that they work to specific sizes, designs and materials. In rural areas in South Africa, many women make bread, raise chickens or make handicrafts to sell to other local women or shops. Similarly, in poor, urban areas of Chile, women sell their products to friends and neighbours; and when the whole community is poor, women are forced to sell at low prices, sometimes not even recovering their costs (HWW, 2003; 2004).

The implications of this debate remain crucial in policy terms since many development agencies and national governments see business support as being the appropriate response for micro-entrepreneurs. In both poor rural and urban communities, programs relating to credit, product development and design, and for access to markets, may all be of relevance and useful to own-account homeworkers. However, it is still crucial that they are acknowledged first as workers, in the broad sense of the term, meaning working people who contribute to the economy through their own labour even though they remain in poverty, or living at subsistence level. Being classified as a worker implies an entitlement to recognition and protection from society in the form of national programs and policies directed to homeworkers in their capacity as working people, and citizens, rather than as small business people. Acknowledging, accepting and recognising the common ground between dependent and own-account homeworkers may encourage governments to accept responsibility for their inclusion in policies addressed at ensuring minimum safety nets, or levels of employment and social protection for all informal workers.

Looking at who is served by the 'dependent/own-account' distinction provides another way of analysing it. For homeworkers, there may not be any significant difference between doing dependent and own-account work. The precariousness of homework in general means that many homeworkers take on whatever kind of work is available, both dependent or own-account, often switching between the two (Beneria and Floro, 2004); as one source of work dries up they may move to another, if and when available.

By contrast, employers and the state may benefit by segmenting homework. In many countries, homeworkers are classified as self-employed, independent, or micro-entrepreneurs, even when they are clearly dependent and doing work for factories or agents (HWW, 2004). For example, in Ica, in South Peru, there is a factory that uses thousands of homeworkers to assemble gold chains. Workers for this factory were told that they would only continue to receive work if they registered as micro-entrepreneurs (CECAM, 2004). In 2007, a new law was passed in Turkey which exempted informal workers from paying tax on condition that they declared themselves self-employed. This seemed to be an attempt to formalise the informal economy, which is large in Turkey, but it was to the detriment of homeworkers who registered themselves as self-employed, not as workers.[1] In the 1970s, new legislation was passed in Italy giving homeworkers the same protection as other workers. One of the ways that employers used to get around the law was to refuse to give out work to anyone not registered as a cooperative. Members of cooperatives were not treated as workers and this was a way around the new law (Conroy Jackson, 1990). These examples illustrate a misclassification in order to avoid the costs of employer/state responsibilities for workers according to existing laws. They also illustrate the social construction of homeworker invisibility – in this case, specifically, the greater invisibility of 'own-account' homework, as discussed earlier.

In general, most homeworkers, both dependent and own-account, have difficulty winning recognition as workers from employers, government and in many cases, from trade unions (Prügl, 1999; Boris and Daniels, 1989; Allen, 1989). In the case of dependent workers, this lack of recognition is a way to place homeworkers outside the responsibility of employers, removing the responsibility to governments, in terms of national legislation protecting workers' rights, level of wages and non-wage benefits, as well as security of employment and formal working relations. Yet, these homeworkers do very similar work to those working in factories or workshops, with the single main difference being that their workplace is their home. In the case of own-account homeworkers, the determination of 'independence' places them outside the responsibility of either employer or the state. They may not have a clearly identifiable employer, they may be working for an agent, intermediary or subcontractor, but the goods they produce, the raw materials, the design and methods of working as well as the final markets are all outside their control.

The categories of 'dependent' and 'own-account' homework are used in mechanisms of institutional recognition of homeworkers, such as standards and regulation to determine compensatory responsibility for homeworkers (see Chapter 3 on regulation). However, the 'dependent/own-account' distinction can result in excluding 'own-account' homeworkers from their rights and entitlements as workers. Throughout this book, we use the term homework for both types of work, based on the numerous commonalities already discussed throughout this chapter.

Conclusion

In this chapter we have highlighted the major characteristics and features of homework as an initial step in *recognising* homework, a key dimension of gender justice. Homeworkers, both dependent and own-account, are present across all the regions of the world, in both rural and urban settings, engaged in informal work across industry sectors, doing an enormous variety of jobs. They are also among the poorest and most vulnerable workers in the world. Their labour is mostly unacknowledged and under-rewarded, their working conditions are sub-minimum standard, precarious, unregulated and largely unorganised, and their social positions and futures are insecure and unprotected.

Although homeworkers are not a homogenous group, there are key commonalities defining homework, principally the gender of homeworkers and the home as the workplace. Socio-political constructions of gender and home-as-workplace explain the conceptual foundations scaffolding various other defining labour conditions of homework: its invisibility, the sub-minimum working conditions and lack of protection and rights. However vital, the gender politics in homework provides only a partial explanation; it does not explain dynamics such as its location in subcontracting chains around the world.

A more complete recognition of homework requires understanding its integration into capitalist production. Our discussion of the features of informal employment as the broader context of homework, and how capital uses homework to create surplus value, highlight the disproportionate benefits for capital of homework. Understanding the relationship between capital, patriarchy, development and homework as three intersectional processes that together contribute to the injustices of homework helps to explain the persistence of homework and its almost unchanged nature in the last two centuries. We identify these as determinant factors in our gender justice framework, introduced in the introduction of this book and discussed in detail in our concluding chapter.

In the final part of our analysis, we examined definitions of homework. A broad definition of homework is discussed in the context of the ILO Convention on Homework (177), the only international standard governing homework. Despite its limited application, convention 177 proposes that homeworkers are to be seen as workers, with rights equivalent to those of other workers. However, persistent classifications of homework remain – in particular, distinctions made between 'dependent/own-account' homeworkers that exclude and pose obstacles to gaining labour rights. This is further discussed in our concluding chapter in relation to change strategies.

We conceptualise gender justice in relation to homework as homeworkers gaining full recognition and rights. This requires considering and challenging dominant paradigms, and their assumptions and dynamics, as discussed in this chapter. The aim of bringing justice to women workers labouring in conditions of poverty and dependency requires taking on the patriarchy and capital together. And we can expect that capital will not easily surrender the long-standing and valuable source of profit that is homework.

Note

1 This was also in contradiction with other laws declaring them workers.

References

Allen, S. (1989) Locating Homework in an Analysis of the Ideological and Material Constraints on Women's Paid Work. In E. Boris and C. Daniels (eds) *Homework: Historical and Contemporary Perspectives on Paid Labor at Home* (pp. 272–291). Urbana and Chicago: University of Illinois Press.

Allen, S. and Wolkowitz, C. (1987) *Homeworking: Myths and Realities*. London: Macmillan.

Bair, J. (2010) On Difference and Capital: Gender and the Globalization of Production. *Signs: Journal of Women in Culture and Society*, 36: 203–226.

Barrientos, S. (2013) Corporate Purchasing Practices in Global Production Networks: A Socially Contested Terrain. *Geoforum* 44: 44–51.

Beneria, L. and Floro, M.S. (2004) Labor Market Informalization and Social Policy: Distributional Links and the Case of Homebased Workers. *Vassar College Economics, Working Paper No 60*, Vassar College, USA.

Bhatt, E. (1989) *Grind of Work*. Ahmedabad, India: SEWA Self Employed Women's Association.

Boris, E. and Daniels, C. (1989) *Homework: Historical and Contemporary Perspectives on Paid Labor at Home*. Urbana and Chicago: University of Illinois Press.

Burchielli, R., Buttigieg, D. and Delaney, A. (2008) Organizing Homeworkers: The Use of Mapping as an Organizing Tool. *Work, Employment and Society*, 22(1): 167–180.

Burchielli, R. and Delaney, A. (2016) The Invisibilization and Denial of Work in Argentinian Garment Homework. *Relations Industrielles/Industrial Relations*, 71(3): 468–493.

Burchielli, R., Delaney, A. and Goren, N. (2014) Garment Homework in Argentina: Drawing Together the Threads of Informal and Precarious Work. *The Economic and Labour Relations Review*, 25(1): 63–80.

Çagatay, N. (2003) Gender and International Labor Standards in the World Economy. In E. Mutari and D. Figart (eds), *Women and the Economy: A Reader* (pp. 305–311). Armonk, New York: M.E. Sharpe, Inc.

CECAM. (2004) Information on Microcredit and Homework. Unpublished personal communication. CECAM.

CEM. (2003) *Caracterizacion del Trabajo a Domicilio y Mujeres (Characteristics of Homework and Women) - Executive Report.* Gobierno de Chile: Centro de Estudios de la Mujer (CEM) – Centre for Women's Studies, and SENCE (National Training and Employment Service).

Conroy Jackson, P. (1990) Beyond Benetton, in Yorkshire & Humberside. *Low Pay Unit Newsletter*, July.

Delaney, A., Burchielli, R. and Connor, T. (2015) Positioning Women Homeworkers in a Global Footwear Production Network: How Can Homeworkers Improve Agency, Influence and Claim Rights? *Journal of Industrial Relations*, 57: 641–659.

Delaney, A., Burchielli, R. and Tate, J. (2017) Corporate CSR Responses to Homework and Child Labour in the Indian and Pakistan Leather Sector. In K. Grosser, L. McCarthy and M. Kilgour (eds), *Gender Equality and Responsible Business: Expanding CSR Horizons* (pp 170–184). London: Routledge.

Dunaway, W. (ed.) (2014) *Gendered Commodity Chains: Seeing Women's Work and Households in Global Production.* Stanford, CA: Stanford University Press.

Fudge, J. and Owens, R. (eds) (2006) *Precarious Work, Women, and the New Economy: The Challenge to Legal Norms.* Oxford: Hart Publishing.

Hill, E. (2005) Organising 'Non-standard' Women Workers for Economic and Social Security in India and Australia. Association of Industrial Relations Academics of Australia and New Zealand (AIRAANZ) 19th Conference Reworking Work, Sydney, 9–11 February.

HomeNet. (1997) *From Embroidery to Footballs: South Asia Report 1997.* Leeds, UK: Home-Net International.

HWW. (2002) *Horizontal Mapping Pack Supplement.* Leeds: Homeworkers Worldwide.

HWW. (2003) On the Edge of Survival: Summary Report of Bulgaria Mapping Meeting: 15–17 March 2002. *HWW Bulgarian Mapping Meeting*: HWW.

HWW. (2004) *Organising for Change: Women Homebased Workers in the Global Economy. Final Report on Mapping Homebased Work.* Leeds, UK: Homeworkers Worldwide.

ILO. (1996a) *Home Work Convention 1996.* Number 177. Geneva: International Labor Organisation. Accessed February 15, 2015.

ILO. (1996b) R 184 *Recommendation on Home Work.* Geneva: International Labor Organisation. Accessed May 1, 2018.

ILO. (2002) *Decent Work and the Informal Economy.* International Labour Conference, 90th session, Report VI. Geneva: ILO.

ILO. (2013) *Women and Men in the Informal Economy: A Statistical Picture* (2nd edition). Geneva: International Labour Organization.

Jütting, J. and de Laiglesia, J.R. (eds) (2009) *Is Informal Normal? Towards More and Better Jobs in Developing Countries,* Paris: OECD Publishing.

Kalleberg, A.L. (2009) Precarious Work, Insecure Workers: Employment Relations in Transition. *American Sociological Review* 74: 1–22.

Kalleberg, A.L. and Hewison, K. (2013) Precarious Work and the Challenge for Asia. *American Behavioral Scientist*, 57: 271–288.

Marx, K. (1990) [1867] *Capital, Volume I.* Trans. B. Fowkes. London: Penguin Books.

Meagher, K. (2013) Unlocking the Informal Economy: A Literature Review on Linkages between Formal and Informal Economies in Developing Countries. *WEIGO Working Papers* No 27. Cambridge, USA: WEIGO.

Mezzadri, A. (2016) Class, Gender and the Sweatshop: on the Nexus Between Labour Commodification and Exploitation. *Third World Quarterly* 37: 1877–1900.

National Sample Survey Organisation. (2007) *Informal Sector and Conditions of Employment in India: 2004–2005* (No. 519). New Delhi: Ministry of Statistics and Programme Implementation; Government of India.

PILER. (2009) *Labour Standards in Football Manufacturing Industry: A Case Study of a Nike Vendor in Sialkot, Pakistan.* Karachi: Pakistan Institute of Labour Education and Research.

Prügl, E. (1999) What Is a Worker? Gender, Global Restructuring, and the ILO Convention on Homework. In M.K. Meyer and E. Prügl (eds), *Gender Politics in Global Governance.* Lanham, Md.: Rowman & Littlefield Publishers.

Prügl, E. and Tinker, I. (1997) Microentrepeneurs and Homeworkers: Convergent Categories. *World Development,* 25:1471–1482.

Rowbotham, S. (1998) Weapons of the Weak. *European Journal of Women's Studies,* 5: 453–463.

TCFUA. (1995) *The Hidden Cost of Fashion: Report on the National Outwork Information Campaign.* Sydney: TCFUA.

Thornton, M. (1991) The Public/Private Dichotomy: Gendered and Discriminatory. *Journal of Law and Society,* 18: 448–463.

Toffanin, T. (2016) *Fabbriche Invisibili: Storie di Donne, Lavoranti a Domicilio.* Verona, Italy: Ombre Corte.

Trebilcock, A. (2005) Decent Work and the Informal Economy. Paper presented at the EGDI-WIDER Conference on Unlocking Human Potential – Linking the Informal and Formal Sectors.

Trebilcock, A. (2006) Using Development Approaches to Address the Challenge of the Informal Economy for Labour Law. In G. Davidov and B. Langille (eds), *Boundaries and Frontiers of Labour Law: Goals and Means in the Regulation of Work* (pp. 63–86). Oxford & Portland: Hart Publishing.

Vosko, L. (2010) *Managing the Margins: Gender, Citizenship, and the International Regulation of Precarious Employment.* Oxford: Oxford University Press.

Wright, E.O. (2000) Working-class Power, Capitalist-class Interests, and Class Compromise. *American Journal of Sociology,* 105: 957–1002.

2

THE INVISIBILISATION OF HOMEWORK

Introduction

A primary feature of homework is its invisibility. This descriptor references the mostly female gender of homeworkers, the home as location of the work, constructed as private and separated from the notion of work. It references the lack of agency, representation and social and political power of the workers that springs from this separation and which, in large measure accounts for the injustices surrounding this work (Allen and Wolkowitz, 1987). Any approach to analysing and addressing injustice in homework must consider the invisibility of homework.

Homework became 'invisible' within capitalist production with the distinction of home and work as 'separate spheres' (Allen and Wolkowitz, 1987: 14) and due to the predominance of women doing homework. With the rise of the factory and wage labour system, the home lost its status as the centre of production, becoming instead the location of women's unpaid, domestic and care work, i.e. of their social reproductive work (Boris and Daniels, 1989). Also deemed as 'unskilled' work, women's paid work at home was, and is presently, remunerated using the piece-rate system, at rates below those paid to factory workers. The use of homework performed by women has thus provided business with a ready source of extremely cheap and extremely flexible labour (Allen and Wolkowitz, 1987; Boris and Daniels, 1989), while the state has benefitted from an abundant supply of caring labour at no cost, exonerating it from the costs of supplying greater social services (Allen and Wolkowitz, 1987; Thornton, 1991). All in all, women's homework has thus had an enormously profitable, enabling effect for capital (Toffanin, 2016).

Feminist debates over the past 50 years propose that work invisibility is a condition brought about by specific social relations, such as gender divisions of labour, social and political neglect, and worker powerlessness. Social relations refer to various types of 'everyday' social interactions between individuals, groups and institutions, that can result in political effects, such as the domination of workers. Invisibility is socially and politically constructed, through the social relations ideologically consistent with capitalism and the patriarchy, using mechanisms of gender and class divisions of labour (Allen and Wolkowitz, 1987; Boris and Daniels, 1989; Thornton, 1991). Recent research builds on these arguments by examining emerging, devalued work categories and precarious modes of employment that are increasingly becoming the norm.

Krinsky and Simonet use the term 'invisibilisation' (2012) to discuss the attainment of invisibility via social processes, arrangements and actors that contribute to recasting work as non-work, 'invisibilising' both work and workers. The authors identify such tactics as renaming, trivialising, normalising, ignoring, denying and justifying, used by governments, political parties and their legal instruments, such as employment contracts, to diminish and devalue work, in order to reduce labour power, and labour and governance costs, in line with a neoliberal agenda.

Applying the concept of invisibilisation to homeworkers means that they have been rendered invisible through similar tactics, observable in the social practices and attitudes enacted in the social relations of gender, work (production and reproduction), class and power. For individual women homeworkers, working from home, this has resulted in a range of inequalities, including an almost total lack of recognition and rights (Burchielli and Delaney, 2016). Understanding the tactics, processes and players that construct invisibility helps to identify alternatives, which may be used to reverse invisibility and bring about the recognition and rights that come with visibility.

Key approaches to tackling homework invisibility include appropriate recognition in laws and regulatory mechanisms, increasing homeworker agency and organising homeworkers (discussed in later chapters). It is interesting to note that since industrialisation, there have been two identifiable periods when homework became more visible: both were linked to periods of organising women workers, including homeworkers. In the early 1900s, there were broad movements of women and workers, linked to a conscious socialist agenda agitating around women's work, including homework. Similarly, in the 1970s, the women's movement again raised issues around women's work, paid and unpaid, and women's homework emerged both in Europe and Asia as an issue, and organising was a key response. Feminist research became an important component of this: these women's movements lobbied statisticians to find ways to count homeworkers.

While we do not suggest that research is the key strategy, it is a recognised means to increase visibility. Empirical evidence acknowledges the existence of homework; it can represent the voices of homeworkers without exposing them to retributions and demonstrate the contribution of homeworkers to industry and economies (Allen and Wolkowitz, 1987). Improving awareness of the size, location, conditions and uses of homework can support homeworker advocacy and inform government policy. However, obtaining or producing empirical evidence is not a straightforward task, as the documenting of homework has been plagued by various obstacles associated with counting informal work. Although the ILO has developed critical definitions and concepts to assist countries gathering statistics about their informal employment (Trebilcock, 2005), there is evidence that deepseated attitudes denying and devaluing women's work at home may continue to result in homeworkers not being counted (Burchielli and Delaney, 2016).

In practice, few countries have prioritised the collection of statistics about homework. This gap in knowledge has largely been addressed by other kinds of empirical research on homework, mostly conducted by feminist scholars, although this has been sporadic. Recent evidence highlights the generalised lack of systematic research on homework, remarking its notable absence from sociology of work texts, despite both the estimated size of this workforce and its longevity as a form of production, suggesting moreover, that it is precisely the predominance of women in homework that explains its marginalisation as a field of enquiry (Toffanin, 2016). Earlier, established texts on homework propose that the absence of a coherent body of empirical evidence on this form of production is a 'symptom' of the dominant ideologies in the relations of production (Allen and Wolkowitz, 1987). In other words, it is but another manifestation of the processes of invisibilisation, or the social construction of the invisible.

Invisibility is only partly constructed by the biases inherent in research assumptions and practices. The critical force driving the persistence of homework, as argued in the previous chapter, is the voraciousness of capitalism that uses patriarchal relations to meet its endless demand for profit. A justice approach suggests the need for representation and recognition of homeworkers and the redistribution of profits. On this basis, we argue that reversing the systemic inequalities inherent in the practices of invisibilisation require homeworker advocacy and organising, where possible, and campaigning to resist neoliberal capitalism and to achieve homeworkers full rights as workers, as suggested in Chapters 6 and 7. Research about homework, although not enough on its own, is an important part of this process. Indeed, some forms of research about homework, such as action research, have built organising and advocacy elements into the research design (Burchielli, et al., 2008).

This chapter starts with a discussion of homework invisibility and invisibilisation and its implications for equality and justice for homeworkers. This is followed by a discussion of large and small-scale research about homework and the types of evidence that each has provided. We argue that there are a range of valid empirical approaches, quantitative and qualitative, large and small-scale, that can deepen our knowledge about homework and homeworkers, that provide adequate relevant knowledge to inform policy development and implementation to support homework advocacy and organising to advance a justice agenda for homeworkers.

Homework invisibility and denial

Key texts about homework establish that homeworker invisibility is ideologically constructed, via the dominant ideologies of patriarchy and capitalism (Allen and Wolkowitz, 1987; Boris and Daniels, 1989). In line with a feminist analysis, these authors argue that homework is not inherently invisible, as demonstrated by the pre-industrial valorising of the home as the centre of production. Rather, its invisibility principally came about post industrialisation, from dominant and discriminatory notions of gender roles. Bringing about current divisions of labour, these include strictly gendered notions of production and the 'breadwinner', and of reproduction and caring as innate women's work, resulting in the separation of work and home (aka the public/private dichotomy).

> As the wage labour system developed outside of the home, the domestic labor of women came to be defined as separate from, and qualitatively different than, 'outside' labor done for a wage. Women's household tasks were systematically undervalued as the idea of 'work' was defined in terms of wage labor done in the public sphere, physically and ideologically separate from home. But while the ideological distinction between home and work reflected real transformations in the nature of production, it also mystified the economic importance of women's work at home, paid or unpaid. Homework, as such, was rendered invisible by this ideology.
>
> *(Boris and Daniels, 1989: 22)*

According to Allen and Wolkowitz (1987), understanding the simultaneous persistence and invisibility of homework entails examining the relationship between the notions of home and work, not as separate concepts and locations, but rather as the intersecting point for the creation of surplus value via the specific form of capitalist production that is homework: 'Tackling the invisibility of homeworking has to begin…by reconsidering the beliefs and theories within which its existence has been denied or ignored' (Allen and Wolkowitz, 1987: 11).

Narrow and discriminatory notions of gender that underpinned the separation of work and home informed, and were subsequently entrenched by key institutional responses, particularly the state with its governance and regulatory powers. These same notions shaped regulatory frameworks and trade unions. Labour laws and unions subsequently contributed to the invisibilisation of homework through the adoption of rigid definitions of work and the worker that marginalised and excluded homeworkers (Prügl and Tinker, 1997; Delaney, Burchielli and Connor, 2015).

Over the past century, capital has sometimes expressed contradictory positions on homework dependent upon what suited it best at the time (Boris and Daniels, 1989) However, capital's most consistent position in relation to homework has been to devalorise its contribution (Allen and Wolkowitz, 1987; Delaney et al., 2015) and deny that it is work. Using such strategies as 'renaming' homework as seasonal, part-time work or housework, or 'normalising' it as an unremarkable fact of history and women's lives, denies it as a form of work and trivialises and denies its contribution to industries and economies (Burchielli and Delaney, 2016). Capital has contributed to homework's invisibility by consistently denying that it is a legitimate form of work and trivialising its contribution as a valuable source of cost-cutting (Delaney et al., 2015) and of competitive advantage (Toffanin, 2016). It has done so by restructuring production, and the extensive use of subcontracting which effectively hides homeworkers at the periphery of production networks (Delaney et al., 2015).

The systematic use of large, invisible, cheap and flexible labour forces of women working from home all around the world has resulted in consistent profit for capital (Mills, 2005; Mezzadri, 2014; Toffanin, 2016). For at least half a century, feminist scholars have argued that specific industry sectors, such as clothing and footwear in Britain and Italy, owe their development and profitability to the cut-price wages of women homeworkers (Allen and Wolkowitz, 1987; Toffanin, 2016). Research in homework has thus highlighted that homework denial and invisibility is no accident. Rather, it has been a foundational principle of capitalist strategy for achieving surplus value (Allen and Wolkowitz, 1987; Toffanin, 2016).

Invisibilisation and visibilisation

A recent conceptualisation of invisibilisation (Krinsky and Simonet, 2012) arises from an examination of current global employment trends, building on knowledge about work invisibility. The work invisibilisation literature refers to precarious and devalorised work, where workers have little or no power or collective identity (Krinsky and Simonet, 2012). The concept of invisibilisation is useful to understand recent trends away from standard work arrangements and protections. Like the precariousness literature (Burchielli, Delaney and Goren, 2014; Kalleberg, 2009), invisibilisation attributes work and employment deviations to changed structural and institutional arrangements, such as reduced labour regulation and union decline. However, invisibilisation primarily focuses on changed social and power relations achieved via political, economic, psychological, and regulatory processes (Krinsky and Simonet, 2012; Renault, 2012; Ainsworth, 2002; Thornton, 1991).

The work invisibilisation concept draws from specific instances of emerging job categories and employment modes, exemplifying diminished and devalorised work, to explain the growth of forms of work that are not paid correctly, are unpaid, are neither professional nor manual, are not properly protected and that ultimately affect whether workers are deemed as such. The invisibilisation concept describes macro political and economic trends and discourses that have justified or otherwise brought about changes in standard employment resulting in diminished work conditions and protections and has also been applied to homework (Burchielli and Delaney, 2016).

The concept of work invisibilisation takes into account the power relations that produce it. It describes the social and political practices adopted by powerful actors such as firms and the State, highlighting discourses that rename, misrepresent, misrecognise, trivialise, deny and ignore work, particularly in the caring, service, and informal sectors. Such practices and discourses diminish and devalorise work, recasting work as non-work, then subsequently denying or justifying diminished work outcomes as necessary collateral damage to achieve broader economic growth agendas (Krinsky and Simonet, 2012). As the number of disempowered workers grow, while capital records ever higher profits, it becomes clear that the collateral damage is disproportionally borne by precarious, low-paid workers, informal workers and homeworkers. These trends blur paid and unpaid work arrangements as well as worker identity, with the effect for many workers of not being recognized as, or not identifying as workers (Krinsky and Simonet, 2012).

The concept of work invisibilisation necessarily invokes the opposite notion of visibilisation. Moreover, there may be degrees of visibilisation/invisibilisation, so these notions are best understood on a spectrum. We understand invisibilisation, on one end of the spectrum, to mean no recognition, no representation and no rights. On the other end of the spectrum, we understand visibilisation to mean the full valorisation of work, including all worker rights, representation and recognition. Partial visibilisation falls then somewhere in between invisibilisation and visibilisation.

At specific points in time and in specific locations, homeworkers have had some degree of visibility. For example, in the early 1900s, there were broad socialist movements in Europe, and Latin America, focusing on women and workers, that agitated around homework, within a broader agenda of women's work rights. In Germany, the UK and Argentina, there were broad socialist women's movements involving homeworkers, linked to mass trade union organising. In Argentina, this resulted in campaigns and parliamentary debates that led to the enactment of the Homework Law that is still current (Lieutier, 2009). Again, in the 1970s and 1980s, homework became more visible as a result of the work of trade unions and the women's movement in Europe. For example, in Madeira, democratisation of the trade unions after the revolution in Portugal led to homeworkers being included in the Embroidery Union by a new all-women leadership. In Italy, the trade unions and women's movement initiated a successful campaign for a law to protect homeworkers (Toffanin, 2016: 140–8).

In Asia too, the issue of women's work was put on the agenda via mobilisation and organising. The Gandhian trade union, the Textile Labour Association, began organising women workers leading to the formation of a new women's union, the Self-Employed Women's Union (SEWA) in Gujarat. It was a long struggle to win recognition for the many informal women workers organised by SEWA – head-loaders, street vendors and homeworkers – as workers. None had formal contracts, and many did not even have a regular employer in contrast to the standard, Western model of an employee or worker. These examples highlight the central role of organising for increasing visibility.

The case of Bolivian garment homeworkers in Argentina, who are prominent in public awareness and have been organized in a small, informal union, provides an example of partial visibilisation (Burchielli, Delaney and Goren, 2014). This case suggests that a degree of work visibilisation has been achieved via regulation together with the advocacy and representation carried out by a specific NGO for these workers. However, other Argentinian homeworkers (the traditional local women working from their homes) continue to work invisibly. Despite national legislation making it illegal for employers to underpay and exploit homeworker labour, current economic and political conditions do not encourage effective use of legislation. Irrespective of different degrees of visibilisation, a range of inequalities continue to exist for all homeworkers in Argentina, in terms of pay, relationship to employer, working conditions, rights and protections (Burchielli et al, 2014). Even though the Bolivian homeworkers are generally acknowledged and thus somewhat visible, by our definition of invisibilisation as reduced rights/protection, they remain in the same category as all Argentinian homeworkers: largely invisibilised (Burchielli and Delaney, 2016).

Invisibilisation is a valuable lens through which to analyse homework. Homework has similar key characteristics with the forms of invisibilised employment described in the invisibilisation literature: both feature irregular and insecure work, irregular/non-existent employment contracts, and irregular/nonexistent employment relationships, i.e. workers are not properly remunerated; they have irregular conditions and are not seen as employees. Invisibilisation frames these conditions as the result of the social relations of domination. A key contribution of the invisibilisation literature is that it reiterates that the diminution of work conditions and protections are part of a political project that serves the dominant interests of capital at the expense of workers (Burchielli and Delaney, 2016); at the same time it demonstrates that increasing numbers of workers are in formal employment whose conditions are closer to those in informal employment, and that a lot of emerging work forms, despite being performed by men, are beginning to look a lot like devalued women's work.

Unlike emerging types of formal employment with diminished standards, homework has not transformed: it has continuously been informal work characterized by inferior standards compared to formal employment. Invisibilisation makes a strong contribution in aiding our understanding of the specific political and social practices and discourses that purposefully construct work invisibility of homework and other kinds of work. It provides continuity to the argument that diminished work creates surplus value for capital and builds on former arguments about homework invisibility by describing the concrete discourses that accomplish it.

Key agents and processes of homeworker invisibilisation

Invisibilisation or the denial of work are socially constructed and accomplished by individuals, various social actors and institutions and their instruments, and by dominant cultural processes (Krinsky and Simonet 2012; Burchielli and Delaney, 2016).

The processes of invisibilisation are observed in the most fundamental forms of worker protection, enshrined within labour laws and contracts. These legal instruments include key definitions, such as who is a worker, and reflect dominant discourses and their constructions (Vosko, 2010). Laws construct the notion of the workplace/non-workplace and perpetuate the public/private dichotomy (Fraser, 2013; Thornton, 1991). Evidence of the continuity of the public/private dichotomy, and its discriminatory effects, can be found in the fact that the concept of work, as described in legislation, refers to 'paid labour emanating from the contract of employment' (Thornton, 1991: 453); this excludes the myriad forms of unpaid labour performed by women in the home (Vosko, 2010; Glenn, 2010) and tends not to cover workers without a formal contract.

Maintaining the demarcation in the public/private dichotomy becomes a political mechanism that enables the state to reduce the number of domains of its responsibility (Fraser, 2013; Thornton, 1991) and allows capital to act without facing regulatory consequences, thus safeguarding the dominant interests of both the state and business (Stone and Arthurs, 2013; Thornton, 1991).

Regulation and labour laws may favour, collude with or confer power to some social actors over others such as corporations and business entities. Regulatory environments are weaker in some countries and may not be adequately enforced. In many parts of the world, a trend has emerged towards reduction of the state's labour inspectorate role and a reluctance to implement labour laws in regard to informal work that contributes to invisibilisation (Krinsky 2012; Krinsky and Simonet 2012). Firms note and take advantage of these local factors by choosing the most favourable regulatory environment for their purposes at the expense of working conditions and worker rights. This is amply documented by the avalanche of reports and publications following the Rana Plaza industrial accident of 2013, where over one thousand workers died following the unfortunate combination of such adverse factors as inadequate law enforcement, international brands seeking the lowest cost at the expense of worker rights, and local firms purposefully ignoring local laws (Human Rights Watch, 2015).

Regulatory environments implicate the State and its legal institutions as key agents and instruments of invisibilisation/visibilisation, depending on whether these institutions maintain or change inequitable constructions defining workers (see Chapter 3). Despite the fact that standard employment, with standard conditions and protections currently represents a minority of workers, labour laws all around the world continue to define work and workers against outdated standards. By the definition of a worker in most labour laws, linking an employee to an employer, all homeworkers are excluded. Dependent homeworkers are excluded via subcontracting chains separating homeworkers from the originating employer. Own-account homeworkers, regardless of their level of dependence, are defined as 'independent contractors' or small business owners and not recognised as workers in standard labour laws. These definitions invisibilise homeworkers by disguising the employment relationship and obscuring who is responsible for homeworkers' actual terms. Invisibilisation of homework also occurs where there are country-specific homework laws, or ratified standards such as the ILO Convention on Home Work, or homework-specific industry codes. Although these may properly define a homeworker, there are insufficient state resources allocated to their enforcement (Delaney et al., 2015).

The Rana Plaza example illustrates that firms too may behave as agents of invisibilisation via some of their business strategies. The common practice of outsourcing is associated with diminished labour standards in terms of pay and conditions and lack of freedom of association (Human Rights Watch, 2015). The role of firms in invisibilisation is also highlighted in specific organisational behaviours. For example, organisational discourses may diminish women's work contribution and status (Ainsworth, 2002). In many countries, homeworkers are renamed by firms in order to trivialise homeworkers' work status and contribution. Rather than being acknowledged as workers, they are renamed by factory owners and brands as housewives and mothers, or a family member, all of which devalues the work, misrepresenting it as part of the reproductive role of women and diminishing women's capacity to seek support, to recognise their own status as workers and to assert their legal rights (Burchielli and Delaney, 2016).

Specific trade unions have been agents in practices of visibilisation/invisibilisation, particularly in relation to informal workers, including homeworkers. Unions in the UK (Allen and Wolkowitz, 1987), US (Boris and Daniels 1989), and Australia publicly advocated against homework in recent history (Delaney, Ng and Venugopal, 2018), while others, such as in Bangladesh (Human Rights Watch, 2015) and Argentina continue to refuse to acknowledge and represent homeworkers (Burchielli et al., 2014).

A philosophy of work perspective proposes that workers internalise these institutional and social messages. When workers accept a devalued perspective of their work and themselves, this affects their ability to associate and collectivise (Renault, 2012). Simultaneously limited by lack of agency and associational power traditionally gained through unions, they are less likely to join together with co-workers to act on feelings of injustice (Renault, 2012). Therefore, the devaluing of certain forms of work perpetuates lack of recognition (Fraser, 2013) and invisibility, via the effect of diminishing worker's capacity to form collective structures and support (Renault, 2012).

The entanglements between governments, laws, firms, and even unions, participating in practices and discourses aligned with the ideologies of capitalism and patriarchy together play a critical role in the attainment of invisibilisation. Achieving a justice agenda for homeworkers includes refusing and resisting invisibility and clearly needs a countervailing power, including alternative, representative organisations for homeworkers. Homeworker visibilisation requires their recognition in the law; functional state monitoring systems; labour organising and activism as well as relevant and appropriate employer initiatives. Worker recognition involves the engagement of institutional and social agents, such as governments, firms, worker advocacy groups together with individual workers, to define, determine and acknowledge all instances of work, regardless of where it sits in the formal/informal continuum. Recognition relies on social relations and processes supportive of recognition, such as regimes that promote worker representation and rights, including state policies in favour of worker advocacy and representation by active unions, functional legislation and monitoring regimes, together with aligned business strategies and behaviours. Visibilisation, defined as both recognition and rights, has yet to be achieved for homeworkers and is discussed elsewhere in this book.

Invisibility, invisibilisation and research

Almost 40 years ago, it was noted that 'the invisibility of homework was, and continues to be, partly constructed by the methods of collecting statistical data used by official bodies' (Allen and Wolkowitz, 1987: 11). Although we know more about homework than we did some decades ago, it is still largely the case that there is almost no large-scale, quantitative data about any of the aspects of homework. 'Relatively few countries produce regular statistics' (ILO, 2014: 6) on informal work and homework: therefore, we do not have any precise data on the size and trends of homework globally. On the one hand, the formal collection of statistics may be subject to financial constraints: for example, the ILO recognises that many countries lack the resources to 'estimate and monitor the informal economy', including homework (ILO, 2014:6). On the other hand, many of the features of homework, such as the invisibility and isolation of homeworkers, the insecurity of the work and the need to combine it with other work, coalesce to create material difficulties for the collection of statistics. However, it is much more likely that the dearth of quantitative data is linked to the political decision to *continue to ignore* these forms of production.

Feminist research in the past has understood the lack of quantitative evidence on homework as a 'symptom' of the dominant ideologies in the relations of production (Allen and Wolkowitz, 1987: 11). As an invisible form of production, homework was widely considered and constructed as marginal compared to other forms of work, such as factory production, which was legitimised in the social relations of production by all manner of instruments (policies, laws and procedures) and institutions (state, political parties, unions, employers). In line with the invisibilisation argument, the invisibility of homework continues to be perpetuated by dominant ideologies and social processes, even in relation to research and knowledge-building.

Current research adopts a similar position, noting the alignment between the systematic marginalisation of homework as a form of production, and the marginalisation of knowledge-building about homework. For example, Toffanin (2016) notes that despite the continuous existence of homework as a form of capitalist production since industrialisation, it is ignored and excluded in sociology of work texts. She also argues that empirical research on homework has been sporadic and piecemeal, and that the study of homework is a marginal, feminised field of enquiry, since women dominate in its research (Toffanin, 2016). According to Toffanin, it is precisely the predominance of women in homework that explains its marginalisation as a field of enquiry, while dominant knowledge-building institutions, such as universities, have done little to challenge this paradigm (2016). Again, these facts underscore the processes and institutions that accomplish the invisibilisation of homework.

An important part of addressing justice issues in homework, including developing appropriate policy and legislation, requires having valid and reliable data (Trebilcock, 2005). Achieving this would constitute powerful evidence that would contribute to homeworker visibility. Homeworkers, their advocates, and governments could use these data to campaign for and promote change to achieve homeworker recognition and rights. Currently, there are some valuable *estimates* of homework, either based on estimates about the broader category of informal work (ILO, 2014), or on such estimates as those projected within specific, national industry sectors, like clothing and footwear, where homework is known to meet a significant part of the demand for production. However, a range of technical difficulties, rooted in the characteristics of homework, have confounded both formal statistics and estimates about homework.

Factors invisibilising homeworkers via estimates and statistics

Many countries do not conduct surveys of the various informal employment categories. *When collected*, data about homeworkers or other informal workers, may be collected via a national Labour Force Survey (LFS), a Household Surveys (HS) or the Population Census (PC). All of which have misrepresented the extent of homework due to inadequate definitions and concepts.

A key problem has been the definition of a homeworker: where homeworkers are mistakenly represented as self-employed or as employers, they are not counted as homeworkers (Trebilcock, 2005). A variety of other factors are associated with survey research conducted about homework within the informal economy resulting in failure to adequately estimate homework for various reasons:

- In LFS questions for firms: the firms may not declare homeworkers.
- In HS, questions regarding forms of remuneration may be interpreted ambiguously as either wages or own-account earnings.
- In PC, 'place of work' may not include the home.
- In LFS and HS, questions on 'working time' may be based on a preceding time-frame (e.g. the preceding week), which may be too narrow to capture all the seasonal and irregular homebased work that women do.
- Homeworkers may not identify as workers and may therefore be unclear as to how to answer questions (HWW, 2004).
- Workers may not know the characteristics of their employing enterprise.
- Workers may be fearful of declaring the work to 'official' data collectors.
- Detailed information is not collected on the firm for which homeworkers work.

The many problems surrounding the validity and reliability of survey methods in research on homework and informal employment continue to be documented. Most recently, it has been noted that the lack of valid and reliable survey data about informal employment 'is only partly due to difficulties in grasping the phenomenon statistically' and that a more general problem lies in erroneous labour market conceptualisation 'resting on the assumption of regular, stable employment arrangements' (Rodgers and Kuptsch, 2008: ix). To counter definitional problems, the ILO published a technical manual (ILO, 2013) that provides the current standards for producing statistics and estimates on informality, including homework.

A positive example of large, survey-based research is the Indian Household Survey conducted in 2004–2005 (NSSO, 2007). The National Sample Survey Organisation (NSSO) found 82% of informal workers in rural areas and 72% in urban areas (NSSO, 2007). This survey, upheld as a successful measurement of the informal economy, adhered closely to recommendations from the 1993 ICLS and included questions on the following key indicators:

- type of enterprise;
- 'status in employment';
- industry of work;
- place of work;
- conditions in employment, including existence of written job contract; nature of employment (permanent or temporary); eligibility for paid leave; eligibility for social security; mode of payment (regular weekly, daily and piece-rate);
- existence of union or association whose main objective was to look after the interests of its members.

Its findings confirmed the predominance of women among informal employment (IE) workers and homeworkers; it located IE workers in every industry and within both rural and urban areas; it highlighted the continuum concept of IE, including the crossing-over by workers between dependent and own-account work; it provided disturbing evidence of the relentless struggle for survival in the well below average incomes of IE workers, and the precarious nature of IE work; it demonstrated the obstacles for overcoming poverty where there is lack of social protection, low education, extremely low on-the-job training and extremely low incidence of social voice via union membership or self-help association, and showed the proportion of women lacking representation being higher than for men.

This survey stands out in terms of documenting the characteristics and conditions of homework, and the informal economy in its many guises in India; it confirms and reiterates findings about homework from small-scale, sectoral or local survey conducted by NGOs and homeworker advocates. Its findings have been used to develop local initiatives for informal workers. Despite technical advances and some, good, large-scale research, there is still reason to remain skeptical about statistics on informal employment and homework. For example, in Argentina, entrenched concepts and attitudes about women's work at home have resulted in local women not being acknowledged or counted as garment homeworkers (Burchielli and Delaney, 2016; Burchielli et al., 2014). There are also compelling arguments for moving beyond statistical measurement for increasing homeworker visibility (Rodgers and Kuptsch, 2008).

Visibilising homework via research

Despite the irregularity and general absence of formal statistical data on homework, a growing body of quantitative and qualitative work around the world has collected information and built key knowledge about homework, some of which may not have been possible via large population surveys. Various existing industry sector and geographic studies have documented the continuities of homework over time, in particular who does homework; the nature of the work and the working conditions that establish that homework is a form of labour segmentation by gender that provides capital with plentiful, flexible and cheap labour. These studies have highlighted the role of subcontracting chains and the complex linkages between large firms, various subcontractors, traders and intermediaries, and homeworkers, revealing key political and economic conditions enabling the persistence of homework as a key form of capitalist production relying on large supplies of women's labour to add value. They have identified critical factors affecting employment and leading to growth in homework and informal employment, in particular the pursuit of regulation by the market and the undermining of labour organisations. Finally, they have documented valuable organising initiatives with homeworkers, showing that with support, homeworkers wish to participate in gaining rights. All of these are important steps in visibilising homeworkers. Some of these studies are outlined below.

The West Yorkshire Studies, UK, 1978–1986

These quantitative studies were conducted to demonstrate the extent and nature of homework in Calderdale and Leeds. Using local knowledge in women's organisations, university and government funding, the West Yorkshire studies surveyed 4,190 households to eventually interview 71 homeworkers (Allen and Wolkowitz, 1987: 45), and some suppliers of homework. These studies represent the voices of homeworkers and expose some of the myths that to this day continue about homework. They reveal the 'realities' of homeworking, which are squarely based on constructed gender divisions of labour, that discriminate against women and devalorise their labour by falsely separating home and work. The research differentiated itself by its strategic focus on suppliers, used to demonstrate that the persistence of homework is less rooted in women's needs and more on the needs of capital for a cheap and flexible labour pool. The findings and analytic approach of these studies informed many subsequent studies on the role of homework in value chains (Delaney et al., 2015; Toffanin, 2016). Importantly, they also led to local government policy and homeworker organising initiatives (Allen and Wolkowitz, 1987).

Human Geography and the chains of production: Thessaloniki, Greece, 1990s

This study was used to capture the extent of homework and other informal work using multiple sources of information, including household and business surveys, to map the chains of subcontracting from outside Greece to subcontractors in the city and from these subcontractors to smaller workshops and homeworkers, both within the city and in surrounding rural areas. One of the strengths of this method was that it did not predetermine the sectors in which homeworking would be located, thus finding multiple layers of homeworking in many different sectors including electronics and vehicle assembly (Chronaki, et al., 1993).

A follow-up study identified the trends and pressures leading to homework that, like other types of informal work, can move from one area to another over time and would otherwise be impossible for researchers to track. A study of trends can show us where to look for homework and why it will inevitably be found in different chains. Through homeworkers and their contacts, it was possible to follow the chains of production upwards to better understand the chains of production. The broader involvement of civil society organisations was another strength of the survey in Thessaloniki: trade union organisers helped researchers establish how the work was moving beyond Greece to Albania and Bulgaria.

A number of similar studies have been conducted globally to identify and track subcontracting chains. Examples include studies of leather footwear in Greece, Italy and Portugal (Tate, 1996). These demonstrated that further subcontracting had moved to Bulgaria, Romania and other countries formerly in the Soviet bloc. Findings from these studies informed various local and international homework related initiatives, including the campaign for the ILO Convention on Homework as well as giving rise to new research linked to organising, such as the International Homework Mapping Program 2001–2006 (Burchielli et al., 2008), discussed further in Chapter 6.

These studies indicate that together, the informality of working relationships and the mobility of the chains of production make it almost impossible for official statistics to capture the full picture of homeworking. Instead, multiple methods are needed to understand homework from different angles. Further, these studies indicate the importance of linking research to contact with homeworkers and their organisations or advocates.

Conclusion

The historic and pervasive invisibility of homework, linked to gender, place of work, and the isolation and dispersal of workers, has been used to create a condition of domination and exploitation of women's labour to advance a neoliberal/capitalist agenda. Homework continues to be socially constructed via the processes and practices of invisibilisation. Invisibilisation refers to the complex social arrangements and processes that are commonly enacted in the social relations of work and gender. Observed in the behaviours and attitudes of dominant and powerful institutions and agents, they deny, diminish and devalue women's work at home, recasting their work as non-work. In terms of the justice framework we propose in this book, invisibilisation represents the means by which the critical determinants – capitalism, gender and development – can influence the gender justice dimensions. This will be further discussed in our concluding chapter. Nonetheless, understanding the processes and players that construct invisibility helps to identify tactics for resistance, which may be used to reverse invisibility, and their corollary inequalities and injustice, to bring about visibilisation.

We define visibilisation as acknowledgement, recognition, and the achievement of workers' rights. Visibilisation refers to achieving justice and redress for homeworkers by way of improvements to their working and living conditions. Very clear implications from our discussion of invisibilisation and visibilisation arise for the millions of unacknowledged and politically neglected informal, home-based workers. By our definition, homework visibilisation, if it is ever to come about, requires concerted efforts from governments, employers, unions and other civil society actors to engage in numerous, simultaneous strategies to reverse gender and class-based inequalities.

Research plays an important role for visibilisation: it provides specific evidence about the nature of homework and its conditions and therefore can inform specific redress strategies. The almost universal, non-collection of regular and reliable, large-scale, statistical data about homework in countries around the world prevents us from making numerical statements about the exact extent, spread and increase of homework over time. However, smaller-scale studies, such as those we have showcased in this chapter, demonstrate its continuing persistence, in significant proportions in specific national contexts, and its movement across geographic locations. These showcase irrefutable evidence that homework is not disappearing and should be sufficient evidence for governments to take local action. Other socio-economic data, particularly about the increase and spread of irregular precarious and informal work support the notion that homework, as a principal form of irregular and precarious work, is probably on the increase. Counting homeworkers is not enough on its own as more detailed information is required to inform redress initiatives. Similarly, research alone, regardless of its quality or scale, is insufficient for visibilisation, which contemplates social relations of recognition, inclusion, and equality. These are the subject of subsequent chapters.

References

Allen, S. and Wolkowitz, C. (1987) *Homeworking: Myths and Realities*. Houndmills, Basingstoke, Hampshire and London: Macmillan Education.

Ainsworth, S. (2002) The 'Feminine Advantage': A Discursive Analysis of the Invisibility of Older Women Workers. *Gender, Work & Organization*, 9(5): 579–601.

Boris, E. and Daniels, C.R. (eds) (1989) *Homework: Historical and Contemporary Perspectives on Paid Labor at Home*. Urbana: University of Illinois Press.

Burchielli, R., Buttigieg, D. and Delaney, A. (2008) Organizing Homeworkers: The Use of Mapping as an Organizing Tool. *Work, Employment and Society*, 22(1): 167–180.

Burchielli, R. and Delaney, A. (2016) The Invisibilisation and Denial of Work in Argentinian Garment Homework. *Relations Industrielles/Industrial Relations*, 71(3): 468–493.

Burchielli, R., Delaney, A., and Coventry, K. (2014) Campaign Strategies to Develop Regulatory Mechanisms: Protecting Australian Homeworkers. *Journal of Industrial Relations*, 56(1): 81–102.

Burchielli, R., Delaney, A. and Goren, N. (2014) Garment Homework in Argentina: Drawing Together the Threads of Invisible and Precarious Work. *Economic and Labour Relations Review*, 25(1): 63–80.

Chen, M., Vanek, J. and Heintz, J. (2006) Informality, Gender and Poverty: A Global Picture. *Economic and Political Weekly*, May 27: 2131–2139.

Chronaki, Z., Hadjimichalis, C., Labrianidis, L., and Vaiou, D. (1993) Diffused Industrialization in Thessaloniki: From Expansion to Crisis. *International Journal of Urban and Regional Research*, 17: 178.

Delaney, A., Burchielli, R. and Connor, T. (2015) Positioning Women Homeworkers in a Global Footwear Production Network: How Can Homeworkers Improve Agency, Influence and Claim Rights? *Journal of Industrial Relations*, 57(4): 641–659.

Delaney, A., Ng, N-F. and Venugopal, V. (2018) Comparing Australian garment and childcare homeworkers' experience of regulation and representation. *The Economic and Labour Relations Review*, 29: 346–364.

Fraser, N. (2005) Reframing Justice in a Globalizing World. *New Left Review*, 36: 1–19.

Fraser, N. (2007) Special Section: Transnational Public Sphere: Transnationalizing the Public Sphere: On the Legitimacy and Efficacy of Public Opinion in a Post-Westphalian World. *Theory, Culture & Society*, 24(4): 7–30.

Fraser, N. (2013) *Fortunes of Feminism: From State-Managed Capitalism to Neoliberal Crisis and Beyond*. New York: Verso.

Glenn, E.N. (2010) *Forced to Care: Coercion and Caregiving in America*. Cambridge, Massachusetts: Harvard University Press.

Harvey, D. (2006) *A Brief History of Neoliberalism*. New York: Oxford University Press.

Hattatoglu, D. and Tate, J. (2016) Home-based Work and New Ways of Organising in the Era of Globalisation, in R. Lambert and A. Herod (eds), *Neoliberal Capitalism and Precarious Work: Ethnographies of Accomodation and Resistance*. UK: Edward Elgar Publishing Limited.

Human Rights Watch. (2015) 'Whoever Raises Their Head': Worker's Rights in Bangladesh's Garment Factories. Accessed online at http://www.hrw.org on 7 March 2016.

HWW. (2004) *Organising for Change: Women Homebased Workers in the Global Economy. Final Report on Mapping Homebased Work*. Leeds, UK: Homeworkers Worldwide.

HWW. (2015) Personal correspondence; 4 June 2015.

ILO. (2013) *Measuring Informality. A Statistical Manual on the Informal Sector and Informal Employment*. Geneva: ILO.

ILO. (2014) *Transitioning from the Informal to the Formal Economy*, Report of the International Labour Conference, 103/V/1. Geneva: ILO.

Kalleberg, A.L. (2009) Precarious Work, Insecure Workers: Employment Relations in Transition. *American Sociological Review* 74: 1–22.

Krinsky, J. and Simonet, M. (2012) Déni de travail: l'invisibilisation du travail aujourd'hui. Introduction. *Sociétés contemporaines*, 87 : 5–23.

Lieutier, A. (2009) *Esclavos: los trabajadores costureros de la cuidad de Buenos Aires* (Slaves: Sewing Workers in the City of Buenos Aires). Buenos Aires: Alameda Centre.

Mills, M.B. (2005) From Nimble Fingers to Raised Fists: Women and Labor Activism in Globalizing Thailand. *Signs: Journal of Women in Culture and Society*, 31:117–144.

Mezzadri, A. (2014) Reflections on Globalisation and Labour Standards in the Indian Garment Industry: Codes of Conduct Versus 'Codes of Practice' Imposed by the Firm. *Global Labour Journal*, 3: 40–62.

NSSO. (2007) *Informal Sector and Conditions of Employment in India: 2004–2005* (No. 519). New Delhi: National Sample Survey Organisation (NSSO); Ministry of Statistics and Programme Implementation; Government of India.

Prügl, E. and Tinker, I. (1997) Microentrepreneurs and Homeworkers: Convergent Categories. *World Development*, 25: 1471–1482.

Renault, E. (2012) The Political Invisibility of Work and its Philosophical Echoes, in N. Smith and J.-P. Deranty (eds). *New Philosophies of Labour: Work and the Social Bond* (pp. 133–150). Netherlands: Brill

Rodgers, G. and Kuptsch, C. (eds) (2008) *Pursuing Decent Work Goals: Priorities for Research* (Research series 115 ed.). Geneva, Switzerland: International Institute for Labour Studies.

Stone, K. and Arthurs, H. (eds) (2013) *Rethinking Workplace Regulation: Beyond the Standard Contract of Employment*. New York: Russell Sage Foundation Press.

Tate, J. (1996) *Every Pair Tells a Story, Report on a Survey of Homeworking and Subcontracting Chains in Six Countries of the European Union*. Leeds: European Homeworking Group.

Thornton, M. (1991) The Public/Private Dichotomy: Gendered and Discriminatory. *Journal of Law and Society*, 18: 448–463.

Toffanin, T. (2016) *Fabbriche Invisibili: Storie di Donne, Lavoranti a Domicilio*. Verona, Italy: Ombre Corte.

Trebilcock, A. (2005) *Decent Work and the Informal Economy*. Geneva: ILO: Expert Group on Development Issues (EGDI) and United Nations University: World Institute for Development Economics Research (UNU-WIDER); Discussion Paper No. 2005/04.

Verdera, F. (2000) *Homeworkers in Peru*. Geneva: ILO.

Vosko, L. (2010) *Managing the Margins: Gender, Citizenship, and the International Regulation of Precarious Employment*. Oxford, UK: Oxford University Press.

3

EXTENSION OF LABOUR REGULATION TO HOMEWORKERS

This chapter describes the application of labour regulation to homeworkers, focused on two aspects of the gender justice approach: recognition and rights. As previous chapters of this book have described in some detail, dependent homeworkers are those who produce, assemble or pack products designed and marketed by others, in a dependent relationship to 'coordinators' in the supply chain. In many cases, the main difference between a homeworker and an equivalent worker in a factory or workshop (where such an equivalent exists) is that her home is her workplace, yet the work is informal. Informal work has become a popular term to define activities that are 'unregulated by the institutions of society, in a legal and social environment in which similar activities are regulated' (Portes, Castells and Benton, 1989).

A particular concern of this chapter is the way that labour laws are the result of, and produce patterns of invisibilisation described in earlier chapters of this book. In these chapters, we showed how different categories and ways of defining work determine workers' status (Krinsky and Simonet, 2012). Invisibilisation offers a lens through which to analyse work – such as homework – that has never been formal or had decent conditions (Burchielli and Delaney, 2016). The term has become synonymous with precarious and devalorised work. Invisibilisation is a powerful device in the diminution of work conditions and protections that is part of a political project that serves the dominant interests of capital and patriarchy at the expense of workers. Homework is spatially invisible, in terms of its 'private' location in the home, away from the public's purview. It is economically invisible, since it is inadequately remunerated as a work activity. It is politically invisible, because what is 'political' continues, despite the great advances of feminism, to be linked with that which is public. It is socio-politically invisible, in the sense that few homeworkers are members of a trade union, self-help group or organisation (Burchielli and Delaney, 2016). Homeworkers most frequently lack a voice in terms of social participation and capacity to improve their own social position.

The law is *shaped* by the invisibility of homework. When work is invisible, it is not in the minds of policy makers when they design labour laws, enforcement mechanisms and social protection. Its spatially hidden nature makes it difficult for policy makers to locate, observe and regulate. This in turn reduces the prospects for collective bargaining and other forms of organising described in Chapter 6 of this book. Invisibilised workers thus face considerable barriers to gaining institutional recognition, legal protection and to claiming rights. The law is also a force in *producing* the invisibility of homework. Invisibility is socially and politically constructed, through social relations ideologically consistent with capitalism and patriarchy (Allen and Wolkowitz, 1987; Boris and Daniels, 1989; Thornton, 1991). This chapter examines the various ways the labour law has rendered workers invisible. In particular, the chapter shows how, when the contract of employment forms the basis of the labour regulation, only a small proportion of the work arrangements conducted at home are visible as work and regulated by law.

In this chapter we assess different legal strategies for improving the conditions of homeworkers by examining the history of regulation of homework over the last century. After a brief description of the regulation of homework in the first half of the 20th century, we assess the effectiveness of labour laws which have been passed in various countries since the ILO Convention and Recommendation on Home Work, adopted in 1996. This labour regulation has mainly taken the form of an extension of the contract of employment to dependent homeworkers. Indeed, most legislation and the ILO Convention is designed to cover one group of homeworkers – those working for an employer in a disguised employment relationship.

Since 1996, and the adoption of ILO Convention 177, we discern two contradictory directions that have been taken in the regulation of homework. On the one hand, the re-regulation of homework is a consequence of destabilisation of the gender contract in recent years (Fudge, 2017: 5). This contract rested upon a sexual division of labour in which women had the primary responsibility for socially necessary, but generally unpaid, labour within the household, and men had the primary responsibility for providing income for the family principally through the wages they earned. As was discussed in considerable detail in Chapter 2 of this book, because this 'domestic' activity was performed almost exclusively by women in the private domain of the household it was not treated as work and its contribution to the economy was rendered invisible (Fudge, 2014: 4). This instability in the current gender contract presents an opportunity for a more egalitarian division of unpaid domestic and paid labour, and, with it, recognition and rights for homeworkers.

On the other hand, because the re-regulation of homework since the 1990s has occurred primarily through the extension of the contract of employment it is a highly precarious path to recognition and rights. The standard employment relationship emerged as one of the key institutions of labour markets in industrialised democracies in the first half of the 20th century, shaping the terms under which labour power is supplied to and utilised within firms. If labour regulation is perceived of as a response to the question of who is responsible for the rights of workers, during this period the answer was 'employers', with some responsibilities for the risks of subordination shared by the state (Hyde, 2012: 84). Labour regulation in this period took the legal/juridical form of the contract of employment, and its function was to link workers' subordination to managerial prerogatives to protections against the abuse of this power. Yet the re-regulation of homework through the extension of the contract of employment occurred just as that 'around the world, workers are embattled, labour markets are in disarray, and labour laws are in flux' (Stone and Arthurs, 2013: 1). For Katherine Stone and Harry Arthurs, the decline of the standard employment contract is 'both a cause and an effect' of these developments. They conclude that it is 'unlikely that the standard employment contract can be revived or that the regulatory regimes once intertwined with it can be resuscitated' (Stone and Arthurs, 2013: 1). Where, then, does this leave homeworkers whose main claim to gender justice hangs on their claim to inclusion in the contract of employment?

This chapter examines country approaches to the regulation of homework through this lens. How much do the regulatory approaches disrupt the gender contract and provide for gender justice?

Part one: late 19th century and early 20th century – trade boards

The extension of the employment contract has not been the only path to recognition and rights over the past century. This section of the chapter shows that the first efforts to regulate homework occurred through localised, participatory structures which avoided many of the problems of the contract of employment.

Legal rights for homeworkers have only occurred following prolonged campaigns and lobbying by homeworkers and their allies. In the second half of the 19th century and early part of the 20th century across the richer countries of the world, a growing movement of manual workers combined with socialist and feminist organisations to fight for better conditions for workers. Within Europe, there were links between these movements in different countries and with similar movements in Australia and the USA. Women's organisations at that time took up the issue of 'sweated labour' of women (Adler and Tawny, 1909; Amsterdam, 1982; Women's Industrial Council; Women's Industrial Council, 1907; Women's Industrial Council, 1907–1908;Prügl, 1999), particularly the situation of homeworkers (or outworkers as they were often known) with the result that the first legislation was brought in to protect women homeworkers.

In 1896 in Victoria, Australia, an amendment to the Factories Act provided for the creation of a wages board (Starr, 1993). The wages board did not set a universal minimum wage; rather it set basic wages for six industries that were considered to pay low wages (Waltman, 2000). The UK's version of the wage boards, created through the Trade Boards Act, were introduced in 1909 after years of lobbying by the Women's Trade Union League, the Women's Industrial Council, and the Anti-Sweating League, as well as numerous commissions of inquiry and reports which assessed the success of the Australian and New Zealand models. The Trades

Board Act of 1909 was an experiment designed for particularly unfortunate female workers (Bean and Boyer, 2009: 258). It was not an attempt to eliminate working-class poverty. Winston Churchill, who as President of the Board of Trade introduced the Trade Boards Bill to Parliament, emphasised that 'these methods of regulating wages by law are only defensible as exceptional measures to deal with diseased and parasitic trades' (Churchill, 1969: 879).[1]

The Trade Boards in the UK had a number of regulatory features that made them effective in improving the conditions of this feminised workforce. We list them here, as they address many of the regulatory characteristics that we describe closer to the end of this chapter as being important for successful regulation (Anonymous, 1938):

- they entailed local tripartite representation;
- they conducted trade based, localised wage setting through a consultation process;
- they applied regardless of whether the worker worked in the factory or at home;
- they provided a process for the adaption of piece rates to the minimum wage;
- and the wage rates applied to all workers regardless of employment status (through 'deeming' provisions);
- once fixed by the trade board, the minimum wages were subject to confirmation by a Minister of Government and enforceable either by civil or criminal proceedings.

One of the most innovative features was the requirement that women were included on the tripartite boards. In the case of a trade in which women are largely employed at least one of the appointed members acting on the board was required to be a woman. Homeworkers had to be directly represented when they formed a considerable proportion of persons employed. In other words, the structure of the Trade Boards facilitated *representation* – one of our four dimensions of gender justice. Representation was built into the architecture of the Trade Boards. The Trade Boards themselves both represented and mediated the collective interests of homeworkers.

A further important aspect of the Trade Boards is that they provided a means for translating hourly rates to piece rates. As we discuss later in this chapter, this aspect of implementation of minimum wages is lacking from most contemporary home-worker protection regulation. If the workers were paid by piece for doing work for which a minimum time rate, but no general minimum piece rate had been fixed, two courses were open to the employer: (a) the employer could establish the rate and be prepared to show, if challenged, that the rate would yield to an ordinary worker in the same circumstances at least as much money as the time rate fixed by the trade board; or (b) apply to the trade board to fix a special minimum piece rate for workers.

The Act included 'deeming provisions' which assumed that any arrangement with a worker was a contract of employment. In order to prevent evasion of the law by the substitution for the contract of employment of some other relation between the parties, any trader, who by way of trade made any arrangement, express or implied, with any worker, in pursuance of which the worker performs any work for which a minimum rate of wages has been fixed, was deemed to be the employer of the worker and liable for the payment of wages at not less than the minimum rate (Wise, 1912: 7). Both these 'deeming provisions' and the fact that Trade Boards were themselves designed with homeworkers in mind is a crucial form of *recognition* for homeworkers. It deemed work conducted by women in the home visible, legitimate and, thus, regulated, even where their work did not resemble traditional, factory based work.

Perhaps because the UK Trade Boards performed these important aspects of gender justice, they were highly effective in alleviating household poverty (Bean and Boyer, 2009). Statistical research by Bean and Boyer found that the Trade Boards Act was successful not only at raising the wages of women who worked in the 'sweated' trades it applied to, but also at alleviating their families' poverty.

Similar regulatory interventions were enacted elsewhere in the world. One of the earliest pieces of legislation targeting homeworkers was the Argentinian Home Work Act adopted in October 1918: Law No. 10505 (4). The law empowered the National Department of Labour to appoint wage boards, composed of an equal number of representatives of employers and of workers and an independent chairman appointed by the Department of Labour, whose duties were to fix minimum rates for home workers, taking into consideration the following: the nature of the work, the price of the articles in the locality, the sums necessary for the living expenses of the workers, the lowest salaries earned by factory workers on the same or similar articles, local customs, the price of articles of prime necessity in the locality, and the value of accessories needed for the work. Employers who paid a lower wage than that fixed as the minimum were liable to a fine of 300 pesos. The law also set specific rules and regulations concerning hygiene and safety in domestic workshops. The 1918 Act began a long period of leadership by Argentina in the regulation of homework, which shall be revisited in later sections of this chapter.

Trade and Wage Boards enjoyed a long period of expansion in the first half of the 20th century as the idea of labour market regulation gained traction. The Trade Boards formed the basis for the UK's Wage Councils (Blackburn, 1988; Blackburn, 2009; Kahn-Freund, 1949; Deakin and Green, 2009) which set minimum wages until their abolition in the 1980s as part of the de-regulation described in the next section of this chapter. They acted as a model for minimum wage setting across much of the Organisation of Economic Coordination, also.

Yet by the post war period, they were no longer as strong a tool for the recognition and rights of women workers. This may be because the post-war gender contract in the developed world undermined the progress that had been made through the Trade Boards and their corollaries. As Judy Fudge (2017: 4) explains:

[The gender contract] rested upon a sexual division of labour in which women had the primary responsibility for socially necessary, but generally unpaid, labour within the household, and men had the primary responsibility for providing income for the family principally through the wages they earned.

As minimum wage setting, and labour regulation more broadly, expanded to regulate 'all workers' as part of the post war social pact, it enacted an erasure of the visibility of women. The supposed universalising of the contract of employment was in fact a masculinisation of this cornerstone of labour protections. As they expanded in coverage, minimum wage setting mechanisms became less about addressing the problems of a disadvantaged, female workforce and more a tool of economic management for the state.

Part two: deregulation from the 1970s

Two trends led to the further de-regulation of homework, alongside a great deal of other work, beginning in the 1970s and 1980s across the OECD, and accelerating in the 1990s. The first trend was related to beliefs about industrialisation and modernism held jointly by workers and capital for much of the 20th century. It had generally been assumed that homework would die out as an outmoded form of employment in a modern industrial society. Part of the movement towards the de-regulation of homework in the 1970s was the consequence of advocating by trade unions for the form of work to be stamped out (Boris, 1994). Homework was seen to be a threat to this system of co-regulation by unions and capital. To hold this view, however, required a gendered myopia which allowed union leaders to assume that this march to progress would result in all work taking a masculine form – away from home, on a full-time basis, free of the constraints of child care and housework.

The second trend was a contradictory and slightly later movement to the first: the emergence of neo-liberal doctrines. This trend took two forms identified by Deakin and Wilkinson (Deakin and Wilkinson, 1991; 2005). One was a strategy of out-and-out neo-liberalism which sought to bring about a fundamental transformation in the relationship between the state and the labour market 'and to restore freedom of contract as the basis for economic relations'. The aim was a marketised form of labour relations. The other was a less ambitious program of 'dualism' in labour and social law that aimed to enhance flexibility in the labour supply. This form of neo-liberalism blamed excessive state regulation of the labour market in the post-war period for the growth in structural unemployment in the late 1970s and 1980s. This less extreme (Deakin and Wilkinson, 1991: 43) version of neo-liberalism entailed a strategy of 'dualism'. Changes in labour regulation in Anglo-American countries, in particular, did not see the wholesale removal of employment protection rights; on the contrary, large parts of the law on dismissal, redundancy and income security remained intact. What has happened instead is a partial withdrawal of protection which focused on 'atypical' work while leaving intact the rights of existing job holders. It was believed this would serve to stimulate labour demand and re-integrate the unemployed into paid employment. This second version was consistent with the existence of homeworkers as a peripheral workforce.

One instance of this withdrawal of protections occurred in the UK, which was at the vanguard of neo-liberal reform. The Wage Councils that were birthed from the original Trade Boards, establishing minimum wages for all workers in the UK, were abolished. When announcing the Bill that would abolish the Wage Councils, the Employment Secretary said that the Bill (1993) would 'increase the competitiveness of the economy and remove obstacles to the creation of new jobs'. Similar forms of deregulation occurred across the OECD, with a shift to enterprise-based collective bargaining in Australia, for example, which excluded homeworkers who were located outside of enterprises, and a preference for individualised contracts rather than collective forms of labour regulation.

Outside the OECD, informal work that was outside the scope of labour regulation and social protection remained the norm. The great social pact of the post-war period had little relevance for most workers. Homework was a common feature of both traditional and industrial production. These workers toiled both as 'own account' workers and also as dependent homeworkers within supply chains. As industrialised sectors grew, particularly in the easy to enter garment sector, homeworkers increasingly worked within globalised supply chains as dependent homeworkers (Hockling and Wilding, 2004; Freeman, 2004; Chen, Sebstad and O'Connell, 1999).

By the 1990s, feminist researchers and activists were highlighting the continued prevalence of homework and arguing for the need for legislation giving rights to homeworkers. By this time, the movement was truly global, with activists and researchers in developing countries highlighting the large numbers of homeworkers, arguing for new laws and policies and for an international movement focused on the International Labour Organization for recognition for homeworkers. As discussed in greater detail in Chapter 6 of this volume, a key part of this international campaign was the demand for better more effective legislation to protect homeworkers.

Part three: 1990s – partial re-regulation

A critical mass of homework and union organisations focused on homework had coalesced by the late 1980s (Boris and Prügl, 1996), and turned their attention to lobbying the ILO for a Convention on Homework. This resulted in an Experts Meeting on homework, held in 1990 at the ILO (International Labour Organization, 1990). Galvanised by the hope of an international standard, a coalition of homework groups, unions and researchers joined forces to improve homework visibility and protection. The International Labour Organization responded to concern about homework with a number of research studies and technical assistance programs supporting work with homeworkers in Asia. These efforts led eventually to formal discussions on the adoption of a Convention and Recommendation on Home Work, held at the annual conference of the ILO in 1995 and 1996 (International Labour Organization, 1996a).

The ILO prepared extensive background materials for the discussion leading up the conferences of 1995 and 1996; it drafted questionnaires and compiled the responses from employers, trade unions and governments and published detailed reports and conclusions of the discussions held at the two conferences in 1995 and 1996 (International Labour Organization, 1996b). The technical committee on homework at the ILO Conference discussed the draft Convention and Recommendation clause by clause, using the detailed preparation conducted by officers from the ILO in preparation for the debate. There was a great deal of debate about the ideal approach to regulating homework.

In addition to the extensive preparation conducted by the ILO itself, the meetings of the trade union group of the committee brought together a number of official delegates and observers with extensive experience of homeworking. Official delegations from Canada and Portugal, for example, included trade union leaders with experience of organising homeworkers. Others were able to participate as observers included as part of the delegation of international trade unions, as advisers or as observers. In this way, extensive practical experience was brought into the discussions. The text was finally adopted by a narrow margin in 1996.

The resulting framework was based largely on extending and adapting labour and social protection to homeworkers based on the standard employment relationship. Though the Convention and Recommendations propose that homeworkers should enjoy freedom of association, and the Recommendation included some measures that reflected a wider approach, the basis of the regulatory model is an atomised model of labour regulation: a bilateral relationship between an employer and an employee.

Regardless of the limitations of a legal approach, adoption of the ILO Convention on Home Work was an important step in winning recognition for homeworkers as part of the workforce, entitled to the same rights as other workers. The remainder of this part of the chapter will explore how effective such a framework can be in protecting the rights of homeworkers, even for those working for piece rates in a disguised employment relationship, who most closely resemble standard employees.

The standard employment relationship

Expressed simply, the standard employment relationship is a full-time continuous employment relationship where the worker has one employer, works on his or her employer's premises under the employer's direct supervision, normally in a unionised sector, and has access to social benefits and entitlements that complete the social wage (Vosko, 2007: 132). This system grew out of negotiations in industrialised countries based on the model of a male worker, in full-time and permanent employment over his lifetime, and, as Judy Fudge observes, the 'boundaries between home/market and public/private became deeply inscribed in contemporary legal doctrines, discourses, and institutions such that the initial jurisdictional classification appeared natural and inevitable and not political and ideological' (Fudge, 2014: 11).

The term 'employee' is used to refer to a person who performs services in an employment relationship. Frequently the terms 'employee' or 'worker' are defined by reference to a range of factors including dependency, subjugation or, in other cases, the idea of direction, authority, control or supervision (International Labour Organization, 2003). In most jurisdictions, the concept of an employee is contrasted with a self-employed or non-dependent worker. The 'employer' is generally defined as the person who employs the worker or uses the worker's services. The 'employer' is however an under-defined concept compared with the term 'worker' or 'employee', and has generally been understood as 'a corporate person' or single entity. The model envisages the employer as the conduit for a range of benefits and protections, in return for subjugation and dependence by the employee. It reinforces a marketised vision of labour regulation in which the freedom for an employer to contract with an employee is modified only marginally by state intervention. As such, it was a very different form of labour regulation from the Trade Boards of the early 20th century that targeted sweated work, discussed earlier in this chapter.

What this means is that, to the extent that homework arrangements mirror the employment norm most closely (where there is a long-term relationship with a single, identifiable employer), this model of regulation is most likely to improve the situation of workers. In contrast, the model is least likely to afford protection and mitigate labour market insecurity for those who do not resemble full-time, permanent, standard employees. For these workers, labour regulation based on the standard employment relationship risks reproducing gendered precariousness (Vosko, 2007). Because various social protections are linked to the contract of employment, exclusion from labour protections can have a considerable financial impact in terms of unpaid social security contributions and taxes.

Exclusion from such protections runs counter to most ILO Conventions, which generally refer to 'workers' rather than 'employees'. In particular, this approach is contrary to the ILO Declaration on Fundamental Principles and Rights at Work, which recognises the fundamental rights of *all* workers (International Labour Organization, 1998). It is also inconsistent with a number of important development goals (United Nations, 2015: goal 8). Over the last ten years, the ILO has undertaken a number of programs and discussions addressing key issues for all workers, including informal or precarious workers, regardless of employment status (International Labour Organization, 1998; International Labour Organization, 2006; International Labour Organization, 2011). These discussions have not necessarily been consistent in their approach. One strand has occurred around the employment relationship, while another has been specifically around informal work leading to the concept of Decent Work which has incorporated a much wider strategy of ensuring minimum standards than simply of extending laws and regulations to include informal work (International Labour Organization, 2013). The development of the Decent Work strategy occurred after passing of Convention 177, however, which has been highly influential in shaping national laws for homeworkers.

DEFINITION OF HOMEWORKER IN C177 – HOME WORK CONVENTION, 1996 (NO. 177)

For the purposes of this Convention:

a   (a) the term *home work* means work carried out by a person, to be referred to as a homeworker,

i   in his or her home or in other premises of his or her choice, other than the workplace of the employer;
ii   for remuneration;
iii   which results in a product or service as specified by the employer, irrespective of who provides the equipment, materials or other inputs used,

unless this person has the degree of autonomy and of economic independence necessary to be considered an independent worker under national laws, regulations or court decisions;

(b) persons with employee status do not become homeworkers within the meaning of this Convention simply by occasionally performing their work as employees at home, rather than at their usual workplaces;

(c) the term *employer* means a person, natural or legal, who, either directly or through an intermediary, whether or not intermediaries are provided for in national legislation, gives out home work in pursuance of his or her business activity.

Extension of the contract of employment to homeworkers following the ILO Homework Convention

Since the mid-1990s, laws passed in various countries extended the standard employment relationship to workers through various methods. As we discuss in greater length later in this section, the only example of legislation we know of which did not perform an extension of the contract of employment, and thus only covered dependent, disguised employment, was in Tamil Nadu, India.

Five methods of extending the standard contract of employment to homeworkers

Dependent homeworkers are treated as regular employees if they can prove that they have an employment contract or are an employee. They are then covered by national employment laws. Examples of this method include the United Kingdom (with some recent changes) and Brazil. In this model, there is no specific law on homework but specific clauses have been inserted in the main labour regulations to the effect that homeworkers are included if they are employees or workers (Government of the United Kingdom, 1996; Government of Brazil, 1943, last amended in 2017; Lavinas, Sorj, Linhares and Jorge, 2011).

CASE STUDY: UK

In the United Kingdom, the law differentiates between five categories: (1) employees, (2) workers, (3) professionals, (4) dependent entrepreneurs, and (5) self-employed persons. The legal definition of a 'worker' (section 230(3) **Employment Rights Act 1996**) is a broader category than that of an 'employee' (section 230(1) Employment Rights Act 1996), which is limited to 'an individual who has entered into or works under (or where the employment has ceased, worked under) a contract of employment'. The concept 'worker' covers those who work under a contract of personal service but do not provide that service in the capacity of a professional or independent business. Such workers are often referred to as 'dependent self-employed', a category that may include freelance workers, sole traders, home-workers and casual workers. Workers do not accrue all the benefits that employees enjoy. Employees are defined by reference to the fact that they are employed under a contract of service, self-employed persons have a contract for services. The mutuality of obligation test is applied in the UK to establish an employment relationship. It tests the existence of an obligation on the employer to provide work to the worker, and an obligation on the worker to perform work. This test has proved particularly pertinent to cases involving 'atypical workers', such as home-workers (1984).

Homeworkers are treated as employees/workers through a specific law that extends general labour laws to homeworkers. This method has been used in Albania, Bosnia and Herzegovina, Bulgaria, Belgium, Italy, France and Finland. The general aim of the legislation is to equalise rights and protection with other workers. Section 1 of Finland's Employment Contracts Act, No. 55 of 2001 specifies that 'Application of the Act is not prevented merely by the fact that the work is performed at the employee's home or at a place chosen by the employee, or by the fact that the work is performed using the employee's implements or machinery'. Amendments of the Bulgarian Labour Code in 2011 explicitly provide for homework, telework and temporary agency work as constituting work performed under an employment relationship (Articles 107b–107y of the Labour Code) (Government of Bulgaria, 1986, last amended 2016). Albania's 1995 Labour Code (Government of Albania, 1995), and Bosnia and Herzegovina's laws are similar (Government of Herzegovina).

Sometimes these amendments to the general labour law include provisions specific to homework (Government of Italy, 1973; Government of France, 2015). For example, in Italian law, the use of intermediaries is forbidden (Government of Italy, 1973: Art. 2(3)). In some Latin America laws, it is specifically forbidden to treat the employment relationship as though it is a trading or commercial relationship. The law on homework in Ontario, Canada, specifies that homeworkers have to be paid the minimum wage plus 10% to allow for their work expenses (Government of Ontario, 2000: Art. 23.1).

CASE STUDY: BELGIUM

Belgium's *Cour de Cassation* decided in November 1999 that the Act of 1978 concerning individual employment contracts did not apply to homeworkers. To remedy this omission, the **1996 Act on Home Working** extended the scope of application of the 1978 Act on Employment Contracts of 3 July 1978 to include home workers. Two factors distinguish the employment contract of home workers from a standard employment contract:

i   work is being performed from home or any other place chosen by the worker, and

ii there is no direct control or supervision of the worker.

The Act on Home Working covers traditional homework as well as newer forms such as telework. It pertains to workers who work under the authority of the employers – i.e. they are employees, not self-employed. It introduces a separate title VI (articles 119.1–12) dealing with homework in the Law of Employment Contracts of 1978 (Government of Belgium, 1978, amended 2011). Article 119.4 regulates the form of the contract, requiring that it is written and include the names and residences of the parties, the remuneration agreed and the basis for the calculation, additional reimbursement for working at home and the agreed schedule for completing the work.

There is a specific category of 'homeworker' and a law regulating homework and spelling out rights of homeworkers. In Germany and Japan (Government of Germany; Zenker, 2014; Government of Japan, 1970) implementation of the law is the responsibility of a dedicated inspectorate. In Portugal, a law specific to homeworkers was adopted which attempted a more flexible approach than was usual in order to attempt to match the precarious and irregular employment of homeworkers (Government of Portugal, 2009). Argentina has a long history of adopting laws specifically to protect homeworkers, as discussed earlier in this chapter. Thailand adopted the Home Worker Protection Act (HWPA) in 2010 which extended obligation on hirers to provide formal documentation of the homeworkers' work orders,[2] the extension of occupational and health safety measures to homeworkers,[3] and the application of minimum wages to homeworker remuneration.[4] The Act does not afford all the rights of employees to homeworkers.

CASE STUDY: ARGENTINA

Homework (*trabajo a domicilio*) is regulated by Law no. 12.713 which was passed in 1941 (Government of Argentina, 1941). It states that homework modality must be 'undertaken for a third party' (*ejecución por cuenta ajena*), restricting the purview of the Act to a relationship of dependency. The Act restricts regulation to those situations where what is produced by the homeworker belongs to 'a third party' (*ajeno*) and not to the homeworker (Jelin, Mercado and Zyczkier, 2001: 5). 'The employer is the person who carries out the manufacture or sale of goods, for profit or not for profit, and who hands out work to a homeworker, workshop owner or intermediary' (Government of Argentina (a)). The Act is wider than some other homeworker protections in that it recognises that homework may occur in either the worker's home (*el domicilio del obrero*) or a workshop-owner's home (Government of Argentina (b)) (Government of Argentina (c)).

As we discuss in greater detail later in this chapter, the Argentinian law is also unique in that it attributes special rights and responsibilities to the workshop owner (*tallerista*) as a worker and employer (*patrono*) (Jelin et al., 2001: 6).

Legislation specific to certain sectors of industry or geographical areas. Homeworkers in the embroidery sector in Madeira, an autonomous region of Portugal, are covered by legislation specific to the sector and geographical area (Regional Government of Madeira, 1993). Some countries have industry-wide legislation for homeworkers, for example, the garment sector in Australia (Government of Australia, 2010; Burchielli, Delaney and Coventry, 2014). In some sectors, the only provision is a ban on homework as exists in some states in the USA where homework in the garment sector is forbidden.

CASE STUDY: AUSTRALIA

Australia's homeworker protections are extensive, but only for the textile, clothing and footwear sector (except in South Australia where the law is not sector specific). The national level collective agreement (called a Federal Award in Australia) (Government of Australia, 2010) and amendments to the Labour Code (the Fair Work Act) contain deeming provisions that seek to overcome efforts to disguise relations of dependence; reverses the onus of proof so that employers have to prove that workers are not employees if they wish to avoid employment obligations; and provides for a registration system as a condition of engaging industrial outworkers, which helps regulators to monitor and track the use of home-based labour. Instead of using the word 'employer', the law uses the term 'principal' described as (someone who engages homeworkers, or whose products are made by homeworkers). The registration system in each state is overseen by a board of reference which is constituted of two union representatives, two principal representatives and one General Manager of the board.

Barriers to effective regulation of homework through laws based on the standard employment relationship model

A range of problems have been identified in the implementation of legislation intended to protect dependent homeworkers. These include calculating minimum rates when payment is made on a piece rate basis; ambiguity about status of homeworkers; danger of losing work as a result of challenging an employer; the burden of proof being often on the homeworker; determining who is the employer where work occurs in a supply chain; the difficulty of organising homeworkers and their lack of representation through formal trade unions; and resources put into a system of inspection. In most countries, significant 'enforcement gaps' persist. Dependent homeworkers have frequently had difficulty proving that they are workers, and even where extensive organising or advocacy has been undertaken, successful claims for employment rights have mainly been after a homeworker has already lost their work, or taking a claim against an employer has directly led to a loss of their work.

These difficulties are particularly acute for homeworkers who are based in their homes or in enterprises which operate wholly or partly in the informal economy. This is because of two related problems: first, it can be difficult to establish the existence of a contractual relationship without documentation (in other words, because of transience and/or informality), and secondly, the flexibility and fluidity of certain labour market transactions challenge the conceptual coherence of the employment relationship.

In some supply chains, a number of intermediaries may be acting in between the worker and the end user of the goods produced, or the 'co-ordinator' in a supply chain. Control or governance is often diffuse within the supply chain that the worker toils within. In previous chapters, we have described the trend in labour market practices towards 'vertical disintegration'. This trend is well documented in the garment sector, and is also found in footwear, electronics, mechanical engineering and other sectors.

Challenges exist to making claims in court even where a work relationship resembles a bilateral employment relationship, it can be difficult to prove the existence of a contract of employment in a court of law or to flesh out the content of that contract. Rarely is adequate documentation such as wage slips provided, wages may have been given in-kind or cash, and employers or their intermediaries frequently do not maintain registers and records, even though they may be required to do so. The court usually makes a determination, subject to a control test, about the nature of the work and relationship to the person giving the work. For example, in the United Kingdom, if a homeworker is told by her employer that she is self-employed, she must go to an employment tribunal who will decide whether she is an employee, a worker or self-employed, with consequent different levels of protection. A number of homeworkers have taken such cases and established that they are either employees or workers, and received compensation awards as a result (NGH, 2003; NGH, 2007). However, they almost invariably lose their supply of work when they challenge their employer in this way.

Enforcement gap

A more general problem is the lack of resources invested in any form of labour inspectorate appropriate to homeworkers by most governments (Davidov, 2006; Davidov, 2010). In most countries, there are currently inadequate resources available for general labour inspectors, let alone inspectors who can visit women in their homes. The many problems around inspection and implementation of the law are greatly increased when a chain of subcontracting is involved, even when this is within one national area.

Lack of representation through formal trade unions

As was described in Chapter 2 of this book, in many countries around the world, trade unions are not active in representing homeworkers. Important exceptions exist, such as the Textile, Clothing and Footwear Union of Australia. This lack of representation is sometimes due to legal barriers resulting from union membership being restricted to 'employees'. Union membership is therefore linked to the success in extending the contract of employment to homeworkers. In other cases, it is due to a view by union leaders that homeworkers are not true workers. At other times, it is because homeworkers do not form the basis of the membership – because they cannot afford union membership fees, for example – and thus are not an influential force within the union.

Because unions are the only representative body apart from the state with the power to enforce labour laws in most countries, with inspection powers, this limits third party monitoring and enforcement of laws. Furthermore, because unions are the only party to bargaining around labour conditions, homeworker interests are frequently not represented in collective bargaining and wage setting.

We can see, then, that the regulation of homework based on the contract of employment which followed the ILO Convention on Homework is consistent with the neo-liberal form of labour regulation in that it furthers a dualist labour market. This system protects only a core workforce of standard workers. Atypical, non-standard workers are largely without protections, or afforded far fewer protections. In order to be protected by labour law, homeworkers have to prove that they are standard employees. Yet, at the same time, the neo-liberal economic structures of vertical disintegration make homeworkers more and more peripheral from the core workforce who toil in lead firms in these increasingly complex supply chains. Because control in these supply chains is so diffuse, it is difficult for homeworkers to show sufficient dependence and subjugation on a single employer (Marshall, 2006; Marshall, 2010).

Part four: alternative models of labour regulation for homeworkers

Given the significant barriers to homeworkers realising rights and recognition based on the standard employment relationship model discussed in the previous section, how, then, can labour law be differently designed? This part of the chapter proposes various ways in which labour rights and protections can be extended to homeworkers through labour regulation. We discuss existing regulations, and show how these could be extended so as to provide stronger and more secure rights for homeworkers.

The options outlined in this section progress from the most readily realisable, and most consistent with the standard employment relationship, to those which depart more significantly from this model.

Documentation

Although administrative formality may seem like a negligible regulatory intervention, it functions as a pre-condition as the realisation of a range of other labour rights and entitlements. A robust formalisation process can be pivotal in empowering home-based workers to make distributional demands against the entities higher in their supply chains, described in the joint liability section later in this section. ILO Recommendation 184 urges that 'homeworkers should be kept informed of his or her specific conditions of employment in writing' (R184 article 5(1)), that 'competent authorities … should provide for registration of employers of homeworkers and of any intermediaries used by such employers' (R184 article 6). This is a limited intervention, though even identifying the identity of the immediate contractor, intermediary and employer at the first level and second level in the supply chain can assist homeworkers in the event that they need to make a claim for unpaid entitlements.

We propose that laws should go further than the lowest rungs of the supply chain, and instead require vertical mapping of the supply chain that the homeworker toils within. Vertical mapping is concerned with tracing the supply chains within which homeworkers' labour is embedded. As we have noted, supply chains may be global – such as those that are typical of the international garment industry, or domestic, involving only very short chains that do not articulate further than a local market. As an organising technique, vertical mapping is a central part of enabling homeworkers to see how their work fits into broader production patterns, but also in revealing possible organisational strategies or points of leverage (see Chapter 4).

Under Australian law, businesses that have homeworkers in their supply chains must lodge records of supply chains with the labour ministry's registration board, and the Textile, Clothing and Footwear Union, providing the contact details of all intermediaries and homeworkers. Such registration means that both the labour inspectorate, and unions, are able to identify homeworkers. From the labour inspectorate's perspective, registration is the most effective way that homeworkers can be located, and their workplaces/homes can be inspected. Without registration, labour inspectors must conduct the onerous task of identifying and visiting individual hirer establishments and demanding to see records of work contracts. From the perspective of worker organisations, registration processes could be pivotal in overcoming one of the key structural conditions that inhibits homeworker organising, namely, that homeworkers tend to be invisible within their spatially dispersed and private places of work.[5]

Translation of hourly rates to piece rates

Most homeworkers around the world are paid by the piece, not by the hour. There is an absence, however, of guidance within homeworker laws about how to translate national minima into piece rates. We propose that as long as piece rates are the norm, this is a crucial aspect of labour regulation for homeworkers.

In the UK, regardless of their employment status homeworkers now in principle have the right to minimum wages and the law establishes a procedure for establishing a fair piece rate. Piece workers are paid by the **number of items they produce** or tasks they perform rather than the number of hours they work. Often piece workers work at home or in factories. Piece workers must be paid at least the National Minimum Wage or National Living Wage for every hour they work unless they are a rated output worker for minimum wage purposes. If they are rated output workers, they can be paid a 'fair' piece rate for each piece produced or task performed. Homeworkers must receive at least the minimum wage, even if they pass some of the work to others, such as close friends or family.

Deeming provisions

ILO Convention 198 on the Employment Relationship provides guidance for policymakers on how to define an employment relationship, suggesting broadening the scope of the application of national labour laws. Though this provides important guidance, it does not overcome the most significant barriers to enjoyment of labour rights for homeworkers. As discussed in the previous section of this chapter, a barrier to the extension of labour regulation to homeworkers is the requirement that homeworkers show that they are employees. One way to achieve this is by changing the onus of proof on the employer and 'deeming' that homeworkers are employees. Deeming provisions state that homeworkers are employees in legislation and have the same rights as an employee. The effect is to reduce ambiguities in law around the status of a homeworker. The Australian labour code – the Fair Work Act – includes such provisions for apparel homeworkers (at section 789BB). This section provides that even where workers are 'contractors' who have registered businesses, for example, they are still considered employees for the purposes of the provisions covering homeworkers. Recent legislation on minimum wages in the UK has proved that this approach is more effective than when the onus of proof remains with the homeworker. Deeming provisions eliminate the need for homeworkers to apply to a court to determine the employment status of the homeworker, and therefore increase the likelihood that a homeworker will be protected and have rights in law.

A supply chain approach to apportioning responsibility for homeworker rights

A further barrier to extending protections to homeworkers is the problem of diffuse control within contracting relations. While the employment contract makes only those who directly contract with the worker responsible for their rights and conditions, we propose that a better approach would be to develop a supply chain approach to apportioning responsibility for homeworker rights and protections. Various jurisdictions provide joint and several liability along the chains of production, making all those involved in the production or sourcing of goods jointly responsible for workers' conditions. This was not provided for in the ILO Convention on Home Work. However, the Recommendation that accompanied the Convention made a reference to joint and several liability for payment only where intermediaries are involved but without reference to subcontractors or international chains (International Labour Organization Recommendation on Home Work, VI, 19). Indeed, the capacity to bring claims against buyers and parties high in the supply chain is a vital step in reducing downwards pressure from within supply chains and promoting living wages. As Alessandra Mezzadri points out, 'a solid theorization of labour contracting networks, and of the role of the [sub]contractor, or the broker, in shaping them, can only start from the recognition of the great heterogeneity and differentiation of these networks' (Mezzadri, 2014: 137). She highlights that subcontractors may themselves be 'aspiring workers', or else 'petty capitalists' participating in a joint enterprise aimed at extracting labour surplus from the working poor not as mere intermediaries but as key players (Mezzadri, 2014). In the latter instance, such a role 'far exceeds intermediation, and extends instead to the organization of entire segments of the production and labour process' (Mezzadri, 2014).

Most homeworker laws do not recognise the varied roles that parties in supply chains play in any given supply chain linked to homeworker production. However, there are examples of labour laws that at least provide some means for homeworker to bring claims against parties other than the direct contractor/employer.

Australian labour laws allow apparel homeworkers to address the uneven distribution of risk throughout the supply chain under Division 3 of the Fair Work Act (the Australian Labour Law Code). Homeworkers can make claims against parties higher in the supply chain for unpaid pay including remuneration, leave, superannuation or reimbursements.[6] No requirement exists to show knowledge or intentional participation (Marshall, 2006; Marshall, 2010; Marshall, 2014; Rawlings and Howe, 2013).

Argentinian legislation recognises these distinctions in the roles of intermediaries and regulates the 'workshop owner' (*tallerista*). National legislation attributes to this one person the dual categories of the work-giver/work-taker relationship. Workshop owners are considered to be 'homeworkers' (*obrero a domicilio*) in the sense of taking work handed out by an employer; meanwhile, since they have products manufactured in their home by workers under their supervision, they are also considered to be 'employers' (*patrono*) who are subject to the obligations contained in law and in the regulations governing those who give out work (Jelin et al., 2001: 6).

Other countries distribute liability throughout supply chains in various ways. Law No 20 123 in Chile establishes vicariously liability for 'recipient companies' for the obligations of contract workers. 'Hot Goods' or 'Hot Cargo' provisions in Section 15(a) of the U.S. *Fair Labour Standards Act* provide another model for joint liability.[7] The Californian 'brother's keeper' law makes liable for labour code violations anyone who enters 'into a contract or agreement for labor or services … where the contract agreement does not include sufficient funds to allow the contractor to comply with all applicable local, state and federal laws or regulations governing the labor or services to be provided' (California Labor Code s.2810(a)). Similarly, the state of New York does so when the manufacturer knew or should have known of the contractor's violations (New York Labor Law, s 345a(1)) (Anner, Blair and Blasi, 2013–2014: 41). These examples show that vicarious liability can be achieved by various means.

There are also historical precedents for mechanisms of this type. Barraud de Lagerie argues that improvements to the conditions of outsourced labour have historically occurred when legislatures have recognised the necessity of regulating the entire integrated productive chain, rather than just the direct employer–employee relationship. Changes to articles L. 721–1ff. of the French Labour Code in 1957 extended liability for home-based worker conditions to principal employers in a manner similar to the Australian expansion of the definition of employer (Barraud de Lagerie, 2013: e8).

The point is to avoid arguments about employment status which preoccupy labour lawyers and instead develop an assignment of 'responsibility" commended by Alan Hyde (2012: 84). In place of the contract of employment, we propose the development of a supply chain approach to regulating homework with its acknowledgement that there may be a number of entities above the homeworker that leverage control over the labour process, and against whom it would be fair and reasonable to make distributional claims. These claims could be proportionate to the control wielded by the party over the homeworker's conditions. Such a supply chain approach to regulating homework would conduct the *redistribution* described in the gender justice approach framing this book. Given that often the 'co-ordinator' or responsible entity in a supply chain is in a different country from the homeworker or the place where the harm occurs, supply chain approaches are more effective achieving gender justice if they are extra-territorial in nature.

Decouple labour protections and employment

ILO Recommendation No. 198 on the Employment Relationship provides guidance for policymakers on how to define an employment relationship, suggesting the broadening the scope of the application of national labour laws. A more radical option for reforming labour law aims to lessen the hold of the employment contract on the form of labour market regulation so as to overcome the barriers to the enjoyment of rights described earlier in this chapter. The Supiot Report (Supiot, 1999), for example, proposes establishing a common labour law, certain branches of which could be developed to cover different kinds of work relationships. According to this report, the scope of labour law should cover not only wage work, but also other types of contract entailing the performance of work for others and even non-market forms of work. It contends that labour market regulation should encompass breaks in paid work and changes of occupation.

Living wage legislation

It is close to 100 years since the Treaty of Versailles (1919) was enacted creating the International Labour Organization and enshrining the principle of a living wage in international law (Shotwell, 1934). The Declaration concerning the aims and purposes of the ILO (Declaration of Philadelphia, III) stresses the 'solemn obligation of the ILO to further among nations programmes that will achieve … a minimum living wage to all employed and in need of such protection'. The right to a living wage is, in addition, established in the following ILO declarations and conventions:

- Constitution of the ILO, 1919: Preamble of the Charter;
- Convention 131 and 156 (indirectly) and Recommendations 131 and 135 (indirectly);
- ILO Tripartite Declaration of Principles concerning Multinational Enterprises and Social Policy in 2006;
- ILO Declaration on Social Justice for a Fair Globalization, 2008. *(International Labour Organization, 2008)*

A number of other international instruments call for the payment of a living wage to all workers in some sense, without employing the phrase 'living wage'.

The adoption of 'minimum wages', regardless of employment status, is a common method of decoupling pay rates from employment status found around the world. This has occurred in India (Chen, Jhabvala and Lund, 2002). Uruguay, likewise, has established minimum wages for a range of previously informal workers such as domestic workers. Less than 20,000 domestic workers were registered in 2005 compared with over 60,000 in 2012 (Marshall and Fenwick, 2016: 195). In the UK, the National Group on Homeworking campaigned from 1984 for equal rights for homeworkers with other workers. As a result of the campaign, when a national minimum wage was introduced in the UK in 1998 specific provisions were set for homeworkers to be covered by the minimum wage (UK Department for Business, 2017; UK Department for Business, 2018). This means that homeworkers, whatever their employment status, now in principle have the right to minimum wages. The system for enforcing minimum wages depends on individual complaints, in the first place, and secondly through an industrial tribunal where the complaint cannot be resolved satisfactorily. As a consequence, there are still problems with homeworkers fearing loss of their work if they make a complaint and the current system makes it difficult for a collective approach to be adopted. Problems of representation and enforcement can therefore be seen to be a further crucial aspect of labour regulation to be remedied in the design of minimum wage legislation.

Despite their widespread adoption, in many countries, government-set minimum wages fall far short of what many estimate to be a living wage (Bolwell, 2016: 9; Ethical Trading Initiative, 2008: 1). According to one calculation, half of all countries set a minimum wage at less than the global poverty level (Bolwell, 2016: 9). We suggest, therefore, that the emphasis be on the provision of living wages, using calculations developed by the International Labour organization (Anker, 2005; Anker and Anker, 2017). There is no reason why approaches which set minima regardless of employment status cannot be coupled with the assignment of 'responsibility' through the development of a supply chain approach to regulating homework proposed in the previous section.

Trade and Welfare boards

The Trade or Welfare Board model seen in the early 20th century in many countries of the world continues to act as a useful model for regulating homework. In India, such boards continue to act as a powerful means of providing rights and recognition for homeworkers and other informal workers. For example, in Tamil Nadu, both dependent and own-account garment workers can register with the Manual Workers Welfare Board, pay a small contribution and in return are entitled to social welfare benefits (Government of Tamil Nadu). The Bidi Boards are a further example of a regulatory approach based on Welfare boards.

The example of the Indian boards is important because it demonstrates that a number of the difficulties in improving conditions for homeworkers can in practice be overcome. Firstly, the boards overcome barriers created by the standard employment relationship described earlier in this chapter, as both dependent and own-account workers can be registered and are included in the provision of a number of benefits, without a complicated procedure to prove employee status. Secondly, the model set by the Welfare Board in Tamil Nadu and of the Bidi Boards (Government of India, 1976) shows that there are alternative ways to financing welfare schemes than the normal means of funding social insurance seen in most states around the world.

The Bidi Board is implemented by the labour departments of the central and state governments. Bidi companies (of branded items) must contribute Rs 2 per one thousand bidis to the welfare board. Workers pay Rs 25 to become members of a Board, and the central and state governments make varying contributions. This overcomes the problem of collecting taxes throughout complex supply chains. Instead of the relevant national authority attempting to track down direct employers or subcontractors to pay taxes, the Bidi Boards tax the end user. The payment of benefits to workers is decoupled from the employment relationship. Workers are paid regardless of who the employer is and board funds have been used for broader social welfare such as hospitals and housing projects (Agarwala and Herring, 2008: 102–103).

A third feature of the boards that is particularly important is that there is a degree of decentralisation and localisation, with workers' representatives being present on the board to have their voices heard. This can be seen in representation of home-workers by SEWA in the Bidi Workers Welfare Board. A fourth feature is that it is not only for homeworkers, but for atypical and informal workers more broadly.

Unlike the UK Trade Boards of the early 20th century, these boards do not set wages. However, there are examples of boards that play this extended role in India. The Mathadi Boards set up under The Maharashtra Mathadi Hamal and other Manual Workers (Regulation of Employment and Welfare) Act, 1969 are an important example which has been explored by one of the authors elsewhere (Marshall, 2014). Concern exists that by regulating work through separate mechanisms like these, instead of universal labour laws, these workers are treated as a second class of worker. However, the success of these models in improving the conditions of workers suggests that targeted regulatory approaches of this type might be required to overcome the barriers described earlier in this chapter.

Conclusion

At the beginning of this chapter, we identified two contradictory trends associated with the regulation of homework. We celebrated the considerable achievement of homeworker organisations in achieving the regulation of homework in many countries around the world after the passing of ILO Convention 177, based on the extension of the contract of employment. We described the application of labour regulation to homeworkers, focussed on two aspects of the gender justice approach: recognition and rights. The regulatory achievements of local and international homeworker networks (described in Chapter 6 of this book) can be understood as part of the women's movement's destabilisation of the gender contract (Fudge, 2017: 5). This instability presented an opportunity for a more egalitarian division of unpaid domestic and paid labour, and, with it, recognition and rights for homeworkers who were previously invisible. Yet in the same period that homeworker laws have been in place, income inequality has increased markedly around the world. This inequality has numerous causes. One set of causes relates to the undermining of worker orga-nisations and the decline of the standard employment contract as the cornerstone of labour protections for working people. This was thanks to the success of the neo-liberal project, coupled with the re-organisation of work as the vertical disintegration of production occurred.

Where does this leave homeworkers? In Harry Arthurs' prescription for how to revitalise labour law, he asks us to

> imagine that labour law had never been invented, or having been invented, that it had become one aspect of the broader field of legal learning and prac-tice entitled 'the law of economic resistance' that addressed not only relations

of employment, but all economic relations characterized by comparable asymmetries of wealth and power.

(Arthurs, 2013: 584)

In the final section of this chapter, we have proposed a range of regulatory forms that might lead to stronger forms of gender justice for homeworkers than that seen through the expansion of the contract of employment to include homeworkers. ILO Conventions are crucial tools of the weak, and Convention 177 was a vital step in the recognition of homeworkers. However, it appears to have limited the imagination of policymakers in many countries as they grapple with how to improve the lives of homeworkers. We propose that it is time to experiment with new forms of regulation that better match the realities of working arrangements and redress the distributional asymmetries of wealth and power in the supply chains in which homeworkers toil. We propose that it is time for a new legislative program that assigns responsibility for homeworker rights through supply chains. This would go some way toward visibilising homework and aiding the stronger bargaining power of homeworkers against capital as it is currently organised (in supply chains). We further address the question of how power and wealth can be more fairly redistributed to facilitate gender justice in Chapter 7.

Notes

1 True to Churchill's word, the UK Trades Board Act 1909 was a modest reform covering the following workers employed in factory *or* workshop or at home in four industries, covering only 175,000 workers, which accounted for about 10 per cent of the overall female workforce outside of domestic service and agriculture: (1) Ready-made and wholesale bespoke tailoring; (2) Paper box-making; (3) Machine-made lace and net finishing and mending or darning operations of lace curtain finishing; (4) Certain kinds of chain-making (Wise, 1912).
2 HWPA article 9; R184 article 5.
3 HWPA chapter 4; C177 article 7.
4 R184 articles 16.
5 Note that this is not true in all cases: in rural areas where homework is clustered, identifying homework through relational ties and local knowledge is a much simpler task.
6 Section 789 CA, CB and CC stated that when a TCF outworker performs TCF work for a person, and that responsible person does not pay an amount that is payable, in relation to the TCF work, an indirectly responsible entity (higher in the supply chain) is liable to pay the unpaid amount.
7 29 U.S.C. § 215(a)(1) (2012) ('[I]t shall be unlawful for any person to transport, offer for transport, ship, deliver, or sell in commerce, or to ship, deliver, or sell with knowledge that shipment or delivery or sale thereof in commerce is intended any goods in the production of which any employee was employed in violation of section 206 [statutory minimum wage] or 207 [maximum hours]').

References

(1984) Nethermere (St.Neots) Ltd v. Taverna and Gardiner
(1993) Wage Councils to be Abolished (United Kingdom). *Commonwealth Law Bulletin* 19.

Adler, N. and Tawny, R.H. (1909) *Boy and Girl Labour*. London: Womens Industrial Council.

Agarwala, R. and Herring, R.J. (2008) *Whatever Happened to Class? Reflections from South Asia*. Routledge: London

Allen, S. and Wolkowitz, C. (1987) *Homeworking: Myths and Realities*. Houndmills, Basingstoke, Hampshire and London: Macmillan Education.

Amsterdam, S. (1982) The National Women's Trade Union League. *Social Service Review* 56: 259–272.

Anker, R. (2005) *A New Methodology for Estimating Internationally Comparable Poverty Lines and Living Wage Rates*. Geneva: Policy Integration Department Statistical Development and Analysis Group International Labour Office.

Anker, R. and Anker, M. (2017) *Living Wages Around the World: Manual for Measurement*. Northampton, MA: Edward Elgar.

Anner, M., Bair, J. and Blasi, J. (2013–2014) Toward Joint Liability in Global Supply Chains: Addressing the Root Causes of Labor Violations in International Subcontracting Networks. *Comparative Labor Law & Policy Journal* 35: 1.

Anonymous. (1938) The British Trade Boards System. *Monthly Labor Review (pre-1986)* 46.

Arthurs, H. (2013) Labor Law as the Law of Economic Subordination and Resistance: A Thought Experiment. *Comparative Labor Law and Policy Journal* 34(3): 585–604.

Barraud de Lagerie, P. (2013) The Wages of Sweat: A Social History Perspective on the Fight Against Sweatshops. *Sociologie du Travail* 55, Supplement 1: e1–e23.

Bean, J.S. and Boyer, G.R.. (2009) The Trade Boards Act of 1909 and the Alleviation of Household Poverty. *British Journal of Industrial Relations* 47: 240–264.

Blackburn, S. (1988) The Problem of Riches: From Trade Boards to a National Minimum Wage. *Industrial Relations Journal* 19: 124–138.

Blackburn, S. (2009) Curse or Cure? Why Was the Enactment of Britain's 1909 Trade Boards Act so Controversial? *British Journal of Industrial Relations* 47: 214–239.

Bolwell, D. (2016) To the Lighthouse Towards a Global Minimum Wage: Building on the International Poverty Line. *Australian Bulletin of Labour* 42: 1–37.

Boris, E. (1994) *Home to Work: Motherhood and the Politics of Industrial Homework in the United States*. New York: Cambridge University Press.

Boris, E. and Daniels, C.R. (eds) (1989) *Homework: Historical and Contemporary Perspectives on Paid Labor at Home*. Urbana: University of Illinois Press.

Boris, E. and Prügl, E. (eds) (1996) *Homeworkers in Global Perspective: Invisible No More*, New York: Routledge.

Burchielli, R. and Delaney, A. (2016) The Invisibilization and Denial of Work in Argentinian Garment Homework. *Relations Industrielles/Industrial Relations*, 71(3): 468–493.

Burchielli, R., Delaney, A. and Coventry, K. (2014) Campaign Strategies to Develop Regulatory Mechanisms: Protecting Australian Garment Homeworkers. *Journal of Industrial Relations* 56: 81–102.

Chen, M., Sebstad, J. and O'Connell, L. (1999) Counting the Invisible Workforce: The Case of Homebased Workers. *World Development* 27: 603–610.

Chen, M.A., Jhabvala, R. and Lund, F. (2002) *Supporting Workers in the Informal Economy: A Policy Framework*. Geneva: ILO.

Churchill, R.S. (1969) *Winston S. Churchill*, Boston: Houghton Mifflin.

Davidov, G. (2006) Enforcement Problems in "Informal" Labor Markets: A View from Israel. *Comparative Labor Law & Policy Journal* 27: 3–26.

Davidov, G. (2010) The Enforcement Crisis in Labour Law and the Fallacy of Voluntarist Solutions. *The International Journal of Comparative Labour Law and Industrial Relations* 26(1): 61–81.

Deakin, S. and Green, F. (2009) One Hundred Years of British Minimum Wage Legislation. *British Journal of Industrial Relations* 47: 205-213.

Deakin, S. and Wilkinson, F. (1991) Social Policy and Economic Efficiency: The Deregulation of the Labour Market in Britain. *Critical Social Policy* 11.

Deakin, S. and Wilkinson, F. (2005) *The Law of The Labour Market: Industrialization, Employment and Legal Evolution*. Oxford: Oxford University Press.

Ethical Trading Initiative. (2008) Living Wage: Make It a Reality. ETI Conference 2008 Workshop 5.

Freeman, D. (2004) Homeworkers in Global Supply Chains. *Greener Management International* 43.

Fudge, J. (2014) Feminist Reflections on the Scope of Labour Law: Domestic Work, Social Reproduction, and Jurisdiction. *Feminist Legal Studies* 22: 1–23.

Fudge, J. (2017) The Future of the Standard Employment Relationship: Labour Law, New Institutional Economics and Old Power Resource Theory. *Journal of Industrial Relations* 59: 374–392.

Government of Albania. (1995) Code of Labour, Law no. 7961 of 12 July 1995, as amended.

Government of Argentina (a). Act 12.713

Government of Argentina (b). Reg.118.755/42.

Government of Argentina (c). Regulatory Decree 118.755/42.

Government of Argentina. (1941) Ley 12713, 'Reglamentacion del Trabajo a Domicilio', *Boletín Oficial*, 15 November 1941, Número: 14171.

Government of Australia. (2010) Textile, Clothing, Footwear and Associated Industries Award 2010.

Government of Belgium. (1978, amended 2011) Loi relative aux contrats de travail.

Government of Brazil. (1943, last amended in 2017) Consolidação das Leis do Trabalho, approved by Decreto-Lei no. 5.452 de 1 de maio de 1943, amended by Lei no. 13.467 de 2017.

Government of Bulgaria (1986) Labour Code.

Government of California, United States of America (2011) Labour Code.

Government of France. (2015) Arrêté du 24 mars 2015 relatif aux critères ouvrant droit à l'aide au poste et à la subvention spécifique dans le cadre des recrutements opérés directement par les entreprises adaptées et les centres de distribution de travail à domicile.

Government of Germany. Homework Act.

Government of India. (1976) Beedi Workers Welfare Fund Act 1976 (No. 62 of 1976) as amended and with references to cases up to 1990.

Government of Japan (1970) Industrial Homework Law.

Government of Ontario, Canada. (2000) Employment Standards Act, 2000, S.O. 2000, c. 41.

Government of New York, United States (1921) Labor Law.

Government of Portugal. (2009) Ley núm. 101/2009 de 8 de septiembre por la que se establece el régimen jurídico del trabajo a domicilio1.

Government of Tamil Nadu. Manual Workers Welfare Board. http://www.labour.tn.gov.in/Labour/tnmanwork.jsp

Government of Thailand (2010) Home Worker Protection Act.

Government of the United Kingdom. (1996) Employment Rights Act.

Government of Herzegovina. Labor Law, *Official Gazette of FBiH* no. 62/15.

Hockling, G. and Wilding, M. (2004) Made at Home: British Homeworkers in the Global Supply Chain. *Oxfam Policy and Practice: Private Sector.* 53–90.

Hyde, A. (2012) Legal Responsibility for Labour Conditions Down the Production Chain. In J. Fudge, S. McCrystal and K. Sankaran (eds) *Challenging the Legal Boundaries of Work Regulation*. United Kingdom: Hart Publishing, 83–99.

International Labour Office. (1999) *Report VI: Dilemma of the Informal Sector.* Geneva: ILO.

International Labour Office. (2002) Decent Work and the Informal Economy, Report VI. In *International Labour Conference, 90th Session.*

International Labour Organization. (1990) Documents of the Meeting of Experts on the Social Protection of Homeworkers. *Social Protection of Homeworkers.* Geneva.

International Labour Organization. (1996a) C177 – Home Work Convention, 1996 (No. 177). Geneva.

International Labour Organization. (1996b) Delegates to International Labour Conference to Focus on Child Labour, Homeworkers and the Unemployed.

International Labour Organization. (1996c) Recommendation on Home Work, VI, Geneva.

International Labour Organization. (1998) ILO Declaration on Fundamental Principles and Rights at Work. Geneva.

International Labour Organization. (2003) The Scope of the Employment Relationship. *International Labour Conference, 91st Session, Report V, fifth item on the agenda.*

International Labour Organization. (2006) Extending Labour Law to All Workers: Promoting Decent Work in the Informal Economy in Cambodia, Thailand and Mongolia.

International Labour Organization. (2011) 100th ILO annual Conference decides to bring an estimated 53 to 100 million domestic workers worldwide under the realm of labour standards.

International Labour Organization. (2013) Decent Work Indicators.

Jelin, E., Mercado, M. and Wyczykier, G. (2001) *Home Work in Argentina.* Series on Homeworkers in the Global Economy. Geneva: International Labour Office.

Kahn-Freund, O. (1949) Minimum Wage Legislation in Great Britain. *University of Pennsylvania Law Review* 97.

Krinsky, J. and Simonet, M. (2012) Déni de travail : l'invisibilisation du travail aujourd'hui. Introduction. *Sociétés contemporaines,* 87 : 5–23.

Lavinas, L., Sorj, B., Linhares, L and Jorge, A. (2011) *Home Work in Brazil: New Contractual Arrangements.* Geneva: International Labour Office.

Marshall, S. (2006) An Exploration of Control in the Context of Vertical Disintegration, and Regulatory Responses. In C. Arup, J. Howe, R. Mitchell et al. (eds) *Labour Law and Labour Market Regulation: Essays in the Construction, Constitution, and Regulation of Labour Markets and Work Relationships.* Sydney: Federation Press, 542–560.

Marshall, S. (2010) Australian Textile Clothing and Footwear Supply Chain Regulation. In *Human Rights at Work: Perspectives on Law and Regulation,* eds C. Fenwick and T. Novitz. Oxford: Hart, 555–585.

Marshall, S. (2014) How Does Institutional Change Occur? Two Strategies for Reforming the Scope of Labour Law. *Industrial Law Journal 43:253-285.*

Marshall, S. and Fenwick, C. (2016) *Labour Regulation and Development.* London/Geneva: Edward Elgar/ILO.

Mezzadri, A. (2014) Backshoring: Local Sweatshop Regimes and CSR in India. *Competition & Change* 18: 327–344.

NGH. (2003) *Organising Homeworkers in the UK: An NGH Interim Report on Trade Union Policies and the Collective Organisation Needs of UK Homeworkers.* Leeds: National Group on Homeworking, 70.

NGH. (2007) *Subject to Status: An Investigation into the Working Lives of Homeworkers in the UK.* Leeds: National Group on Homeworking.

OECD. (2011) *OECD Guidelines for Multinational Enterprises.* OECD.

Portes, A., Castells, M. and Benton, L.A. (1989) *The Informal Economy: Studies in Advanced and Less Developed Countries.* Baltimore, Md.: Johns Hopkins University Press.

Prügl, E. (1999) *The Global Construction of Gender, Home-Based Work in the Political Economy of the 20th Century:* Columbia University Press.

Rawlings, M. and Howe, J. (2013) The Regulation of Supply Chains: An Australian Contribution to Cross-National Legal Learning. In K.V.W. Stone (ed.) *Rethinking Workplace Regulation: Beyond the Standard Contract of Employment*. Russell Sage Foundation.

Regional Government of Madeira. (1993) Regional Decree-Law no. 12/93M of 23 July 1993.

Shotwell, J.T. (1934) *The Origins of the International Labor Organization*. New York: Columbia University Press.

Starr, G. (1993) Minimum Wage Fixing: An International Review of Practices and Problems. In *Office IL* 2nd ed. Geneva.

Stone, K. and Arthurs, H. (2013) The Transformation of Employment Regimes: A Worldwide Challenge. In K. Stone, and H. Arthurs, (eds) *Rethinking Workplace Regulation: Beyond the Standard Contract of Employment*. New York: Russell Sage Foundation, 1–20.

Supiot, A. (1999) Introduction. In *Au-dela de l'Emploi, Transformations du Travail et Devenir du Droit du Travail en Europe*, ed. A. Supiot. Paris: Flammarion, 7–24.

Thornton, M. (1991) The Public/Private Dichotomy: Gendered and Discriminatory. *Journal of Law and Society*, 18: 448–463.

UK Department for Business EaIS. (2017) *National Minimum Wage Law: Enforcement – Policy on HM Revenue & Customs Enforcement, Prosecutions and Naming Employers who Break National Minimum Wage Law*. UK Department for Business EaIS, UK.

UK Department for Business EaIS. (2018) *National Minimum Wage and National Living Wage: Calculating the Minimum Wage*. UK Department for Business EaIS, UK.

United Nations. (2015) Sustainable Development Goals.

Vosko, L.F. (2007) Precarious Part-Time Work in Australia and in Transnational Labour Regulation: The Gendered Limits of SER-Centrism. *Labour & Industry: A Journal of the Social and Economic Relations of Work* 17: 45–70.

Waltman, J. (2000) *The Politics of the Minimum Wage*. University of Illinois Press.

Wise, E. (1912) Wage Boards in England. *The American Economic Review* 2: 1–20.

Women's Industrial Council. (1907) Report of the National Conference on the Unemployment of Women. London.

Women's Industrial Council. (1907–1908) Eight Reasons Why You Should Support the Council. London.

Women's Industrial Council. *Annual Report* 1894–1912. London.

Zenker, I. (2014) *Basics of German Labour Law: The Employment Relationship*. Germany: Books on Demand.

4

CORPORATE SOCIAL RESPONSIBILITY

Improving homeworkers' recognition?

Introduction

Coinciding with the shift in production to the global south, corporate social responsibility (CSR) initiatives began to emerge in the 1990s. CSR is a general term covering different aspects of a corporate business practice and relate to a range of issues including employment practice, environmental impact or issues such as corruption and charitable giving. These voluntary mechanisms have emerged at a time of deregulation of labour standards, increased informalisation and feminisation of production. We analyse CSR from a gender perspective, arguing that the systemic undervaluation of women's social reproductive role, which explains the undervaluing of their productive role, can also explain characteristic approaches to CSR as observed in most initiatives in relation to homework. This aligns to recognition in the gender justice framework since it is about access to the work-related right of freedom of association and collective bargaining. The representation dimension overlaps with issues discussed under recognition about acknowledging, valuing and visibility of homework, as a means to representation and rights.

In this chapter, we refer to CSR to encompass company, industry and broader multi-stakeholder initiatives that incorporate standards, policies and obligations around human and labour rights to workers in their supply chains. We discuss CSR in relation to the rising expectations of civil society for company responsibility towards workers in their supply chains, whether national or global, and the development over the last 20 years of codes of conduct and multi-stakeholder initiatives. We examine the limitations of the voluntary nature of these codes, and their capacity to address the position of women workers, specifically informal women homeworkers. We draw on three case examples from India, Pakistan and Australia to demonstrate various types of CSR responses to homework in the garment and footwear sectors, these approaches we categorise as prohibition, tolerance and engagement (Delaney, Burchielli and Tate, 2017). Further, we explore the use by firms of compartmentalisation as a method to create boundaries against which they can shield themselves from addressing systemic labour rights problems in the supply chain. These, we argue, allow them to avoid taking responsibility for the practices of their own making, such as corporate purchasing practices that undermine CSR aims and impact negatively on workers across the supply chain.

We use the term supply chains rather than value chains or production networks for simplicity, and to avoid distinctions and assumptions between the ways of categorising and analysing global production we find in some literature. The use of subcontracting in a range of industry sectors is now more common than ever before. The common separation of workers from their direct and apparent employers (lead firms), using subcontracting, labour hire and recruitment agents, often transnational, with many intermediaries and other forms of informal employment, leaves workers beyond the traditional forms of labour regulation.

Our analysis begins with the reality that CSR voluntary mechanisms now occupy a significant part of the transnational regulatory space. The effectiveness of voluntary mechanisms such as corporate codes and multi-stakeholder initiatives therefore, remain an important consideration as do the tensions between legal standards and voluntary standards. To date, no effective global regulatory schema to regulate global labour in global corporations has emerged to regulate how transnational corporations (TNCs) function across global boundaries. Global corporate led CSR responses may contribute to the failure of, or obstruct, the development of homework recognition and potential for collective agency. This is explored in the following sections.

The rise of voluntary CSR and homework

Increasingly, corporations are dependent upon women workers to supply goods and services across global production geographic sites, yet their CSR initiatives remain focused on the corporation's priorities – tending to consist of profit driven outcomes or one-off CSR projects aimed to depict the corporation in a good light, as a display of its 'good' corporate citizenship (Jenkins, 2001; Mezzadri, 2014). Feminist scholars have highlighted the link between gender and labour rights and argue for the inseparability of production and reproduction (Pearson, 2014; Prieto-Carrón, 2014). Social and industrial organisation persists in separating these functions, such that work, paid and unpaid, undertaken in the home is unvalued, undervalued and devalued (Boris and Prügl, 1996; Mohanty, 2006). We have already argued extensively that homework is undervalued and devalorised work, and survival is a challenge for homeworkers due to poverty and low wages (see Chapter 2). Simultaneously, traditional labour strategies, such as union representation, are often unavailable to them (Balakrishnan 2002; Elias 2004).

Homeworkers commonly are not employed directly by large corporations, but through a chain of subcontractors and intermediaries, the immediate employer often classifying homeworkers as self-employed (Burchielli, Delaney, Tate and

Coventry, 2009). Lead corporations deny responsibility as the homeworkers work for a subcontractor, not the company itself, and the subcontractors are often small businesses who themselves are not making large profits. The large companies control the supply chain and can extract the most value and profit from low wages of homeworkers (Elias, 2004; 2011; Hale and Wills, 2005).

There is a long history of NGO and campaign groups working to make links between workers' conditions in the global South and brands in the global North. For example, SOMO, based in the Netherlands, was one of the pioneers to publish studies on poor labour conditions in global brand supply chains, including homeworkers in Europe; they argued that brands should be responsible for the conditions of their subcontractor's workers. This campaign approach contributed to the establishment of Clean Clothes Campaign, a global campaign focused on improving workers' conditions in the global garment sector. In the UK, Women Working Worldwide conducted a solidarity campaign with women garment workers in the Philippines that led to one company taking responsibility for its subcontractor there (Hale and Turner, 2005). Another strand was solidarity campaigns with garment workers highlighting that exposure of bad conditions and the discovery that boycott of retailers was not what women workers in producer countries wanted; this provided impetus for campaigns to engage with companies to persuade them to improve conditions. Campaigns were sometimes effective in strategies to 'name and shame' companies to address the homeworkers' situation, but in general large companies refused to take responsibility for labour conditions of workers not directly employed by them. This changed in the 1990s as, parallel to homeworker campaigns, Unions, other labour rights groups, media organisations and non-government organisation (NGOs) highlighted abuses of labour rights in the production of goods in the global South. These were then sold in the North, particularly in the fashion industry (Seidman, 2005; Brooks, 2007).

In the 1990s, the trend for companies to take some responsibility for their supply chains, even when they were subcontracting to independent companies, took hold. The main tool used was a code of practice, usually drawn up and monitored by the company itself. Auditing of supplier factories would be conducted internally and sometimes by third-party auditors (Jenkins, Pearson and Seyfang, 2002). Later developments involved the establishment of multi-stakeholder initiatives – for example, in the US, the Fair Labour Association (FLA), and in the UK, the Ethical Trading Initiative (ETI).

Homeworkers were usually ignored in the corporate codes and most companies denied that homeworkers were in their supply chain (Brill, 2002; Delaney, Burchielli and Connor, 2015. Homeworker groups continued campaigning and learned from each other's experience; in 1990s garment unions in Canada (UNITE) and Australia (TCFUA) took up the issue of homeworking. These unions combined different elements of legal protection and voluntary codes; union organising and supply chain monitoring, and social movement campaigning to put pressure on brand names. In Toronto, Canada, for several years the union prioritised building an association of homeworkers linked to the union structure, public campaigning on brands and the implementation of existing laws, though this approach was not sustained (HomeNet, 1998). In Australia, the TCFUA adopted a similar approach, organising of homeworkers, negotiating rights and collective bargaining approaches through a code of practice and legislative protection for garment homeworkers. The union worked closely with the community campaign, FairWear, established with the specific purpose of addressing the exploitation of garment homeworkers in the fashion industry. The important development which emerged from this campaign approach in Australia and discussed later in this chapter was the Homeworkers' Code of Practice and legislation specific to garment homeworkers (Rowbotham, 1999; Burchielli, Delaney, and Coventry, 2014).

Globally there are few examples of CSR initiatives that highlight and recognise the needs of homeworkers. Homework groups such as HomeNet international, the European homework group, the UK national group on homework, and later, Homeworkers Worldwide and the Federation of Homeworkers Worldwide, have made an important contribution toward raising awareness of homework issues and CSR, promoting the inclusion and recognition of homework. Apart from the ILO convention on Homework (no. 177) passed in 1996, and later inclusion of a homework policy in the Ethical Trading Initiative (ETI), few companies or multi-stakeholder initiatives (MSIs) have incorporated the principles of the ILO Convention on Homework into CSR policy and practice. There are few examples of CSR codes and multi-stakeholder mechanisms that incorporate the international standards of the homework convention or demonstrate recognition of homework. We further explore this in the next section through a focus on gender, homework and CSR.

Gender, homework and CSR

Homework is frequently viewed by corporations and governments as 'just women's work', that justifies devalorising this work, and in turn, making space away from the likelihood of recognition, legal protection and worker rights (Barrientos and Evers, 2014; Pearson, 2014; Burchielli and Delaney, 2016).

Homeworkers are predominantly women, are the least organised and experience the greatest disadvantage because of limited legal recognition and protection, and the disintegration of national policies, laws and services, which further distance the possibility of such protection. Current trends in world trade are towards the opening of markets for manufactured goods and services at the same time as priority is given to export markets by national governments in developing countries (Delaney, Tate and Burchielli, 2016). This creates a situation in which low paid women own account homeworkers often experience loss of their traditional markets at the same time as they lose access to land and raw resources. In Tamil Nadu, for example, agricultural land was decimated due to tanning operations, which forced people off the land and into footwear factories and homebased work in order to survive. Artisan and traditional craft workers may face downturn, as machined products become available at cheaper prices.

Simultaneously, homeworkers rarely have access to technology or infrastructure, credit or training to enable them to shift to other means of earning an income. For rural homeworkers, this is aggravated by the impact of globalisation on agriculture particularly the traditional subsistence sector. While most trade agreements are negotiated behind closed doors, with little attention paid to the impact on workers in general, homeworkers and other informal workers are still unrecognised and without a voice in the processes, despite the existence of strong social movements active around the issues affecting workers (Lambert and Herod, 2016). The absence of any recognition of the value and benefits of reproductive activities of women further highlights the divide between the public and private spheres (Burchielli and Delaney, 2016). Business focuses on what is economically valuable to them. In contrast, women workers have a broader notion of benefits in both the private and public spheres, and what they consider economically and socially valuable. The universal undervaluing of women's unpaid labour denies the benefits that women's social reproductive labour contributes to society and the extent that production activities are dependent upon women performing these tasks (Elias, 2011; Prieto-Carrón, 2014).

The notion of women's social reproductive contribution is rarely considered by corporations or governments since it is assumed that unpaid labour performed by women will continue to support the 'productive' roles beneficial to capital and society (Mies, 2014). Such unpaid reproductive activities function to ensure the household functions, that the family is fed, children are born and reared, that future workers are nurtured and educated, and other caring responsibilities are fulfilled (Mies, 2014; Delaney, 2017; Boeri, 2016). When women are working from home, they are forced to combine the two roles, one of producing goods for employers to accumulate value and profit, and the other, tasks that we define as socially reproductive such as child rearing, educating children, caring for relatives, growing food and rearing animals, unpaid housework, and work in the community. These reproductive tasks are not attributed 'economic or social' value and have implications in how their women's reproductive and productive work is undervalued (Elias, 2011; Mies, 2014).

The lack of recognition of women's reproductive role extends to where women workers are consulted by corporations in the development and implementation of corporate codes (Pearson, 2007; Prieto-Carrón, 2014). The focus of CSR and private corporate mechanisms often encompass global standards such as the ILO core labour standards, yet in practice, corporate CSR responses frequently focus on a narrow range of labour conditions, such as child labour and the worst forms of labour abuse, often driven by consumer demands and firm responses (Pearson, 2007; Pearson, 2014). Frequently, corporate led CSR has been accused of being a corporate managed agenda that focuses on what benefits the corporation; the use of language or narrative of CSR; the propensity to be voluntary; the lack of independent monitoring; lack of sanctions or penalties for non-compliance; and lack of accountability around the practices that contribute to human and labour rights abuses, for example corporate purchasing practices and failure to address conditions beyond the first tier supplier (Mezzadri, 2012; Locke, Rissing and Pal, 2013).

The struggle to be paid fair remuneration for work performed in the home has often centred on the nature of the relationship of the homeworker to the person giving the work. National laws have often excluded homeworkers from receiving wages equivalent to workers performing the same work in a factory location because homeworkers have not been included in the definitions of worker within the labour legislation (Boris and Prügl, 1996; Burchielli, Buttigieg and Delaney, 2008) (see Chapter 3). Traditionally workers would be represented by unions, but in many countries, workers face employer and government supported repression and lack the rights associated with freedom of association – the very same rights enshrined in many CSR codes and mechanisms. For homeworkers, this is even a greater challenge since they are rarely collectively organised. Few unions have been willing or able to focus organising efforts to get to the point where groups such as homeworkers have a seat at the table and sufficient leverage to negotiate with national or global corporations.

Available evidence suggests that corporations have been unwilling to acknowledge the existence of homeworkers in the production chain (Burchielli et al., 2014; Delaney et al., 2017). The lack of recognition of homeworkers' involvement in production, the failure to recognise them as workers and the failure to take responsibility for all workers involved in production entrenches their position as exploited workers, creating barriers to exercise freedom of association (Prieto-Carrón, Lund-Thomsen, Chan et al., 2006; Lund-Thomsen and Coe, 2013). At the same time, CSR strategies reinforce gender stereotypes based upon concepts that women will accept any work at any price, without complaint (Bair, 2010). Many assumptions exist relating to work provision to women workers, wages and other conditions (Balakrishnan, 2002). A dominant narrative has emerged from government, brands and employers that giving women jobs will contribute to their economic empowerment (Prügl, 2017). The logic that follows from this is that homeworkers should be grateful for any work they have (this issue is explored in Chapter 5). The 'jobs at any price' rationale translates to reluctance by governments and companies reluctant to acknowledge and uphold respect for freedom of association. This ultimately only comes about when unions are able to initiate collective solutions to improve workers' income and work situation. Contractors and intermediaries reinforce this narrative by low piece-work rates to homeworkers on a 'take it or leave it' basis; that's the price they are paying. The ILO rejects these jobs at any price view, as outlined in the decent work and informal employment conclusions (ILO, 2002; ILO, 2016).

CSR in relation to homework requires consideration of numerous factors. First, issues exist concerning the more traditional approach of labour regulation at the national level by states and at the transnational level, and whether these can be complemented by CSR initiatives. Options such as multi-stakeholder agreements may not adequately address homeworkers' priorities. A second issue relates to the nature of national and international laws and policies that can operate in tandem to support legal standards when they exist. These factors are critical to the extent that homeworkers may be recognised, and their work considered worthy of protection and value (HWW, 2004).

A third factor considers access to land and raw resources as important: home-workers commonly collect and supply natural products, such as seaweed, shea butter, medicinal herbs, rattan, mushrooms or berries to TNCs for export to use in food, medicinal, cosmetic and furniture products. Many of these women live in isolated areas and are dependent on traders who buy their products for low prices; they are not generally dependent waged workers, but rather own-account workers, economically dependent on global supply chains and markets. Other, more indirect mechanisms that impact on women homeworkers' lives and work include the priority given to the use of natural resources, such as bamboo or leather for export production which deprives own-account homeworkers of sources of raw materials, or at best increases the cost; the destruction of natural resources, for example, by logging and loss of water resources leading to loss of raw materials; the subsidies given by governments to production for export at the expense of production for local markets (HWW, 2004). Whilst we focus on the broader features of CSR and in particular the impact on dependent homework in national and global supply chains, the interrelation of own-account workers is relevant, since they are becoming more frequently entwined with global brands and markets. The broader argument around CSR – that it can help to address poverty alleviation in the global South – needs to be considered in light of the fact that CSR may cause more harm than good and potential benefits are scarce (Prieto-Carrón et al., 2006). We explore this further in the next section.

The limits of CSR

CSR has become a mainstream response to make corporations accountable and supply chains more transparent to enable labour conditions to be better monitored. There are large numbers of corporations involved in many different types of CSR initiatives globally. However, many commentators note that the majority of cor-porations interpret CSR responsibility to mean 'do good' in the community, and to support philanthropic causes, rather than to take seriously the task of ensuring they do no harm through the production or provision of goods and services they supply for profit (Utting, 2005).

Another argument suggests that the discourse of CSR has been diverted by corporations to advance their own agenda of gaining reputational outcomes, which explains their failure to address labour rights abuse or environmental harm. They focus instead on maintaining profit maximisation strategies (Mezzadri, 2012; et al., 2013). Corporations are often involved in CSR programs to reduce public pres-sure, to engage in reputation saving, and to attain some social legitimacy. They can assert their ethical CSR credentials to push their competitive advantage and entry to new markets (Mezzadri, 2014). Considerable debate amongst civil society actors, unions and labour rights activists has focused on the limitations of CSR programs and the effect, if any, they are having on worker conditions (Jenkins et al., 2002).

Generally, studies conclude that very few workers benefit from CSR initiatives and that they fail to deliver any improvement in relation to process rights such as freedom of association and collective bargaining (Barrientos and Smith, 2007; Rennie, Connor, Delaney & Marshall, 2017). Some evidence is available that CSR can support improvements in outcome standards such as occupational health and safety, but the instances of improvements have only been found to be relevant to workers in first-tier supplier factories. Even these improvements are rare (Barrientos and Smith, 2007). This has important implications for workers in second and third-tier suppliers and home-workers, rarely acknowledged by lead firms and suppliers as being part of the workforce (Barrientos, 2013; Delaney et al., 2016). Overall, CSR is not linked to improvements for informal workers at the furthest fields of the supply chain. Homework is more likely to be ignored (Barrientos, Gereffi and Rossi, 2011). The lack of worker involvement at any stage of the negotiation of conditions of codes is also of concern (Jenkins, 2001; Preto-Carrón, 2014), as is the lack of gender awareness around CSR initiatives, and the failure to address the concerns of the feminised workforce particularly in labour inten-sive sectors such as footwear, garments and electronics.

The extent that CSR initiatives tackle the substantial causes of labour rights abuses in the supply chain needs to be considered. Recent debates look at the 'sphere of influence' of firms, and their 'complicity' in so far as it is recognised that firm's actions have consequences beyond their immediate stakeholders. These reach to their supply chains, local communities and the natural environment (IILS, 2008). Further, various analysts suggest that firms have yet to incorporate ethical principles in their core busi-ness (Vilanova, Lozano and Arenas, 2009). Research suggests there is a diminishing responsibility towards stakeholders such as workers in the supply chain (Locke et al., 2013; Ruggie, 2015; Ruggie, 2018). Failure to respect freedom of association and ensure living wages, the rights enshrined in most codes and multi-stakeholder initia-tives, indicates a fissure between CSR ethical principles and the extent that such standards become part of corporate practice in the supply chain (Mezzadri, 2012).

A glaring lack of any CSR approach to improving labour standards then is visible. Research into global value chains demonstrates that CSR efforts from lead firms can lead to some technical improvements, concerning first tier suppliers, referred to as economic upgrading. The debate around economic and social upgrading asserts that as suppliers in host countries increase their technical and economic standards improved social conditions of workers as articulated by the ILO decent work con-cept will become evident (ILO, 2002). (This is discussed further in Chapter 5.) Evi-dence indicates that workers in the first-tier supplier factories have some, though limited, benefits as a consequence of economic upgrading (Barrientos et al., 2011). In contrast, in labour intensive industries such as garments, textile and footwear, work-ers beyond the first-tier supplier are often employed in contract, home-based and forced labour arrangements (Delaney and Tate, 2015; Delaney and Connor, 2016; Barrientos et al., 2011) where there are no CSR efforts.

Compartmentalisation, firm purchasing practices and CSR

A crucial criticism of CSR concerns global firm purchasing practices, based on out-sourcing. These often lead to numerous subcontracting events, such as where a brand may outsource to one, first-tier supplier, who may then outsource to numerous factories and small enterprises that may then further subcontract to homeworkers. Firm purchasing practices are frequently cited in the garment industry, then, as a contributor to the failure to implement CSR. Corporations may place 'ethical' conditions on their suppliers, while at the same time leaning on them for the lowest price and imposing tight delivery deadlines. Although CSR efforts are intended to apply throughout transnational corporations (TNCs), including their supply chains, it is recognised that the various business units of a given firm may behave differently in terms of CSR: 'one subsidiary of an organization [may] engage in a responsible activity, while another may act irresponsibly; TNCs may be simultaneously socially responsible and irresponsible' (Strike, Gao and Bansai, 2006: 851).

The duplicitous personality of the global corporation is frequently revealed by the tensions between different firm departments/functions: the CSR team may place 'ethical' or CSR compliance conditions on their suppliers, and at the same time, the buyer team squeezes suppliers to attain the lowest purchase price (Barrientos, 2013; Locke et al., 2013; Anner, 2018). Misalignment between departments/functions is a recognised structural problem in the strategic management literature. However, we refer to this moral or values-based contradiction as a form of compartmentalisation, and suggest that it is a method corporations intentionally utilise. It allows them to separate certain practice and behaviour from ethical standards or separate different functions within the organisation, such as purchasing practices that can be distanced from adherence to ethical principles through CSR compliance or regulatory obligations (McBarnet, 2009; Rozuel, 2011). Compartmentalisation quarantines responsibility, by being selective in how profit maximisation is prioritised over other ethical norms and responsibilities (MacIntyre (1984) cited in MacNeil and O'Brien, 2010: 16). We use the term compartmentalisation here to describe a technique created by the corporation to avoid having to address systemic problems related to worker labour rights and human rights across the supply chain, as illustrated by the barriers it creates for homeworkers in terms of decent work conditions, including a living wage.

A further example is corporate action to protect brand reputation at the expense of addressing workers and human rights' abuses, and workers having a transparent process for redress. Compartmentalisation is commonly practiced through brands being selective in how they may address a systemic problem, for example, paying below minimum wages or failure to respect freedom of association. Rather than putting in place CSR measures across the whole organisation and supply chain, they compartmentalise their CSR strategy and response, often to one supplier or section of the supply chain. Many examples exist in the garment industry illustrating firms focusing on a single supplier that may have not complied with the firm's CSR standard. The typical firm response is to end the contract, and subsequently declare they are no longer working with the particular supplier, so have no case to answer to.

Compartmentalisation of responsibility results in the failure by brands to improve wages and address core concerns of workers at all levels of the supply chain. Due to its influence across the supply chain, compartmentalisation ultimately impacts negatively on women workers' capacity to develop agency and any potential to propose an agenda that meets their social production priorities; particularly for home-workers (Barrientos, 2013; Mezzadri, 2012; Delaney, Burchielli & Connor 2015. Compartmentalisation highlights the elite power and control of corporations over the supply chain, while creating the pretence that they are doing their best to address labour rights abuses – typically in response to poor audit reports, or civil society agitation over worker's rights in the supply chain. Even when positive CSR responses are initiated by brands, usually in response to labour campaigns or media exposure of labour rights abuses, their responses always align with the compartmentalisation principle that enables prioritising reputation concerns over worker conditions. In the following section, we discuss three types of CSR responses to homework.

Corporate CSR responses to homework in the supply chain

Corporate led codes, or multi-stakeholder initiatives, as primary approaches to CSR rarely make mention of homeworkers – despite the accumulating evidence that home workers are often producing goods which are sold by TNCs (Brill, 2002; Jenkins, 2001; Barrientos, 2013; Delaney et al., 2016). The linkages across own account work and global supply chains have increased; work produced by home-workers often involves traditional crafts and handiwork such as embroidery, weaving and carpetmaking turning out products sold directly to markets and local buyers. For example, fashion brands may source embroidery work from homeworkers to be incorporated into contemporary garment styles. The shift in own account work being sourced in supply chains creates a case for brands to distinguish the use of homework as an occasional occurrence. Yet, brands are less likely to recognise the presence of dependent homework embedded in their supply chains, because workers are working for small contractors on piece rates (Delaney et al., 2016).

The other reason that brands are less likely to acknowledge homework in the supply chain is that, universally, homeworkers' work conditions have been found to be well below minimum labour standards. Since CSR is commonly used to respond to corporate reputational concerns and vulnerabilities in corporate supply chains, public reporting of adverse conditions on labour rights can encourage brands to shorten supply chains and bring work into factories where working conditions are easier to monitor, thus adversely affecting homeworkers who may lose their livelihoods (Brill, 2002; Delaney et al., 2016). Despite the problems besetting homework, we do not advocate for the abolition of homework, which is frequently the only available source of income for homeworkers; rather we advocate for bringing equality and justice to homework.

Reports of child labour have frequently been linked to homework, and many examples can be found where brands have distanced themselves from instances of child labour by ending the relationship with a supplier, which has negatively impacted on homeworkers. A consequence of brands associating homework with child labour is that they have become reluctant to acknowledge homework in their supply chain (Delaney et al., 2016). Homeworkers face a constant threat from corporations to relocate; in this way, corporations regularly use 'economic blackmail' against workers trying to use collective bargaining to improve their conditions (Brill, 2002). Codes may assist in acknowledging the rights of homeworkers on paper, but this would not necessarily negate corporations using economic threats, such as ceasing to outsource the work, or to relocate production to another area. Furthermore, most codes are implemented in a 'top down' fashion, with minimal consultation or involvement on the part of the factory workers, let alone those within the informal sector, working in small workshops or in their own homes (Jenkins, 2001; Pearson, 2007).

Codes and publicity around CSR often focus on consumer-weighted issues – for example, environmental issues, and the worst forms of exploitation such as child labour, rather than the problems prioritised by the workers making the products (Seidman, 2005; Collins, 2003). Homework advocates suggest it is vital that workers have a say in formulating campaigns; in articulating their demands to companies, and in code development (HWW, 2004). From the perspective of homeworkers, the major limitations of CSR include: initiatives that are not binding or difficult to enforce; initiatives that are not linked to national and local union organising efforts (Stevis and Boswell 2007), which may limit their scope and application to informal workers; and initiatives which do not equally apply to all business units in the supply chain (Delaney et al., 2016), as in compartmentalisation. Corporate CSR responses to labour rights abuse currently contribute to maintaining the status quo by failing to address the poor working conditions of homeworkers. We explore this further in the following section through examples of three types of CSR approaches to homework.

Common CSR approaches to homework

In previously published research, we discussed two common CSR responses by lead corporations to the detection of adverse conditions associated with homework in the supply chain (Delaney et al., 2016). One response is *rejection*: the firm *rejects* homework either through 'cutting and running' or banning homework, resulting in homeworkers losing their work and income. The rejection response is often demonstrated through prohibiting contractors to give work to homeworkers or insisting that all work is performed within factory premises or small workshops. The second type of response is *tolerance*, where the corporation accepts that homework is present in the production chain without making any improvements to the workers working conditions. We propose that both rejection and tolerance are inadequate to address the work condition of homeworkers (Delaney et al. 2016). We propose a third CSR approach – engagement – to explain CSR responses beyond tolerance. The following examples highlight features of these three approaches.

CSR response: prohibition of homework in the Football stitching in Pakistan and India

Before campaigns against child labour in Sialkot, Pakistan and in Jalandhar, India, in the late 1990s, homeworkers made up the main workforce assembling footballs (BBA, 2009; Lund-Thomsen, 2013). Work was given out, both directly, by factories and through subcontractors to men and women to do at home. The homeworkers were paid low piece-rates and were not given any of the benefits of factory work such as social insurance, bonus or pension rights. Many children in these families worked alongside their parents to increase production and income. Following the campaigns against child labour, some brands insisted that work should be brought into factories and homework abolished, as child labour was associated with homework (thus demonstrating rejection). A more common solution was to establish stitching centres, which became the norm in both Sialkot and Jalandhar – the rationale for stitching centres being they could more easily be monitored for child labour (ILRF, 2010).

Major issues and findings identified in these studies relate to the loss of work for homeworkers, particularly for women, due to the emergence of the stitching centres. Many of the homeworkers lived in villages, at a distance from the city. If work was brought into the factories away from the village, it was impossible for homeworkers to travel there for work (Delaney et al., 2017). Reports compiled by a number of NGOs refer to 12 relatively large stitching centres, set up by Saga Sports in response to Nike's demands for child-free production (STC, 1997; STC, 1999). The workforce of 4,500 were mainly men although eventually, one women-only centre was established with transport provided for women from surrounding villages. However, it was reported that the majority of the women workers at this centre were young, single women. Women with children were not in a position to leave their homes and travel to the centres (PILER, 2009). The implications for the women homeworkers unable to relocate to the stitching centres were a loss of work and income and becoming more invisible by being vulnerable to even more precarious and lower paid work available through subcontractors (Delaney et al., 2017).

The corporate responses to media reports of child labour in soccer stitching which led to the establishment of stitching centres have become a standard response by many companies. Stitching centres meet the risk management requirements of brands and offer contractors a means to retain a low paid workforce. From our research, we have found no evidence of stitching centres, and the banning of homework, leading to improvements in workers conditions; rather, they have invariably further disadvantaged women homeworkers. The response to prohibit homework and establish stitching centres was a response by brands to avoid taking responsibility for the low wages and poor working conditions that contributed to child labour. This example demonstrates a form of compartmentalisation to justify lack of action in improving wages for homeworkers and workers in stitching centres. Further, brands' failure to consult the homeworkers indicates a failure to incorporate gender dimensions within CSR strategies. Importantly, banning homework has become a standard response by many brands following public exposure about homework and/or child labour.

CSR homework responses: prohibition, tolerance and engagement – responses to child labour and the footwear supply chain in India

The footwear sector in Tamil Nadu supplies many UK, European and North American firms, and the industry is structured around homework, where the process of hand-stitching shoes continues to take place alongside machine production. Certain styles of shoes require this kind of hand-stitching work which is commonly carried out by homeworkers all over the world (HWW, 2008).

Women homeworkers described very low piece rates (Delaney et al., 2015), earning an average of 5 rupees per pair of shoes and usually making 10 pairs per day, giving them an average earning of 50 rupees a day. The women estimated needing a minimum of 150 rupees a day for the family to survive, hence their 50-rupee daily earnings fell significantly short of basic requirements for survival. They also indicated that they did this work because they were poor, with little choice and did not have benefits that factory workers received.

> We don't have any other choice, so we choose to do this work, so I cannot complain to anyone. We have to do this work because of the poverty in our families.
>
> *(Mathivathane homeworker 2013)*

> We don't have any rights. No, there is no such thing, if we have problems we women just get together and talk that is all. We don't come under the union; if we work then we get paid our wages. I don't know anything about the company. I am just at home doing this work.
>
> *(Prathanya homeworker 2011)*

> We have to bear the (medical) expenses ourselves, we have to shell out our own money, we have heard that those who work in the company have health insurance and a pension. But we don't have any of these things. We don't get those benefits, those working in the companies get, he (the middle man) just goes around and collects the uppers and we stitch it; that is all.
>
> *(Gokilamani homeworker 2011)*

In 2011, an international NGO published a report on the Indian leather footwear industry highlighting the existence of child labour in production, stating that child labour was a common phenomenon and that it was very likely that Indian children were participating in the production of hand stitched shoes for the European market (HIVOS, 2012). Despite the significant evidence that the Indian footwear industry is structured around and is reliant on homeworkers for production, manufacturers tended to downplay the existence of homework and to trivialise its contribution to production, representing homework as a minor and insignificant part of their production process, demonstrating tolerance of homework (Delaney et al., 2017). One supplier interviewed in 2015 stated they had opened a stitching centre so that they could showcase to brands 'effective monitoring' of homework and ensure no child labour was involved, but they also admitted that they continued to subcontract work to intermediaries that they acknowledged used homeworkers.

Global footwear brands identified by the Stop Child Labour campaign (SOMO, 2012; HIVOS, 2012; HIVOS, 2013) indicated that they were addressing homework and child labour issues in their production network. However, a number of brands formally responded to claims of child labour in their supply chains. One brand, Deichmann, a member of the Business Social Compliance Initiative (BSCI), sourcing mainly in the North of India, had requested that all work be moved into stitching centres. Similar to an earlier response by Nike in relation to soccer balls in Sialkot and Jalandhar, the establishment of stitching centres was driven by corporate risk concerns (thus demonstrating homework rejection), such as protecting brand reputation, and prioritised suppliers meeting normative CSR standards. More recently Business Social Compliance Initiative (BSCI) and Danish brand ECCO have declared homework a 'critical issue' which determines it to be 'high risk' leading to them placing a ban on homework (Tate, email communication 2017). For example, BSCI recommended that homework be treated as a critical issue – 'high risk' since it is likely to be linked to child labour (BSCI, email communication 2013).

In response to the Stop Child Labour report, examples of international brands sourcing from Tamil Nadu, South India, demonstrated a different response to homework. The responses by these brands, while limited, can be considered a step forward compared to those that respond by prohibiting homework. A relatively few brands, acting in conjunction with the BSCI industry initiative in response to the Stop Child Labour report, appeared to have openly recognised the use of homework as part of the footwear production process in India, therefore, showing some tolerance of homework. Following from this, they began to formulate some responses, for example, conducting stakeholder meetings and initiating a small research project on homework.

There is no evidence of any improvement in homeworker's conditions coming out of these brand initiatives; it is rather business as usual. The primary change identifiable in the Tamil Nadu footwear production region was some suppliers establishing stitching centres. Suppliers stated that stitching centres were the best way to respond to brand concerns about child labour (Delaney, 2016). One supplier had established over 20 stitching centres, located in the villages where the women lived; women were therefore able to attend the centres without risk of losing their work. We spoke to several homeworkers working in the stitching centres. Overall, they reported that the piece rates and other conditions were the same, except that they went and sat together in the centre to work. This further confirms the adoption of a tolerance approach. Similar to the soccer ball CSR response, it demonstrates brands' compartmentalisation of CSR aims, prioritising reputational concerns, but a failure to implement minimum wages amongst homeworkers.

In another example of the footwear sector in Tamil Nadu, one brand chose a different course of action. Homeworkers Worldwide (HWW) had published a report on the Tamil Nadu footwear homework situation and requested the ETI take up the issue (HWW, 2017). Little came out of approaches to the ETI, but they were able to begin a dialogue with Pentland, a footwear brand and an ETI member. Pentland, having previous experience in the soccer ball case, and in response to reports detailing homeworkers' poor working conditions, agreed to participate in a supply chain project with HWW in the UK, and CIVIDEP a broad-based NGO based in Bangalore, India. The pilot supply chain project's current aim is to work with one supplier to map the supply chain and explore options for ensuring homeworkers receive equity of wages and other benefits.

The footwear homeworkers supply chain pilot is one of the most positive initiatives adopted by a brand in recent times. In comparison, other UK based footwear brands and ETI members have done little in response to reports of homework labour rights abuses in their supply chains (HWW et al., 2016). The homework supply chain project demonstrates a CSR engagement approach because it sets out to address fundamental causes for homeworkers' low pay and other equity issues (Pentland, 2017; HWW, 2017). The project began in 2016, and it is too early to claim this initiative as a success. It does, however, show promise. By collaborating with HWW and CIVIDEP, Pentland is supporting local work with homeworkers to enable their participation in the project.

An important element of the development and ongoing progress of the homework supply chain project is the involvement of stakeholders: the brand, suppliers, and transnational and local NGOs. The local NGO is working to support the homeworkers to develop collective strategies to participate in the process. The supply chain project has begun to trace the supply chain and to document working conditions with the purpose of increasing transparency. It is exploring the possibility of how to formalise the link between the homeworker and the factory, regularising work and improving piece-rates.

From the NGO's perspective, the priorities and aims of the project include improving recognition of homeworkers in the industry and actively involving them in production so that they have a say in the conditions of their work; tracing agents and homeworkers and documenting their situation; assessing what a fair piece-rate should be and improving transparency in the supply chain so that homeworkers know where the work comes from; and, forming a collective organisation of the homeworkers. The project is also anticipated to contribute to introducing social protection measures for homeworkers and focus on homeworkers health concerns (HWW, 2017).

The homeworker supply chain project brings together various types of expertise. HWW brings experience in organising homeworkers; developing training materials; developing policy and experience in working with brands, regulators and local NGOs. HWW has within its international network researchers with expertise on gender, supply chains, informal employment and homeworking. CIVIDEP has expertise in supporting the establishment of a new garment union; is familiar with working with brands, suppliers and regulators and can support new organising of homeworkers. The combination of transnational and national experience of both HWW and CIVIDEP presents a complementary force to collaborate with willing brands to achieve substantive improvements for homeworkers.

In addition to the supply chain project, our research on homework in the footwear sector in Tamil Nadu (Delaney, 2016) led to industry stakeholders being invited to a meeting in December 2017, bringing together brands, suppliers, NGOs and homeworkers in the footwear sector for the first time. Discussion over two days, including homeworkers addressing the meeting, and working in small groups with suppliers and brands, led to the meeting endorsing the establishment of a Tamil Nadu multi-stakeholder, industry working group to focus on three key issues: establishment of a fair piece-rate for homeworkers, improving work conditions in stitching centres, and expanding the supply chain project to other suppliers and brands. If this multi-stakeholder group's work progresses and the supply chain project is successful, it will become a positive model for improvements in homeworkers' work conditions and support for freedom of association and collective bargaining. Therefore, indicating the potential for homeworkers to utilise multi-stakeholder engagement processes that may improve awareness about their representation and rights, but there remains some way to go for this to be realised.

While this is an encouraging development in CSR engagement, it is currently confined to one small part of the supply chain. The challenge for brands working on such initiatives is to extend the knowledge and lessons gained to other parts of the supply chain and move beyond compartmentalisation and siloed responses. We suggest it requires more than a self-regulatory regime for compartmentalisation to be overcome. The following example in the garment sector in North India highlights the limitations of CSR initiatives when there is failure to change purchasing practices.

A CSR homework response: tolerance – the ETI homework project in North India

Evidence to date indicates that CSR initiatives have had little impact in relation to regulating and improving conditions of homeworkers. However, some positive and other initiatives with mixed outcomes exist that have incorporated homework protection into code mechanisms. The Ethical Trading Initiative (ETI) based in the United Kingdom has developed policy on homework and been involved in specific projects focusing on homework in production networks. The ETI example highlights the fact that policy development can improve recognition of homeworkers. Equally, corporations may adopt a homeworker policy, but it will only exist at the level of tolerance, with little done to address the injustices that homeworkers experience.

An ETI pilot project in the North of India brought together a number of retailers, exporters, subcontractors, trade unions, and labour rights organisations to collaborate in a pilot project with people doing embroidery for the export garment sector. This project has demonstrated clearly the large numbers of homeworkers involved in the sector, and the many problems associated with their employment. It has begun to trace parts of the supply chain in order to identify homeworkers and improve their recognition (Delaney, 2016; Mezzadri, 2016). An NGO for homeworkers was established in Bareilly, where thousands of embroidery and embellishment homeworkers are found. Reports appeared of moderate increases in piece-rate payments, although well below the minimum wage rate. In addition, some improvements in subcontractors paying homeworkers the piece-rate owed to them were achieved through use of a 'yellow book' where homeworkers recorded the amounts they sewed, and payment owed (interviews with brands and NGOs 2014; 2015).

While many companies remark that it is almost impossible to trace the supply chain beyond the first tier – in particular, where homeworkers are involved – a positive consequence from the ETI homework project demonstrated that the supply chain can be mapped. Participants in the project mentioned various improvements for homeworkers over the life of the project, such as access to crèche facilities, the formation of self-help groups, and training and registration with government artisanal schemes. Some brands opted for working with the Self-Employed Women's Association's (SEWA) controlled distribution centres as a solution to monitoring conditions (Archana and Dickson, 2017). However, interviews with a number of the brands and NGO participants in the project indicate this is not the best way to solve the issue of homeworkers' pay and conditions in general (Delaney, 2016). After the project ended, many of these brands ceased providing work to the SEWA distribution centres, citing reasons such as lack of capacity and quality issues for discontinuation of orders (Delaney, 2016). Brands also shifted production to areas closer to Delhi for reasons of being easier to audit. Consequently, some women homeworkers experienced loss of or reduction in work (Delaney, 2016).

Some ETI corporate members have introduced homework policies, for example, Monsoon, (2008). The Monsoon policy states that there is acceptance of homework; it includes a broad definition of homework and a commitment to improving labour conditions of homeworkers by the corporation and by suppliers. Whereas the intention of the policy is clear, uncertainty remains in how the ETI base code can deliver any improvements. The ETI project was conducted over ten years, and some progress was made with addressing issues for subcontractors, documenting the supply chain, but was not able to assert sufficient pressure for brands (lead firms) to commit to guaranteeing payment of minimum wages to homeworkers, despite a commitment through the ETI to pay a living wage (Delaney, 2016).

The UK-based ETI has developed a base code that companies can implement across national and international supply chains. Compared with other similar CSR initiatives, the key achievement of the ETI in relation to homeworkers has been that the ETI has recognised homework as an important equality and justice issue, because of the consistent input into the initiative over the last decade from Homeworkers Worldwide and the National Group on Homeworking in the UK.

The ETI's tolerance approach contributed to an increased recognition of homework in the supply chain but failed to deliver substantial improvements to homeworkers. The ETI approach does not stipulate how corporations should implement the base code inclusive of core labour standards, nor are there any consequences for non-compliance. However, a failure to tackle systemic justice and human rights problems in the garment supply chain indicates a significant gap in CSR approaches to homework. Despite the positive outcomes, such as NGOs and unions working to improve the regularity of work for homeworkers and evidence of the early stages of organising homeworkers, brands' decisions to shift the location of production indicates the project had little influence on changing brand business practice. A significant insight arising from the ETI homework project is that CSR representatives of global brands have insignificant influence within their organisations to change corporate purchasing practices. This point is made in the comments of one brand's CSR representative:

> There has to be integration between the CSR compliance and the purchasing teams. If that's not happening in the organization, then what you have created is two different, parallel-run organizations, which is not going to work out.
>
> *(Brand interview, 2014)*

A conclusion we draw from the ETI project example is that separation and compartmentalization of CSR and buying practices within garment brand organisations effectively thwarts making systemic change in the supply chain. The following example from Australia provides evidence of a co-regulatory approach that contributed to a sustained engagement response to homework.

A CSR homework response: engagement: the Australian homeworkers' code of practice and homework specific legislation

The example of the homeworkers' code of practice from Australia demonstrates an innovative strategy that combines a voluntary and legal approach to regulate homework in the supply chain. The Australian example demonstrates that legislation and a code of practice specific to garment homework conditions provides comprehensive levels of protection to homeworkers. A key feature is that it incorporates a method of joint liability and accountability of lead firms in the supply chain. This initiative is a shift away from 'simple' codes to combinations of hard/soft mechanisms or a co-regulation initiative for homework protection and transparency through the supply chain.

The homeworkers' code of practice (HWCP) (now known as Ethical Clothing Australia (ECA)) is a national voluntary code that applies to homework in the Australian garment industry. The Textile, Clothing & Footwear Union of Australia (TCFUA) and employer representatives, the Textile Fashion Industry of Australia (TFIA) jointly constitute and manage the code committee which is administered by ECA. The code applies to corporations producing garments in Australia (Burchielli et al., 2014). Different to corporate codes, it stipulates specific requirements for accredited companies to comply with, such as work-order records corporations are required to keep, including minute rates for garment sewing times; standard contracts they must enter with their subcontractors, and it recognises the role the TCFUA has in monitoring the code.

The ECA requires corporations, retailers and suppliers to seek accreditation. The corporation seeking accreditation must provide a list of all suppliers and secure from each supplier, and any of their supplier's subcontractors, evidence of homeworking, and evidence that the homeworkers in the supply chain are being paid legal minimum conditions. The accredited corporation (usually a retailer or brand owner, herein lead firm) shares a joint liability with their subcontractors. If a subcontractor is found in breach of the code, then the accredited corporation is found in breach of the code and is therefore obligated to remedy the situation. Failure to remedy the situation in a required period results in the loss of accreditation of the lead firm. Though accreditation only brings a 'moral and ethical' status as the code is not legally binding, firms have been keen to gain the tick of approval from union and consumer campaigners to indicate to consumers they comply with the code.

A co-regulatory model

The background to the Australian homeworkers' code lies in the strong regulatory schema associated with industry awards and state and national labour regulation. The homeworkers' code, while voluntary, mirrors the industry wide, national legislation, called the Clothing Trades Award (now the Clothing Industry Modern Award), underpinned by mandatory codes enacted by state governments, which replicate and complement contents of the voluntary code (Burchielli et al., 2014). In 2012, amendments were passed in the national labour law to strengthen garment homework protection and rights, including a deeming provision that defines them as employees.

The strength of the code exists in the reporting, contract and joint liability provisions, that corporations must provide evidence of meeting before becoming accredited. The code strengthens the legislative provisions since it mirrors the legal requirements and therefore a company that meets the code conditions is credited to be meeting their legislative requirements. One of the weaknesses is the limited resources and capacity for the union to effectively monitor the supply chain, whilst over 80 companies have become accredited to the Code, this only covers a small percentage of their garment production. The Code has increased the visibility and recognition of homework in the supply chain and increased the industry adherence to legislation regarding homework (Burchielli et al., 2014).

The social movement strategies used by the TCFUA, the NGO, Asian Women at Work (AWATW), and the FairWear campaign were effective in establishing the code and legislative reform (Burchielli et al., 2014). Securing protections for homeworkers combined strategies to pressure brands and suppliers to join the Code and collaborate on industry initiatives to stop sweatshop conditions; for example, the Code is administered by a joint union and employer committee. The Australian code demonstrates improvement in corporate compliance and application of both voluntary and regulatory mechanisms to improve homeworkers' conditions. This can be partly attributed to the participation by corporations in the voluntary code, but it only applies to production in Australia, which is now only a small percentage of garments sales, and the majority of garments are now produced at overseas locations.

This co-regulatory approach goes beyond tolerance to an engagement CSR approach to homework. This engagement approach enabled incremental improvements being secured for garment homeworkers, such as the inclusion in national labour laws as employees, and an increased capacity of homeworkers to access these rights. Importantly, in the Australian national context, the interrelationship between the legal and voluntary mechanisms – the co-regulatory approach – relies upon national labour regulation and industry regulation for it to work.

We note that the CSR engagement approach relies upon union and NGO's continuous involvement to agitate and pressure industry, to collaborate with industry, and to support homeworkers to participate and organise. Importantly, it requires connections being made between women workers' rights and women consumers for such campaign strategies to be effective (Burchielli et al., 2009). This places a great burden on unions and NGOs in regard to resources and commitment to ensure any improvements for homeworkers are implemented and sustained. Australian brands have moved the majority of production offshore to countries such as Bangladesh, China, and India, where legal and voluntary obligations are laxer, and women continue to labour in factories and their homes under poor conditions. Shifting production to host countries with less developed labour regimes and limited resources to monitor labour conditions demonstrates another category of compartmentalisation, since brands may get some 'good will' from CSR initiatives in their home country, yet the majority of their supply chain is deliberately sourced from locations where wages are very low, and brands are not held accountable for the labour rights' abuses that occur there. In the next section, we discuss international standards in relation to homework.

The need for international legal standards to regulate TNCs to protect homeworkers

The CSR approaches discussed above need to be assessed in relation to how they may contribute to improving working conditions and or protections to homeworkers. Gender specific issues need to be considered since codes and other mechanisms developed from the top down do not reflect concerns of women workers (Pearson, 2007).

International institutions, employer groups and many NGOs have defined or accepted CSR programs as voluntary initiatives. The United Nations Guiding Principles on Business and Human Rights (Guiding Principles) posit that all firms, regardless of size, location or industry devise and implement activities, measures and processes, to meet their 'responsibility to respect human rights' (Ruggie, 2011). The Guiding Principles have emerged as a response to the failure of regulatory standards applying to TNCs and constitute the most recent attempt to improve human rights' outcomes resulting from the business activity. The Guiding Principles stewarded by John Ruggie (2011) further cemented a voluntary approach to state and corporate responses to human rights at the international level. The guiding principles are framed by three conceptual pillars: 'respect, protect and remedy', and largely depend upon national action plans by each nation state to operationalise them (Ruggie, 2011). Not long after the endorsement by the UN Council of the Guiding Principles there came a strong push from a group of states backed by transnational civil society, for a legally binding treaty.

In June 2014, the Human Rights Council adopted a resolution that paved the way for an intergovernmental working group to explore the scope and form of a legally binding instrument to the regulation of business in international human rights law (A/HRC/32/19, 2014). A key argument put forward by the proponents of a legally binding instrument is that it is necessary to regulate TNCs, and to provide adequate protection, justice and remedy to victims of human rights abuse; to improve state responses on human rights, and address gaps in regulatory regimes (Deva and Bilchitz, 2017). Both optimism and scepticism continue to co-exist around how this can be achieved. Ruggie (2015) argues that too many obstacles stand in the way to implement a legally binding instrument, but many scholars and activists are also proponents of a legal instrument to govern global corporations (Simmons, 2012; Deva and Bilchitz, 2017).

Whilst unions have had varying responses to CSR initiatives, they continue to participate in a range of multi-stakeholder processes. At the same time, unions have begun to commit to other processes to improve workers' conditions and core labour standards. Global Union Federations (GUFs) are promoting International Framework Agreements (IFAs) as an alternative to the corporate social responsibility (CSR) approach. The IFAs have some advantages over mainstreamed self-regulated CSR strategies: they are legally binding and may offer a way to improve the visibility of homeworkers in the supply chain, though this may depend upon local union affiliates to GUFs being able to make links to organising strategies with homeworkers. It remains to be seen how inclusive of gender and homeworkers IFAs can be. Even with a potential for greater emphasis on regulation alongside voluntary mechanisms, it remains unclear how informal homeworkers can benefit from such initiatives without organising initiatives; this is discussed further in the following chapters.

The tensions between the current limitations of CSR initiatives and the barriers to achieving transnational legal and accountability options continue to exist. Consequently, the work of holding corporations to account through CSR mechanisms continues to be the main avenue for civil society to engage with transnational and national firms to effect change, despite many union and NGO representatives frequently stating their frustration at how little has been achieved since the inception of CSR initiatives (Delaney and Connor, 2016).

Conclusion

We have argued that voluntary codes rarely include homework and other informal work arrangements, nor have they delivered improvements concerning core labour standards. CSR voluntary standards remain discretionary regarding corporations' involvement, and even when TNC's intentions are genuine, there are no sanctions or accountability if they do not meet the standards of a code they agree to implement. The dilemma of how homeworkers can be adequately recognised and represented, their work valued and protected through CSR approaches remains a significant challenge. The compartmentalisation of responsibility by corporations limits the potential for systemic remedy of labour and human rights' abuses identified in the supply chain; many would argue that such barriers cannot be resolved without regulation in place.

This chapter discussed three CSR approaches by corporations which either ignore or respond in various ways to the poor conditions of homeworkers. The prohibition and tolerance examples discussed highlight many of the limitations of CSR responses. The examples of engagement as in Australia, offer important lessons in homeworker recognition in the supply chain. Recognition is essential as a first step but alone cannot change homeworkers' context. Workers need to collectively organise to be able to assert collective agency and demands. Regardless of the nature of voluntary or legally binding mechanisms or a combination of both, CSR needs to be inclusive of the gender dimensions that incorporate factors affecting homeworkers and other informal workers in supply chains. CSR appears to have some potential to facilitate worker recognition but has limited impact on improving homework representation. This issue is taken up in the next chapter.

References

A/HRC/32/19. (2014) *Human Rights and Transnational Corporations and Other Business Enterprises.* United Nations Office of the High Commissioner for Human Rights: New York.

Anner, M. (2018) CSR Participation Committees, Wildcat Strikes and the Sourcing Squeeze in Global Supply Chains. *British Journal of Industrial Relations* 56: 75–98.

Archana, and Dickson, M. (2017) Social Sustainability in Apparel Supply Chains: Organizational Practices for Managing Sub-Contracted Homework. In C. Henninger, P. Alevizou, H. Gowerek, et al. (eds) *Sustainability in Fashion: A Cradle to Upcycle Approach.* Houndmills, Basingstoke: Palgrave Macmillan, 267.

Bair, J. (2010) On Difference and Capital: Gender and the Globalization of Production. *Signs* 36: 203–226.

Balakrishnan, R. (2002) *The Hidden Assembly Line: Gender Dynamics of Subcontracting in a Global Economy.* Bloomfield: Kumarian Press.

Barrientos, S and Ware, S (2013) Labour Chains: Analysing the Role of Labour Contractors in Global Production Networks. *Journal of Development Studies* 49: 1058-1071.

Barrientos, S. (2013) Corporate Purchasing Practices in Global Production Networks: A Socially Contested Terrain. *Geoforum* 44: 44–51.

Barrientos, S. and Smith, S. (2007) Do Workers Benefit from Ethical Trade? Assessing Codes of Labour Practice in Global Production Systems. *Third World Quarterly* 28: 713–729.

Barrientos, S., Gereffi, G. and Rossi, A. (2011) Economic and Social Upgrading in Global Production Networks: A New Paradigm for a Changing World. *International Labour Review* 150: 319–340.

Barrientos, S. and Evers, B. (2014) Gendered Production Networks: Push and Pull on Corporate Responsibility? In S. Rai and G. Waylen (eds) *New Frontiers in Feminist Political Economy* (pp. 43-61). London and New York: Routledge.

BBA. (2009) *Offside: Child Labour in Football Stitching*. New Delhi: Bachpan Bachao Andolan.

Boeri, N. (2016) Boundaries of Home and Work: Social Reproduction and Home-Based Workers in Ahmedabad, India. *CUNY Academic Works*. New York: City University of New York, 229.

Boris, E. and Prügl, E. (1996) *Homeworkers in Global Perspective: Invisible No More*. New York: Routledge.

Burchielli, R., Buttigieg, D. and Delaney, A. (2008) Organizing Homeworkers: The Use of Mapping as an Organizing Tool. *Work, Employment & Society* 22: 167–180.

Burchielli, R., Delaney, A. and Coventry, K. (2014) Campaign Strategies to Develop Regulatory Mechanisms: Protecting Australian Garment Homeworkers. *Journal of Industrial Relations* 56: 81–102.

Burchielli, R., Delaney, A., Tate, J. and Coventry, K. (2009) The FairWear Campaign: An Ethical Network in the Australian Garment Industry. *Journal of Business Ethics* 90: 575–588.

Burchielli, R. and Delaney, A. (2016) The Invisibilization and Denial of Work in Argentinian Garment Homework. *Relations Industrielles/Industrial Relations* 71: 468–493.

Brill, L. (2002) I'll Tell You What I Want…Women and Codes of Conduct. In R. Jenkins, R. Pearson and G. Seyfang (eds), *Corporate Responsibility and Labour Rights* (pp. 113–123). London: Earthscan.

Brooks, E. (2007) *Unraveling the Garment Industry: Transnational Organising and Women's Work*. Minneapolis, London: University of Minnesota Press.

Collins, J. (2003) *Threads: Gender, Labor, and Power in the Global Apparel Industry*. Chicago and London: The University of Chicago Press.

Delaney, A. (2016) Barriers to Redress: Leather Footwear Workers in Tamil Nadu, South India. *Non-Judicial Redress Mechanism Report Series 12*. Melbourne: Corporate Accountability Research.

Delaney, A. and Tate, J. (2015) Forced Labour and Ethical Trade in the Indian Textile Industry. In L. Waite, G. Craig, H. Lewis and K. Skrivankova. *Vulnerability, Exploitation and Migrants: Insecure Work in a Globalised Economy* (pp. 244–255). Basingstoke: Palgrave.

Delaney, A. and Connor, T. (2016) *Forced Labour in the Textile and Garment Sector in Tamil Nadu, South India: Strategies for Redress*. Melbourne: Corporate Accountability Research, 66.

Delaney, A., Burchielli, R. and Connor, T. (2015) Positioning Women Homeworkers in a Global Footwear Production Network: How Can Homeworkers Improve Agency, Influence and Claim Rights? *Journal of Industrial Relations* 57: 641–659.

Delaney, A., Tate, J. and Burchielli, R. (2016) Homeworkers Organizing for Recognition and Rights: Can International Standards Assist Them? In J. Jensen and N. Lichtenstein (eds) *The ILO From Geneva to the Pacific Rim (pp.159-179)*. Houndmills, Basingstoke: Palgrave Macmillan and the International Labour Office.

Delaney, A., Burchielli, R. and Tate, J. (2017) Corporate CSR Responses to Homework and Child Labour in the Indian and Pakistan Leather Sector. In K. Grosser, L. McCarthy and M. Kilmore (eds), *Gender Equality and Responsible Business: Expanding CSR Horizons (pp. 170-184)*. London New York: Routledge.

Deva, S. and Bilchitz, D. (2017) Building a Treaty on Business and Human Rights. In *Building a Treaty on Business and Human Rights: Context and Contours*. Cambridge: Cambridge University Press.

Elias, J. (2004) *Fashioning Inequality? The Multinational Company and Gendered Employment in a Globalising World.* Burlington: Ashgate.

Elias, J. (2011) The Gender Politics of Economic Competitiveness in Malaysia's Transition to a Knowledge Economy. *The Pacific Review* 24: 529–552.

Hale, A. and Turner, J. (2005) Codes of Conduct through a Gender Lens. In N. Ascoby and C. Finney (eds), *Made by Women* (pp. 75–83). Amsterdam: Clean Clothes Campaign.

Hale, A. and Wills, J. (2005) *THREADS OF LABOUR: Garment Industry Supply Chains from the Workers' Perspective.* Antipode Book Series. Maldon: Blackwell Publishers, 266.

HIVOS. (2012) *Child Labour in the Leather Footwear Industry: An Overview and Assessment of Policies and Implementation of 28 Footwear Companies.* Report, Hivos, Netherlands, November.

HIVOS. (2013) *Working on the Right Shoes.* Report, Hivos, Netherlands, November.

HomeNet. (1998) Special Issue on Consumer Campaigns and Homework. *The Newsletter of the International Network for Homebased Workers* 10: 15.

HWW. (2004) *Organising for Change: Women Homebased Workers in the Global Economy. Final Report on Mapping Homebased Work.* J. Tate (ed.). Leeds, UK: Homeworkers Worldwide.

HWW. (2008) *Who Foots the Bill?* Leeds: HomeWorkers Worldwide.

HWW, CIVIDEP & LBL. (2016) *Stitching Our Shoes: Homeworkers in South India.* Leeds: Homeworkers Worldwide.

HWW. (2017) *Homeworking in Global Value Chains: A Case Study of Leather Footwear.* Leeds: Homeworkers Worldwide.

ILO. (2002a) *Decent Work and the Informal Economy: Report VI.* Geneva: International Labour Office.

ILO. (2016) *Decent Work in Global Supply Chains.* Geneva: International Labour Office.

IILS. (2008) *Governance, International Law & Corporate Social Responsibility: Research Series 116.* International Labour Organization: International Institute for Labour Studies 207.

ILRF. (2010) *Missed the Goal for Workers: The Reality of Soccer Ball Stitchers in Pakistan, India, China and Thailand.* Washington: International Labour Rights Forum.

Jenkins, R. (2001) *Corporate Codes of Conduct: Self-Regulation in a Global Economy.* Technology BaSPpn (ed.). Geneva: UNRISD. United Nations Research Institute for Social Development.

Jenkins, R., Pearson, R. and Seyfang, G. (2002) *Corporate Responsibility and Labour Rights.* London: Earthscan.

Lambert, R. and Herod, A. (2016) (eds) *Neoliberal Capitalism and Precarious Work: Ethnographies of Accommodation and Resistance.* Cheltenham: Edward Elgar Publishing.

Locke, R., Rissing, B. and Pal, T. (2013) Complements or Substitutes? Private Codes, State Regulation and the Enforcement of Labour Standards in Global Supply Chains. *British Journal of Industrial Relations* 51: 519–552.

Lund-Thomsen, P. (2013) Labor Agency in the Football Manufacturing Industry of Sialkot, Pakistan. *Geoforum* 44: 71–81.

Lund-Thomsen, P. and Coe, N. (2013) Corporate Social Responsibility and Labour Agency: The Case of Nike in Pakistan. *Journal of Economic Geography* 16 December: 1–22.

MacIntyre, A. (1984) *After Virtue: A Study in Moral Theory.* Notre Dame IN: Notre Dame University Press.

MacNeil, I. and O'Brien, J. (2010) *The Future of Financial Regulation.* Portland: Hart Publishing.

Mezzadri, A. (2012) Reflections on Globalisation and Labour Standards in the Indian Garment Industry: Codes of Conduct Versus 'Codes of Practice' Imposed by the Firm. *Global Labour Journal* 3: 40–62.

Mezzadri, A. (2014) Indian Garment Clusters and CSR Norms: Incompatible Agendas at the Bottom of the Garment Commodity Chain. *Oxford Development Studies* 42: 217–237.

Mezzadri, A. (2016) Class, Gender and the Sweatshop: On the Nexus Between Labour Commodification and Exploitation. *Third World Quarterly* 37: 1877–1900.

Mies, M. (2014) *Patriarchy and Accumulation on a World Scale: Women in the International Division of Labour.* London: Zed Books.

McBarnet, D. (2009) *Corporate Responsibility Beyond Law, through Law, for Law.* Edinburgh: University of Edinburgh.

Mohanty, C.T. (2006) *Feminism without Borders: Decolonizing Theory, Practicing Solidarity.* Durham and London: Duke University Press.

Monsoon. (2008) *Monsoon Accessorize Homeworking Policy* [Electronic Version]. Available at: http://www.monsoon.co.uk/page/ethicaltrading/.

Pearson, R. (2007) Beyond Women Workers: Gendering CSR. *Third World Quarterly* 28: 731–749.

Pearson, R. (2014) Gender, Globalization and the Reproduction of Labour: Bringing the State Back. In S. Rai and G. Waylen (eds) *New Frontiers in Feminist Political Economy* (pp.19-42). London and New York: Routledge.

Pentland. (2017) *Pentland Group 2017 Corporate Responsibility Review.* Available at: http://www.pentland.com/downloads/cr-reviews/Pentland-Group-CR-Review-2017.pdf

PILER. (2009) *Labour Standards in Football Manufacturing Industry: A Case Study of a Nike Vender in Sialkot, Pakistan.* Karachi: Pakistan Institute of Labour Education and Research.

Prieto-Carrón, M. (2014), Bringing Resistance to the Conceptual Centre: Threats to Social Reproduction and Feminist Activism in Nicaraguan Commodity Chains. In W. Dunaway (ed.), *Gendered Commodity Chains: Seeing Women's Work and Households in Global Production* (pp.225-240). Stanford: Stanford University Press.

Prieto-Carrón, M., Lund-Thomsen, P., Chan, A., et al. (2006) Critical Perspectives on CSR and Development: What We Know, What We Don't Know, and What We Need to Know. *International Affairs* 82: 977–987.

Prügl, E. (2017) Corporate Social Responsibility and the Neoliberalization of Feminism. In K. Grosser, L. McCarthy and M. Kilmore (eds), *Can CSR Responses be Inclusive of Informal Women Worker Rights and Priorities? (pp.46-55).* London: Routledge.

Rennie, S., Connor, T., Delaney, A. and Marshall, S. (2017) Orchestration from Below? Trade Unions in the Global South, Transnational Business and Efforts to Orchestrate Continuous Improvement in Non- State Regulatory Initiatives. *UNSW Law Journal* 40: 1275–1309.

Rowbotham, S. (1999) *New Ways of Organising in the Informal Sector: Four Case Studies of Trade Union Activity.* Leeds: HomeNet.

Rozuel, C. (2011) The Moral Threat of Compartmentalization: Self, Roles and Responsibility. *Journal of Business Ethics* 102: 685–697.

Ruggie, J. (2011) Report of the Special Representative of the Secretary-General on the Issue of Human Rights and Transnational Corporations and Other Business Enterprises: Guiding Principles on Business and Human Rights: Implementing the United Nations 'Protect, Respect and Remedy' Framework, UN Doc A/HRC/17/31 (21 March 2011) annex. New York: United Nations Office of the High Commissioner for Human Rights.

Ruggie, J. (2015) Regulating Multinationals: The UN Guiding Principles, Civil Society, and International Legalization. Regulatory Policy Program Working Paper RPP-2015–2004. Cambridge, MA: Mossavar-Rahmani Center for Business and Government, Harvard Kennedy School, Harvard University.

Seidman, G. (2005) Monitoring Multinationals: Corporate Codes of Conduct. In J. Bandy and J. Smith (eds), *Coalitions Across Borders: Transnational Protest and the Neoliberal Order* (163-186). Lanham: Rowman & Littlefield.

Simmons, P. (2012) International Law's Invisible Hand and the Future of Corporate Accountability for Violations on Human Rights. *Journal of Human Rights and the Environment* 3: 5–43.

SOMO. (2012) *Where the Shoe Pinches: Child Labour in the Production of Brand Name Leather Shoes*. Netherlands: SOMO.

STC. (1997) *Stitching Footballs: Voices of Children in Sialkot, Pakistan*. Save the Children.

STC. (1999) *Child Labour Project, Sialkot, Social Monitoring Report*. Save the Children.

Stevis, D. and Boswell, T. (2007) International Framework Agreements: Opportunities and Challenges for Global Unionism. In K. Bronfenbrenner (ed.), *Global Unions* (pp. 174–194). Ithaca and London: Cornell University Press.

Strike, V.M., Gao, J. and Bansai, P. (2006) Being Good While Being Bad: Social Responsibility and the International Diversification of US Firms. *Journal of International Business Studies* 37: 850–862.

Utting, P. (2005) Corporate Responsibility and the Movement of Business. *Development in Practice* 15: 375–388.

Vilanova, M., Lozano, J.M. and Arenas, D. (2009) Exploring the Nature of the Relationship Between CSR and Competitiveness. *Journal of Business Ethics* 87: 57–69.

5

THE LOGIC OF THE SUPPLY CHAIN

Barriers and strategies for homeworker representation

Homework has long been an integral part of supply chains. Since the 1880s employers have established 'putting out' or contracting systems for garment production, evident across the United Kingdom, Europe, Australia, North America, Asia and Latin America. In the 20th century, the use of homework surged from the 1970s to the 1990s in garments, footwear, automobiles and electronics. Homework was also detected in engineering sectors and packaging, and the provision of services, such as administration and telemarketing. Homework became embedded in these diverse national and global supply chains.

Whilst the use of homework has ebbed and flowed with the needs of capital, homework has flourished under 21st century capitalism. Capital has continued to incorporate dependent homework into labour intensive garment and footwear sector supply chains where the trend for cheap, informal and unorganised labour is a predominant characteristic of globalised production. Similarly, own account homework is increasingly being incorporated into global supply chains, such as agribusiness for food (e.g., shea butter), cosmetics (e.g., seaweed collection) and furniture (e.g., rattan), packaging and service provision and traditional textiles such as embroidery, weaving and carpets. Homework makes it possible for women to work and earn an income from home. Yet, homework is embedded in supply chains that make use of historical and geographic inequalities based on gendered constructs of social reproductive labour, class, race, and colonisation. The social relations of production through supply chains maintain cheap and flexible production, and lock homeworkers, fearful of losing their work, into irregular work on low piece rates, whilst limiting opportunities for workers to collectively organise.

Representation of homeworkers by unions has been spasmodic; few unions are dedicated to being inclusive of homework (Burchielli, Buttigieg and Delaney, 2008). Others have focused on supporting policy and regulation reform around homework yet have had limited success in organising homeworkers. More often, homeworkers have found support and allies through forming new organisations through women's groups and NGOs, some of which have developed into unions and membership organisations. Consumer campaigns have played an important role in highlighting homeworkers' situation and pressuring transnational corporations directly and through multi-stakeholder initiatives to address the dire work conditions of homeworkers in global supply chains. Yet, solidarity activity to support worker organisation and collective bargaining has rarely been a focus of such campaigns (Delaney, Burchielli and Tate, 2017).

In this chapter, we adopt a broad definition of representation as in advocacy 'on behalf of', collective bargaining and capacity-building in relation to homeworkers. As such, our notion of access to work-related freedoms, such as freedom from discrimination and freedom of association is conceived as an issue of rights. This concept of rights overlaps with issues discussed under recognition and representation, and is linked to the concept of 'rights' in the gender justice framework because it refers to the fundamental human and labour right of 'freedom of association'. We argue here that homeworkers are constrained to exercise this right because of the many obstacles to their being recognised and represented as workers. Drawing on traditional forms of union collective worker representation and less traditional forms of collective representation through NGOs and women organisations, case study examples and empirical data are drawn from the garment and footwear sector in India, Australia and Myanmar. We explore the concepts of associational and symbolic forms of power (Wright, 2000; Silver, 2003) and the capacity of workers, who face exclusion in society, to understand how they can gain recognition and access to justice.

Given the location of homeworkers in supply chains, we further explore the nexus between inequalities at the local level, and the power asymmetries that exist across geographic and economic boundaries and the various actors across supply chains. We examine the factors that contribute to uneven development and the dynamics of supply chain capitalism to understand the constraints to homeworkers' representation and rights.

We argue throughout this book that homework is frequently an undervalued and invisibilised form of work. The devalorisation of homework's productive labour and women's social reproductive labour, such as childrearing, caring for family, the household and social labour in the community occurs through the relations of patriarchy and capitalism (Delaney, Burchielli and Connor, 2015). This is discussed in Chapters 1 and 2. Homeworkers are predominantly women who are relegated through their work and their reproductive labour to the private sphere. In this chapter, we argue that the location of homework in the private sphere means that homeworkers have low levels of social capital, limited identity as workers, limited collective agency and reduced solidarity, and, in turn, impacts on any potential leverage they may have in the supply chain.

The idea of empowerment is frequently referred to as a means to improve women workers' lives. This empowerment is rarely defined, and more often it relates simplistically to improving economic conditions. We discuss the concept of empowerment in relation to unions and new forms of labour NGOs and development NGOs linked directly or indirectly to supply chains, aiming to investigate what forms of collectivisation can assist women homeworkers to improve a range of conditions through representation in the supply chain. The concept of worker empowerment we propose arises from the individual empowerment that emerges from institutional recognition, representation, rights and redistribution as set out in the gender justice framework in the Introduction. Despite some heartening examples, suggesting both some progress and optimism, the chapter concludes with a sobering assessment of the various serious obstacles for homeworker representation.

Uneven development and unequal exchange

To appreciate the realities of homework, such as the lack of recognition and representation in supply chains, we turn to the circumstances of capitalism that spawn the supply chain power relations and associated social relations of production. The concept of a value chain has been used in development studies to incorporate all the activities required to source, produce, and distribute a product. This includes all the people involved in producing the goods or services, from the farmer that sows the cotton seed, to the consumer that wears a T-shirt. For consistency, in this book we use the term supply chain to refer to the people and activities involved to develop, process, make, distribute and consume goods or services. We incorporate, alongside homeworkers, other key actors: global and local corporations, unions, civil society, states and consumers in our analysis.

The concept of uneven development is a useful way to understand the features of global trade. In particular, it is a useful way for understanding how, over recent decades, the expansion of the industrial organisation – the structure and boundaries between firms and markets – has opened up new trade between North and South economies. The global trade and expansion of global production are often proposed within a frame of development, and as being beneficial for the host economy country.

The global supply chain is a key feature of global capital expansion. Host countries in developing economies, or 'the global South', once peripheral to capital, are now central to the value-creation process of global corporations. Whilst colonial power relations of the recent past remain ensconced in global trade, neoliberal globalisation has facilitated capital to expand into new source locations. Similar to early trends of capitalist expansion, global trade and global supply chain production is dependent upon an unequal exchange across the North–South economies; this is mirrored in the relationship between capital and workers (Amin, 2014). The extension of global trade and globalised production has been enabled by free trade agreements and government regulation supportive of transnational corporations and trade. It has been further facilitated by the support of neoliberal policies and a ready supply of labour to work at low wages, yet rarely have workers shared in the profit of this exchange (Bieler and Morton, 2014).

Many host states compete to offer cheap labour, tax incentives and union suppression to gain the business of global corporations, which is based upon maintaining an unequal exchange (Bieler and Morton, 2014). The unequal exchange becomes evident through different levels of recognition of productivity. Productivity refers to higher volumes of production for the same cost or lower costs. The unequal exchange is where higher productivity of labour occurs in one part of the world, compared to another location, ensuring value creation for capital. To illustrate, the high productivity of homeworkers in India, hand-sewing shoes for a few cents a pair, delivers to corporations the surplus value created by their cheap labour. The profit to the corporation comes from their surplus value being higher than the profit available from workers performing the same work in the corporation's home country. Uneven development also signifies the value attributed to different inputs and outcomes of labour (Elson, 2015; Skeggs, 2014). Value creation for the brand selling the shoes is (unjustly) generated through the commodification of homeworkers' labour and subsistence wages.

The unequal exchange between capital and labour is accentuated through the expansion of capital into new production locations fuelled by global trade, and this dynamic propagates uneven development (Amin, 2013; Bieler & Morton, 2014; Elson, 2015). Alongside the inequalities global trade gives rise to, it also has negative impacts in the national context. Global trade generates 'race to the bottom' strategies, that contribute to the erosion of legal protection of labour standards, the informalisation of jobs previously formal and the creation of new jobs that are informal. Informal work such as homework in supply chains is denied the 'moral right' to bargain with capital because it is invisibilised and not recognised (Burchielli and Delaney, 2016; Chun, 2012; Bowles and Harriss, 2010).

As such, the concept of uneven development captures the inequalities across geographic and economic boundaries that binds states, economies and workers into continuing to serve and promote the capitalist social relations of production (Amin, 2013; Bieler and Morton, 2014; Skeggs, 2014). This is a central feature of labour intensive industries such as garment, textiles and footwear, but also characterises the growth of outsourcing of services to developing countries such as call centres, information technology, care and domestic work.

Labour and the logic of the supply chain

In general, supply chains are based on outsourcing and subcontracting, and entail all the entities and processes involved in the production/consumption of goods and services. In the context of global production, supply chains support the broad neoliberal project of expansion into new markets (Tsing 2009) and constitute the principal mechanism for global capital to create surplus value. The feminised, labour-intensive, global garment industry is characterised by an extremely tight hold on costs and deadlines (Reinecke and Donaghey, 2015; Reinecke and Donaghey, 2018) – evident at every point in the supply chain, from the procurement of raw materials through to the procurement of manufacture. The literature highlights that firms use all 'their political, economic and managerial resources to maximise the efficient operation of their production chains' (Delaney et al., 2015: 643).

The supply chain aim is to accumulate value for capital, primarily through access to labour in host countries, that is cheaper than the lead firm's home country. Tsing (2009) proposed the term *supply chain capitalism* to describe the supply chain as a phenomenon that has emerged from outsourcing as well as global communication and technologies that have improved the capacity to speedily move commodities across the globe. The logic of supply chain capitalism recognises the heterogeneity of supply chains and the diversity of the types of firms in the supply chain. The brand or lead firm creates strict conditions of control through compliance in relation to the price, quality and delivery of the product with a key intention to reduce labour costs. Tsing suggests the dynamics of capital and labour involves the incorporation of rhetorical terms used by brands and lead firms, such as 'consumption and entrepreneurship' to promote the logic to consumers while utilising the existing dynamics of patriarchy, colonialism, social and cultural diversity to privilege and create value through the supply chain (Tsing, 2009: 151). Following Tsing, the idea of supply chain capitalism highlights methods that global firms use to promote positive discourses around the supply chain: for example, bringing cheaper goods to consumers in the North, and jobs to people in the South. This logic supports the benefits they reap from cheap labour, from outsourcing responsibility for labour conditions onto supplier firms, and from placing an increased burden onto workers.

A prevailing belief alleges that the presence of supply chains in a wide range of locations means that job creation and economic development can be achieved effectively. Moreover, that foreign investment in those locations also brings long-term benefits of infrastructure development. Such is the argument of economic upgrading of local suppliers by global corporations in the garment sector: when local firms invest to upgrade infrastructure, the assumption is that this will bring broader societal benefits (Barrientos et al., 2011). For women workers, the benefits are frequently championed as creating empowerment opportunities to explain women being incorporated into the workforce, even at below minimum wages, poor health and safety and precarious work arrangements. At the same time, the supply chain capitalises on local economic, social and political conditions and circumstances to encourage labour mobilisation and maintain discipline and control of workers (Tsing, 2009; Skeggs, 2014).

The use of gendered and racialised conditions to control the workforce can be understood through our case example of garment and footwear supply chains in Tamil Nadu, South India. The garment workforce in Tamil Nadu was previously made up predominantly of male workers but is now largely composed of women, consistent with the feminisation of production over the last three decades (Elson and Pearson, 1981). With neoliberal shifts toward the global export market and increased pressure for lower wages, suppliers have moved to the recruitment of female migrant labour mainly from Dalit, as well as low caste Hindu communities in factories, and homebased workers in the garment sector. Migrant women workers are recruited from impoverished areas of India to factories through bonded labour three-year schemes also called Sumangali schemes that promise young women three years of salary at the end of the term, this promised lump sum payment is promoted to young women as a means to prepare their dowry for marriage. Additionally, many of the same workers are recruited under forced labour arrangements that bind them to hostel accommodation in factory premises that limits their freedom of movement and demands their availability to work around the clock (Delaney and Tate, 2015; Delaney and Connor, 2016).

In the same example, the rhetoric of some brands is showcasing the provision of health programs about individual women's health as 'empowering women' despite the use of bonded and forced labour practice and poor health and safety in the same supply chain being largely ignored (Delaney and Connor, 2016). This illustrates that the management of the supply chain accommodates and perpetuates the social and political features at the local level to maintain poor working conditions, low wages and control over workers.

Similar practices are observed in the Tamil Nadu footwear sector, where worker recruitment targets the same demographic profile (mostly women from Muslim, Dalit and other low caste Hindu communities) for factories, tanneries and home-based production. Again, this utilises the class, race-caste and gender conditions to maintain the low costs that uphold the features of the supply chain. The poverty in the villages where homeworkers are recruited to work for the footwear factories to supply global brands is not new, but the features of work in the supply chain make use of workers' poverty to effectively control the workforce.

In our research in Tamil Nadu, where we talked to hundreds of homeworkers in the leather sector in recent years, the story of low payments and debt is common (Delaney, 2016). Homeworkers are commonly locked into a cycle of low piece rates and debt to survive. This effectively controls workers by keeping them bound to the dynamics of the supply chain. One worker described her circumstances:

> My family forced me to get married, doing the household things, and working making shoes, so each of us has our own problems. I get paid so little money for my sewing work, being Muslim I feel I am treated badly, and the family must borrow money from the middle man, then we pay it back each month. Every day I think about my children's future, will it be great? Then every day when I am about go to sleep I think about my debts; if it is managed for another day I'll be happy.
>
> (Mumaith Beevi, homeworker 2011)

The supply chain logic is reproduced through the process of employers' paying homeworkers low piece rates and forcing them into debt to survive. This same logic is promoted by corporations and nation-states as a means of economic development and growth to host countries. The appeal for sourcing from host locations lies in existing inequalities to extract the most value through exploitation and control over workers. Local management of the supply chain prioritises maintaining control over workers with the consequence of disrupting worker solidarity. The differences and divisions between workers limit worker solidarity and unionisation. While these differences are not impossible to overcome, workers who are marginalised in society struggle to form links across work enterprises within the supply chain and across class, caste and gender divisions, therefore placing them at the margins and outside and beyond the traditional means to collectively bargain (Shamir, 2016).

Contributing to the disruption of worker solidarity are the restrictive anti-union management practices. Workers experience a restraining capacity to form solidarity links across different types of enterprises across the supply chain, despite the commonality of work experience, low wages, lack of work security and poor health and safety conditions (Shamir, 2016). In this sense, the firm strategies described above contribute to the supply chain functioning as an instrument to disrupt worker solidarity.

In the above example of the footwear and garment supply chains, homeworkers already experience marginalisation due to being women, located in their villages and homes, where their work context is shaped by their social reproductive roles. Homeworkers from Dalit communities frequently face discrimination and exclusion in society, further experience barriers to collectively join together and considerably more to unite with other workers to improve conditions. In our examples from India, the recruitment of the marginalised homeworkers into the supply chain utilises the worker's experience of poverty, and discrimination based on gender and caste and lack of social capital. This highlights the challenges workers must address to be able to assert any moral right to bargain with capital (Mezzadri, 2016).

Homeworkers are already isolated and marginalised in society and face further marginalisation due to their position in the supply chain. Being invisible to suppliers and brands, and dependent upon the contractor that supplies the work, leaves them few options to form linkages with other workers.

> I don't know anybody who can help us build a group, but there are many of the women doing this work, but how can we join together? I don't know how to organize. I have no other experience like the factory work, or what the company thinks about homebased workers, I just do the stitching.
>
> *(Aleeza, homeworker 2011)*

The dynamics of the supply chain are conducive to treating and rendering workers as invisible, of disrupting solidarity and forcing them to reinvent how they collectively organise and bargain with capital. Those workers recruited from the marginalised, informal workers working in the low tiers of the supply chain cannot access structural power traditionally aligned with unions and the workplace, so they are forced to look for forms of symbolic or moral power to improve their agency (Chun, 2012; Webster, Lambert and Bezuidenhout, 2008). In other words, the utilisation by capital of patriarchal, colonial, class and race dynamics in the supply chain further disadvantages marginalised workers and limits their capacity to build representative and associational power relational to their labour power in the supply chain.

Some propose that the supply chain can be a positive lever for development in host producer countries. However, we note that the World Bank, an important champion of free trade, states that participation in global supply chains does not automatically improve living standards and social conditions in a country (World Bank, 2018). In their study of global value chains, Taglioni and Winkler observe that the value chain provides opportunities not only for improvements in production outcomes such as quality and scale, but also for 'redressing market failures' (2016: 4). This would entail 'engineering equitable distributions of opportunities and outcomes – including employment, wages, work conditions, economic rights, gender equality, economic security, and protecting the environment' (Taglioni and Winkler 2014: 4). We explore this further in the next section.

Uneven development and economic and social upgrading

Uneven development literature highlights some of the macro conditions that contribute to inequalities between firms, nations and people in the global North and South. The exploration of global production contributing to development in the global South has led to a great deal of scholarly attention on the benefits and pitfalls of supply chains, also referred to as global value chains or global production networks. Earlier research on commodity chains and value chains indicated that the majority of value creation has been in industrialised countries (Gereffi, 1994). Scholars have also focused their attention on a development perspective, concerning themselves with how economic upgrading can bring social benefits to producer country economies (Gereffi, 2014).

Economic upgrading refers to the various processes that create economic value for firms, which may also lead to flow-on benefits for related firms and intermediaries. The focus on economic upgrading highlights the economic benefits for supplier firms, encouraging upgrading of technological processes and work organisation to improve flexibility, quality and speed of production to meet lead firm standards (Posthuma and Nathan, 2010). Economic upgrading is essentially the technical improvements at the first-tier, supplier firm level, usually described as greater efficiencies, improved and updated infrastructure, factory premises and machinery. Many studies have focused on the way production is organised between firms, with less focus on labour and the formation of collective strategies and representation to improve worker conditions. More recently, there has been a noticeable shift toward understanding the dynamics and role of labour in relation to the supply chain (see Rainnie, Herod and McGrath-Champ, 2011) and in particular a focus on gender (Dunaway, 2014; Bair, 2010).

A central argument supporting economic upgrading is that supply chains will bring a range of social benefits to developing countries, based on notions of economic efficiency, These also give rise to claims that supply chains reduce social costs in the South, such as unemployment, and benefit consumers in the North, and the belief that the expansion of supply chains in a wide range of locations means that job creation and economic development can be achieved effectively.

Moreover, foreign investment in those locations is also seen to bring long-term benefits of infrastructure development, such as roads and transport.

Such is the argument made by global corporations about economic upgrading to local suppliers in the garment sector. The assumption is that when local firms invest to upgrade infrastructure, this will bring broader societal benefits (Barrientos et al., 2011). This argument is frequently invoked to support companies' relocation of production to developing countries and used as an example of how global trade brings opportunities to developing economies. The incorporation of up-to-date technology and large shiny, clean factories are ideas frequently used to indicate the positive economic benefits of extension of production and trade into new countries and regions. However, research in economic upgrading in supply chains suggests that it is only first-tier firms that benefit economically from the supply chain structure (Barrientos et al., 2011). Little evidence exists around the economic benefits for first-tier suppliers directly contracting to global firms. Furthermore, there is little evidence of social upgrading, particularly in developing countries (Delaney et al., 2015).

Whilst the literature distinguishes between economic upgrading and social upgrading, it also refers to the possible links between the two (Posthuma and Nathan, 2010). In contrast to economic upgrading, social upgrading is a concept related to 'decent work' as articulated by the ILO (2002; 2016. The concept of social upgrading to address employment standards and rights emerged to tackle the consequences or opportunities brought about by economic and technical upgrading (Barrientos, Kothari and Phillips 2013; Posthuma and Nathan, 2010). The factors that contribute to low wages and precarious work conditions in developing countries are well documented (Phillips, 2011). Evidence also exists indicating that workers in the first-tier supplier factories get some limited benefits as a consequence of economic upgrading, such as occupational health and safety (Barrientos et al., 2011; Selwyn 2011).

But more telling, the evidence shows that particularly in labour intensive industries such as garments, textile and footwear, workers beyond the first-tier supplier, are often employed in informal, short-term contract, homebased and forced labour arrangements (Barrientos et al., 2011; Carswell and De Neve, 2013; Delaney & Tate, 2015; Delaney et al., 2015) and that they have more risks than benefits.

Research from the garment sector suggests that low purchasing prices set by global brands or buyers are the main reason for suppliers to cut costs, creating a price squeeze further down the supply chain (Anner 2011). Suppliers are motivated to remain integrated within the supply chain, and therefore churn workers through on short-term contracts and subcontract work, increasing the level of informality and depriving them of social benefits and potential social production benefits, traditionally linked to formal work. In this way, garment work and the like has become less secure, lower paid, and rather than gaining anything, workers are more likely to be captive to work and have little more than a survival strategy, this is particularly so for women workers (Barrientos et al., 2011; Phillips, 2011; Selwyn,

2011). Whilst local firms contract directly to global corporations, they wield significant power in the local context. Their capacity to yield maximum surplus value from workers is their primary goal to satisfy their global clients. To date, little evidence exists that economic upgrading brings any social upgrading benefits associated with decent work, such as improvements in regulated work conditions, including secure employment, living wages, and social protection to formal sector workers, and no evidence of any benefits to informal workers (Barrientos, 2014).

From the homeworkers' perspective, there is little evidence that sewing leather footwear 'uppers' (the part of the shoe that attaches to the sole) for the export market brings any improvements for them beyond subsistence. Anitha, a homeworker in Chennai, expressed her feelings about her work,

> There is nothing good in my life. My husband is earning little and couldn't support the family. We have nothing, that's why we know this is exploitation. We have no other way, that's why we are involving in this work. If I have any other income definitely I won't do this. So according to my concern, I don't have anything positive for my life.
>
> *(Anitha, homeworker 2012)*

In practice, what this means, on a day to day basis, for homeworkers situated in the margins of the supply chain, is that the irregularity of the work is insufficient to survive, and they remain in poverty.

> We homeworkers are all very poor, often we have little work in the months of May, June, July. We really don't know what the reason is. So we go to the contractor and ask, because we don't have any money to look after the family, 'give us some work'. So they may give us three pairs per day, so then we can get 10 or 20 rupees per day because that's the time when we have an economic crisis at home. We sell our gold rings to look after the family. Once the work starts again, then we stitch more and our situation will improve a little. Sometimes I have to borrow money to keep our family day to day life and all. So when the work comes, we all stitch extra.
>
> *(Divya, homeworker 2011)*

So, whereas the common argument for expansion of production to developing countries is that it brings benefits to those economies and to the workers, the evidence points us to a world of diminishing wealth distribution, greater inequalities and gaps between the rich and poor, and that these workers are not attaining benefits beyond subsistence from their labour. As a consequence, the term 'social downgrading' has been developed as a way to capture some of the differences regarding how inequalities emerge through the supply chain to affect different groups. Precariousness, vulnerability and inequality, and the linkages between them, arise directly from factors such as class, gender and race (Selwyn, 2013; Selwyn, 2014; Beneria & Floro, 2005; Jenkins and Blyton, 2017).

Proponents of economic development through the expansion of global trade and production appear to believe that this is the way to address rising inequalities. However, they fail to concede that the 'jobs at any cost' strategy does not actually bring gains to the millions of workers employed to produce goods and provide services in the South for global corporations. We are not proposing an argument against economic development per se, but we recognise that under the current circumstances, where workers are locked into an unequal exchange, the economic, social and political factors that produce inequalities are *not* being addressed.

Advocates of global trade in the neoliberal market would argue that such trade dynamics are preferable to none; and that workers benefit from low wages by surviving. Some go as far as to promote sweatshops as a good thing, that the market can adjust for these factors. This argument proposes that some wage is better than none (Powell, 2014). The liberalist idea that the market will provide ignores the consequences of uneven development that occur as a result of capital taking advantage of the inequalities that reproduce inequality and disadvantage to workers (Tsing, 2006; Skeggs, 2014). Consequently, the supply chain opens up access to suppliers and workers to be embedded in the reproduction of difference based on gender, class, race and cultural characteristics of the host countries. The logic of the supply chain, therefore maintains differences and reproduces inequalities to suit capital and to disrupt worker solidarity.

We now consider the proposition promoted by capital and capitalists, that labour and capital are equally free to exchange (Skeggs, 2014). We explore this further in relation to homeworkers and turn our attention to representation in the supply chain.

Homework and the logic of the supply chain

As discussed in earlier chapters, the nature of homework is often characterised as invisible, insecure and poorly paid. Women homeworkers work directly for employers on piecework rates, or for subcontractors. When there is work, they struggle to get by, and this is often described as working to survive (Burchielli and Delaney 2016; Boeri, 2016; 2018).

The gendered nature of informal and precarious work has been extensively documented (Fudge and Owens, 2006; Vosko, 2006). Stereotypical notions of women as more compliant, nimble-fingered or less reliant on ongoing employment, contribute to reasons women are over-represented in industries with high levels of precarious and informal work such as production in garments, footwear, textiles and electronics, care and domestic work (Elson and Pearson, 1981; Bair, 2010; Rai and Waylen, 2014).

Women's participation in the labour market has increased, yet they remain responsible for social reproduction, which invariably locates them in the types of work most likely to have a higher concentration of women, lower income-levels and greater levels of precariousness. Despite having some benefits through access to an income, they remain burdened and disadvantaged in the labour market in comparison to men (Barrientos and Evers, 2014). Blurred boundaries between paid and unpaid work, and formal and informal work, are critical to understanding women's involvement in homework: although insecure, unrecognized, low paid and usually unprotected, it provides an opportunity to combine their reproductive roles in the household and the community, with their productive role as workers creating surplus value for capital.

Overall, homeworkers may benefit individually through gaining access to paid work, and this may create opportunities that impact positively on the family relations. For example, women homeworkers describe their work as important for them to have some economic independence and to support their children and family. But at the same time, they are acutely aware of the injustice of their work.

> It is only because of our family's economic situation, why I am doing this, nothing else. It is difficult, I know, but I am in the house, I am doing this to meet the needs for my family, so I am just doing this work. The price is not fair at all, it's not enough because costs of living are always going up. With children, whatever I am earning, it just meets some basic costs, to buy the food for the children only. The middle man also, we may say sometimes, 'why do you give us so little?' He says, 'I am carrying all the way from the company to here and in between, I have to give gate passes and I have to pay and come back. This is what I can give you. What can we do?
>
> *(Venpa, homeworker 2012)*

Clearly, paid work is important to homeworkers; however, this homeworker highlights both the inadequacy of the income and a sense of inability to have any positive influence on price and income. We argue that the logic of the supply chain reinforces the social and political inequalities homeworkers experience. Homeworkers who are marginalised socially and economically require collective strategies, recognition of the value of their work, and collective representation to challenge the power relations of the supply chain.

Recognition and value of homeworkers' work

Work arrangements linked to homework commonly evade rights and protections under traditional models of labour law because of the separation of workers from their employers through the use of subcontracting. The latter are often transnational, with many intermediaries, and they also utilise other forms of informal employment, such as small enterprises and home-based workshops. These nodes in the supply chain disguise the employment relationship and obscure who is responsible for minimum conditions for the worker, effectively enabling invisibilisation. Chapter 2 suggests that the process of invisibilisation not only contributes to the devalorisation of categories of work, but also diminishes workers' connections to each other, and limits recognition via regulatory fields, limiting homeworkers' capacity to seek solidarity amongst each other and to establish spatial solidarity across the production network. The process of invisibilisation not only affects informal workers' capacity to join collectively and to struggle together. The disruption of solidarity amongst workers in general, for example between workers in the North and South, and amongst workers located in different tiers or across enterprises of the same supply chain, discourages solidarity, denies workers a moral right to bargain with capital, and disrupts the potential of spatial solidarity across the production network (Silver, 2003). However, the effects of the disruption of solidarity are magnified for marginalised workers such as homeworkers, as this increases the obstacles they face to enact collective agency and strategies to collectively bargain.

The gendered nature of homework has considerable bearing on traditional union's willingness to engage with them as workers. Invisibilisation, also linked to gender, has contributed to the denial of the work of homeworkers, leading to lack of recognition as workers in the production network and invisible to government regulators, unions and corporations (Burchielli and Delaney, 2016). Therefore, homeworkers' struggle for recognition can be linked to a broader struggle of marginalised and disadvantaged groups who are devalued in society (Fraser, 1996). The invisibilisation of homeworkers has contributed to a symbolic devaluation, politically, economically, socially and culturally, and has impacted on their recognition, personal identity and identity as workers. This devaluation process is central to understanding the limits and potential for homeworkers' capacity to gain representation in the supply chain.

The rise of inequality and union representation

Asymmetric power relations are a central feature of supply chains since the brands at the top of the chain wield the greatest power. The imbalance of power makes it difficult for informal workers to raise their voices (Prieto Carrón, 2014; Pearson, 2014; Barrientos & Evers, 2014) since their livelihoods and survival depend on keeping the work they have. Women carry the burden of this unequal exchange, as the majority of workers employed in the global production of garments, electronics and other sectors are women, and women are the majority in the informal sector. Yet traditional forms of representation still elude most informal women workers.

The trade union movement has been the main mechanism for civil society to represent working people and challenge inequality and injustice. However, the unequal exchange has a detrimental impact on transnational labour movements' capacity to mobilise workers under the present-day social relations of global production (Bieler and Morton, 2014; Webster, 2015; Chun, 2012). Union membership continues to decline and unions in various economies and locations struggle to figure out their role, how or if they will challenge the free trade agenda of global capitalism (Bieler & Morton, 2014; Williams, 2015; Webster, Lambert and Bezuidenhout, 2008). The weakened capacity for innovation by unions to address societal and global inequalities arising from trends of globalized capital (Xhafa, 2014) suggests there are two possible responses from unions – those that side with capital and maintain a role for themselves that does not challenge the status quo, and those that join with social movement struggles that aim to redistribute wealth and rebalance inequalities (Bieler, Hilary and Lindberg, 2014; Webster, 2015). This is not just a struggle between capital and labour, it is an ideological divide that has important implications for large numbers of informal women workers; specifically, to be inclusive of the concerns of informal women workers, and to support and enable their participation in this broader struggle against inequality.

Within the broader socio-political and economic forces of neoliberalism, work inequality has increased, corresponding with the rise in precarious informal work, which has impacted on women disproportionally (Beneria, Berik and Floro, 2016). Specific employment relations' conditions are associated with informal and pre-carious work, including a weak employment relationship and low/no worker access to labour and social protection. In the organisational context, employers continuously seek more flexible and low-road strategies and to shift the risks onto workers. Consequently, in terms of worker representation, informal and precarious work aids the decline of unions, undermining the capacity for workers to collec-tively organise and improve rights (Beneria et al., 2016).

Global corporations purchasing practices are continuously reshaping the structure and characteristics of the supply chain, such as the number of participants or layers and where production tiers extend or contract (Barrientos, 2013). Suppliers who contract directly for global corporations or their agents, often referred to as tier one suppliers, may present as modern production sites, but in order to meet the prices of global corporations, they recreate subcontracted work arrangements. The crea-tion of new layers of informalised work arrangements lends itself to increased marginalisation, invisibility and insecurity (ITUC, 2016).

Despite the shift to more casual, contracted, and precarious forms of work arrangements, the rate of organised informal workers into established unions is nominal. This is occurring alongside the reduction in formal employment workers and union members. Globally, there are numerous examples of unions challenging inequalities, such as the broad movements in Greece and Spain to fight against the austerity programs, and participation in social movement activities around tax equity and women's equity in Brazil (Williams, 2015; Xhafa, 2014). Yet strong arguments remain that more unions need to engage with the broader social, political and economic struggles to tackle the inequal-ities affecting many people. Many unions recognise the necessity to challenge injustice and the key indicators of inequality such as increasing precariousness of work, wage gaps, the rise in profit margins of corporations, and the decline in welfare protections as contributors to inequality (Xhafa, 2014). This would involve a major reorientation towards organising the most marginalised groups, and engagement in political struggles outside formal political structures (Webster, 2015; Chun & Williams, 2013; Fraser, 2008). Yet, many unions continue to be deficient in adopting adequate policies and strategies towards parity participation for women and informal workers, such that they might have the necessary help to improve their capacity to reflect the actual worker demographic (Williams, 2015; Xhafa, 2014).

Homeworkers building associational and symbolic power

Homeworkers are rarely members of traditional unions and have limited structural power or capacity to assert some influence on employers, disrupting production and/or service delivery. We have argued this is largely due to intersectionality of gender, class, race and spatial locations. Being situated at the margins of the supply chain, and often marginalised and excluded in society, makes it more difficult for homeworkers to establish worker identity, collective identity and to build collective representation. Less traditional forms of collective representation have been via NGOs and women's organisations. We explore the concept of associational and symbolic forms of power (Wright, 2000; Silver, 2003) here in relation to homeworkers' efforts to gain recognition and improve their capacity to access rights through collective representation.

The process of forming links with NGOs or unions is a potential means for homeworkers to improve recognition and begin to challenge the asymmetries of power in the supply chain. Associational power refers to the power available through the collective and is generally understood in relation to trade unions since they are participants in national and international tripartite structures and often have ties to political parties. Male-dominated unions have traditionally relied upon structural power, essentially the capacity to stop production, and broader political power through having historical ties to a Labour party or centralist democracy party. In many countries, union affiliation to political parties has led to complex and multiple peak union associations – for example in India, Brazil and Indonesia.

Shifts in production to the global South have influenced these traditional power structures. Whilst some unions have managed to maintain strong structural and associational power even when union membership is quite low, due to alliances with political parties in government, others have had to form new alliances with social movement actors to improve their associational power (Webster et al., 2012). Workers having recognition and influence through unions are more likely to be able to gain legitimacy and assert influence on the state, corporations, and global institutions (Silver, 2003).

Homeworkers have had to look beyond unions to establish means to collectively organise and gain any associational power. This has often involved finding allies in local women or NGO organisations to support the formation of new organisations and collective strategies to amplify their voice. While potential exists for homeworkers to forge solidarity links across production and networks through forming new organisations and unions, another option is to join with NGOs and consumer campaigns in 'buyer countries' to provide the networked symbolic power to facilitate homeworkers empowerment through collective agency. The following section outlines case study examples of different approaches to homework representation by unions and NGOs.

Unions and NGOs working with homeworkers

Despite the general lack of focus by unions to recognise and recruit informal women homeworkers, some unions have been working for many years to incorporate informal workers and homeworkers as members. These have had varying success in representing homeworkers and challenging the power relations of the supply chain (Rowbotham, 1999; Burchielli et al., 2009). We explore case study examples from two unions, with a dedicated focus on homeworkers including the Self-Employed Women's Association (SEWA) in India and the Textile Clothing & Footwear Union (TCFUA) in Australia.

Historically, SEWA has been successful in representing bidi (hand-rolled, tobacco leaf cigarettes) workers in the national supply chain context. Despite decades of struggle, the bidi workers were eventually found by the courts to have an employment relationship with local employers, and so to be entitled to legislated rights (Rowbotham, 1999). SEWA is well known for its combined union and NGO activities, with a broad focus on development and women worker rights. SEWA's more recent work involved homeworkers in global supply chains, including establishing a distribution centre to distribute embroidery work to homeworkers in areas around Delhi, North India. This it did in its capacity as a participant in the Ethical Trading Initiative (ETI) supply chain project described in detail in the previous chapter. At the time this project was documented, the actual homeworker membership of SEWA in the Bareilly area in North India was low, though all workers were able to link into broader services associated to SEWA, for example training and childcare through the Handiwork Foundation established in Bareilly and surrounding areas with brands and the ETI project (Delaney, 2016; Mezzadri, 2016).

SEWA's role through SEWA Bharat (the national federation of SEWA organisations) and Ruaab (established by SEWA as a producer owned company with seven production centres), functioned as both intermediary and worker representative (SEWA, 2016). SEWA's combined role as union and NGO has the potential for the women to gain a better understanding of their rights through training and guidance on such matters as occupational health and safety, but also presents incongruities in trying to represent the competing interests of the brand and the workers. One of the key barriers to improving the situation of homeworkers, identified by brand participants of the ETI project, was the brands' unwillingness to change its buying practices that would lead to homeworkers receiving a piece rate equivalent to the minimum wage (Delaney, 2016; Mezzadri, 2016). Therefore, the project focused activities at the subcontractor level of the supply chain, given it could have little effect on brand behaviour (Delaney, 2016). The homeworkers' piece rates were low and remained so; work continued to be irregular, and even SEWA's attempts to reduce pressure on workers in regard to deadlines and quality had mixed outcomes (Archana and Dickson, 2017).

Although workers acknowledged they preferred to work for the SEWA distribution centres rather than with local subcontractors, despite little difference in the piece rate payments, the case highlights the limitations of negotiating with brands primarily within a business relationship (Archana and Dickson, 2017). It further illustrates the primacy of cost cutting in the logic of the supply chain. NGO–Union involvement in global supply chains highlights the complexity of issues faced by homeworkers producing embroidery for global garment brands, and the structural obstacles in the supply chain that challenge homeworker's wellbeing or economic survival, even with union representation. A positive outcome from the SEWA example is improved visibility of homework with brands that are more willing to acknowledge the presence of homeworkers in their supply chains (Archana and Dickson, 2017).

The embroidery homeworkers do not have a clearly defined legal status and protection, therefore the brands engage in a form of CSR-motivated collective bargaining with SEWA. The idea of eliminating the middle-man and creating opportunities to channel work directly to the women workers has merit. Yet, if workers cannot increase their leverage in the supply chain, the potential to influence brands to maintain orders and improve prices is limited. As such, the case is a perfect example of the fundamental power imbalance between labour and capital, whereby capital needs labour to expand but labour needs capital to survive. The brands can subject the NGO intermediary to the same pressures as any other supplier; they can threaten to leave or limit the supply of production. A development business model without collective bargaining strategies to improve workers conditions, and in the case of homeworkers increase piece rates, limits any prospect to challenge the power relations of the supply chain (Mezzadri, 2016).

In another example, the Textile Clothing and Footwear Union of Australia (TCFUA), has a long history of working to address homework inequality in the garment industry. Homeworkers were low paid, and exploitative practices were extensively documented. A social movement alliance formed by the TCFUA with the FairWear campaign gave homeworkers associational and symbolic moral power with brands and government they would otherwise not have had (Burchielli et al., 2009). A key driver of FairWear NGO Asian Women at Work (AWATW) had established an extensive membership base of homeworkers who worked closely to support the union campaign. Union and AWATW representatives founded the FairWear campaign which attracted a broad range of activist supporters from students, faith groups, women's groups and unionists. This enabled the union to orchestrate a number of wide ranging strategies to improve homeworkers' representation to achieve key outcomes. The union and campaign partners were able to collectively bargain with industry and government actors around homeworkers' conditions and to improve legal protection. The union's alliance with FairWear enabled improvements in supply chain transparency and regulation, and improved legal protection for homeworkers, especially through its campaign activities that shamed firms into becoming accredited by the voluntary code, known as the Home Workers Code of Practice (HWCP). These improvements took many years to achieve and the diverse activities FairWear engaged in proved effective in providing a range of community voices. This community–union campaign successfully broadened the debate beyond traditional industrial relations and union–employer debates, to one of public ethical and moral standards and worker rights (Burchielli et al., 2009; Delaney, 2017).

FairWear created a source of social power for homeworkers who otherwise had no structural or associational power, since very few were union members and were invisible to firms and regulators. The success of gaining improved legal provisions to regulate the supply chain placed greater ethical and legal obligations on firms and led to the moral and legal recognition of homeworkers as employees. The social movement alliance between FairWear and TCFUA was successful in connecting firms to broader social and moral concerns about the work conditions of home-workers in the Australian fashion supply chain (Burchielli et al., 2009). Despite the positive outcomes of the long-term activities to support garment homeworkers in Australia, many homeworkers still face barriers to accessing these rights (Delaney, 2017). As legal and ethical accountability prevailed, the industry increasingly moved production offshore. Not surprisingly, global companies are not seeking to source garment production in Australia and, likewise, Australian brands have relocated pro-duction to Bangladesh, China, India and Myanmar amongst other locations.

Although these union case studies have distinct characteristics, both have worked to improve homeworkers' recognition and rights in the supply chain despite few homeworkers being members. The combination of social movement strategies to gain legislative initiatives, a voluntary code and homeworker recognition in Aus-tralia indicates that social power is an important means to increase recognition of marginalised workers in the supply chain. The successful outcomes of homeworker representation in Australia have been thwarted by corporate strategies to move to low-paid labour host locations with less legal protection or limited capacity of the state to monitor and enforce labour regulation. In contrast, in North India, the strategies to maintain homeworkers' livelihood has not been reconciled with the global brand's strategies to benefit from the exploitation of low paid workers, who are paid below minimum wage and well below a living wage. In each case, the current capitalist supply chain logic demonstrates that the dominant strategies by global corporations are to continue to use spatial divisions of labour, to maintain low standards for impoverished workers, and to avail of societal inequalities to maintain control over workers in the supply chain.

Can homeworkers gain recognition and representation in supply chains?

The key characteristics of homeworkers – isolation, poor labour conditions and lack of social capital – means they need assistance to form groups and build col-lective agency. The lack of recognition and representation of homeworkers by global and local corporations and the marginalised conditions they experience exacerbates their feelings of exclusion.

Lack of recognition and representation create significant barriers to home-workers, by discouraging workers to join together to voice their concerns towards either direct employers or global firms (Purkayastha and Subramaniam, 2004). These barriers contribute to a sense of helplessness, a feeling that no one cares about them and that nothing can change, evident through the many conversations with homeworkers. Our data, collected over recent years, indicates they commonly expressed sentiments such as: 'no one is going to listen to us'; 'we are just doing their work'; 'when we have a problem, we talk together us women'.

An example of an NGO development approach is the ActionAid M'Boutik social enterprise project in Myanmar. From a development perspective, social enterprises are an increasingly popular way to promote new work-income opportunities for women, and for those living in poverty with limited income opportunities. Projects often identify homebased workers fitting this criterion since many women are limited by their reproductive roles and cannot leave the family home. The M'Boutik project by Action Aid Myanmar was formed to create opportunities for women in areas with limited employment options, and as an alternative to leaving the local area and moving to work in garment factories under very poor conditions; it is a women producers' association. This niche enterprise has focussed on working with an Australian-based, ethical fashion business, The Fabric Social 'Fair Couture', to create a market for the women's work. In addition, the women make products for the local Myanmar market. The Fabric Social states on its website 'and remember: destroy the patriarchy, not the planet' (https://thefabricsocial.com). The strong linking of social, political and moral reasons to support ethically made garments links the women's development project to potential social power that, on their own, the workers would not have. The distinguishing feature of the M'Boutik model is the commitment to build the women producer's association to create leadership capacity in the women.

M'Boutik offers each of these women a fair wage, dignified working conditions and the right to organise and voice their demands. ActionAid states "This is what a feminist supply chain looks like and this is what we should demand of every brand we buy from" (http://www.actionaid.org/australia/feminist-supply-chain). This feminist supply chain model relates to better employment conditions and the support offered to the women through the development organisation ActionAid Australia and ActionAid Myanmar. The business partnership between the social enterprise and The Fabric Social is not subject to the tight price and deadline pressures of fast-fashion global brands (http://www.actionaid.org/australia/feminist-supply-chain). The M'Boutik program is in its early days: it is not autonomous; the program relies upon donor support, the ActionAid Myanmar management of the project, and the income generated through the enterprise, but there may be potential for women to take the lead and eventually take control in the long term.

A key characteristic of this ethical social enterprise model is the focus on women building income-capacity. Women workers improving their skills and developing their own association is important and has an empowerment aspect. Though not all social enterprises are equal, and many may provide work and income opportunities, few offer worker control and agency in the process. Lack of worker agency and control can lead to the pattern of unequal exchange in the supply chain.

Therefore, social enterprises may offer individual women homeworkers economic and social improvements, such as a source of income, and it is an option for niche markets, but remains beyond the scope for the majority of workers embedded in the social and political relations of the supply chain. Scope certainly exists for social enterprises to provide an alternative to traditional models of trade and uneven development relations, yet such examples remain very few.

Our focus on labour agency through representation in the supply chain encompasses efforts by workers to draw on networked relationships and social power to advance their cause. Existing evidence of such approaches being used among informal workers, including homeworkers, highlights both the possibilities and challenges of marginalised workers forming transnational linkages and utilising symbolic power to gain agency in the supply chain (Delaney et al., 2015). Our discussion of the CIVIDEP project in India, supported by Homeworkers World-wide (HWW), suggests that it is possible to create new homework organisations and unions but that it takes time. CIVIDEP's work with footwear homeworkers in Tamil Nadu, South India, demonstrates that while the workers do not have any formal links to unions (as in membership), and unions are not actively engaged with the homeworkers, the homeworkers have been able to form relationships with local and international NGOs to increase their recognition in the supply chain and assert some pressure on global corporations drawing on social power.

Based in Bangalore, CIVIDEP has experience supporting women workers to form a new union. Over ten years, they supported garment workers in Bangalore to establish the Garment Labour Union (GLU). This experience provided them many lessons in working with local suppliers and global brands in the garment sector. CIVIDEP's experience negotiating with brands and importantly building the women worker's capacity to take on leadership has been critical to the success of GLU. Homeworkers Worldwide had previously documented the situation of homeworkers in the footwear production cluster of Tamil Nadu and needed a local partner to work with those women workers. HWW had previously worked with a local NGO partner with limited experience of working with employers and brands, and this had negatively affected the success of their work. The NGO partner's limited under-standing of supply chains and their failure to develop leadership skills amongst the women homeworkers also contributed to this NGO's work not progressing.

CIVIDEPs initial aim was to establish a worker's centre employing field workers in the Ambur region of Tamil Nadu. Multiple strategies to engage with the women workers included labour and gender rights training sessions, tutoring for children and dialogues on gender issues and women's health. They also established self-help groups in villages and began to support workers to gain access to Gov-ernment schemes and welfare board registration to access some welfare and health benefits. At the same time, they have been attempting to map the supply chains to find more information on intermediaries and details of prices at each tier of the supply chain but have found it difficult to uncover this information. The coop-eration of intermediaries, manufacturers and brands is crucial to gain a better understanding of the pricing structure and to map the supply chain.

CIVIDEP and HWW have engaged in a supply chain pilot with one UK based brand and one supplier in Tamil Nadu. The project is in its initial stages, has improved communication and discussions around improvements for the workers, but lacks specific details. The pilot project contributed to an industry wide meeting being held in 2017. This was the first time that brands, suppliers NGOs and homeworkers had come together to identify problems and discuss possible solutions. Homeworkers addressed the meeting and detailed the main problems around their work: low piece-rates that do not qualify as a living wage; work-process issues including occupational health problems; the general health of workers and their families and the absence of health insurance; a lack of adequate social benefits; the unequal payment relationship with middlemen/intermediaries, and a lack of legal recognition as workers (along with an absence of benefits). Importantly, suppliers and brands ceased to deny the existence of homeworkers in their supply chain. The meeting engaged in discussions over two days, focusing on four key areas: how to achieve fair piece rates; improving the work conditions in village-based stitching centres; expanding the supply chain pilot to more suppliers and brands; and, establishing a footwear sector, multi-stakeholder group to work on industry responses to these issues.

NGOs noted at the meeting that there remains an urgent need to transform the nature of the employment relationship with manufacturers in the area, to make the latter directly responsible for homeworkers who contribute labour to their businesses. It is early days for footwear homeworkers in Tamil Nadu improving visibility, leverage and bargaining potential in the supply chain. The combined social power of local and international NGOs has made an important contribution to improving their presence and capacity to speak directly to the key stakeholders.

This case indicates that even when homeworkers are considered the most vulnerable and least connected to the networks of production, they can still establish relationships that are of benefit to them. Some pre-conditions are necessary for these relationships to bring about positive outcomes to homeworkers: the NGOs must be committed to empowerment and capacity-building of the workers to improve their potential to collectively organise and bargain (Delaney et al., 2015). The challenge remains for homeworkers to gain any collective representation and bargaining; to do so does challenge the premise and function of contemporary supply chains. Returning to the supply chain logic, supply chain pilots are useful but there is a threat that the response of one brand will make it look good and do little for workers. Siloed, one-off pilots offer important lessons but need to be generalised to production networks to have any real impact. Challenging the existing logic used in the supply chain requires strategies to bring about changes beyond specific locations and actors. This is much more difficult.

Homeworker groups and consumer campaigns: global and local advocacy and representation

Consumer campaigns have been used over the last 40 years to highlight and combat inequities and injustice for workers in various industries. The relationship between consumer campaigns and worker groups is not easy. Many consumer-driven campaigns focus on collecting evidence of corporate brands being linked to poor labour practices but rarely prioritise consultation and follow up with workers.

Although fuelled by good intentions, many campaign groups do not have the connections or the long-term association with groups of workers in specific locations. In relation to homeworkers, it is difficult if they are not organised and do not have established leaders to represent them. In such campaigns, the failure to build support for workers to form their own organisations is common. Similarly, there is no ongoing communication with workers to follow up on any change in corporate practices or any adverse effects of such changes on workers (Delaney, 2016). Homeworkers have particular needs and vulnerabilities; for example, the threat of losing their work is high, and any changes, such as the restructuring of the supply chain, may have adverse effects. Such changes may negatively impact on the formation of new organisations and capacity for the women to establish collective agency to represent themselves. Some child-labour campaigns have targeted brands without talking to homeworkers or considering the impact of the campaign on the women and their children, with detrimental consequences for both (Delaney, 2016; Delaney et al., 2017).

As indicated in the CIVIDEP example, realising the potential for homeworkers to build collective strategies and organisation requires a medium to long-term commitment of time and resources. Homeworkers are less likely to have a union or formal organisation since it may take a very long time for workers to develop agency and be able to build their own organisation. Homeworkers require support to form or register a union, often from NGOs committed to improving the women's leadership capacity and collective agency. Campaigns can contribute a form of social power to marginalised workers and create countervailing forces to improve worker representation in the supply chain, but ideally would involve campaigns being willing to take the lead from the homeworkers' needs and demands, because the implications for homeworkers may include losing their work and livelihood.

Conclusion

In this chapter, we have discussed representation as advocacy and capacity-building and outlined the factors that contribute to power imbalances between capital and workers. Uneven development results from trade based on globalised inequalities, particularly lack of adequate recognition and representation. Uneven development is shaped by the market and contributes to workers in the global South being further disadvantaged despite new work opportunities through global production. In terms of our gender justice framework, our discussion highlights the links between recognition and representation, since uneven development relies on the absence of both and reproduces those as injustice conditions.

The capitalist logic used in supply chains relies upon existing inequalities that can be utilised to maintain control over workers. These constitute critical barriers for homeworkers to gain any representation in the supply chain alongside the barriers already existing in their struggle to balance time, space and productivity between income-generating and caring tasks in the home. The act of providing space to marginalised workers and encouraging their voices to improve their representation in the supply chain is of itself important and is a key contribution of this chapter. In the context of global production, representation intersects with worker recognition and rights. We explore this further in the next chapter on organising.

References

Amin, S. (2013) *The Implosion of Contemporary Capitalism*, New York: Monthly Review Press.

Amin, S. (2014) Imperialist Rent and the Challenges for the Radical Left. *Globalizations* 11: 11–21.

Anner, M. (2011) The Impact of International Outsourcing on Unionization and Wages: Evidence from the Apparel Export Sector in Central America. *Industrial and Labour Relations*.

Anner, M. (2018) CSR Participation Committees, Wildcat Strikes and the Sourcing Squeeze in Global Supply Chains. *British Journal of Industrial Relations* 56: 75–98.

Archana and Dickson, M. (2017) Social Sustainability in Apparel Supply Chains: Organizational Practices for Managing Sub-Contracted Homework. In C. Henninger, P. Alevizou, H. Gowerek et al. (eds), *Sustainability in Fashion: A Cradle to Upcycle Approach*. Houndmills, Basingstoke: Palgrave Macmillan.

Bair, J. (2010) On Difference and Capital: Gender and the Globalization of Production. *Signs* 36: 203–226.

Barrientos, S. (2013) 'Labour Chains': Analysing the Role of Labour Contractors in Global Production Networks. *Journal of Development Studies* 49: 1058–1071.

Barrientos, S. (2014) Gendered Global Production Networks: Analysis of Cocoa–Chocolate Sourcing. *Regional Studies* 48: 791–803.

Barrientos, S. and Evers, B. (2014) Gendered Production Networks: Push and Pull on Corporate Responsibility? In S. Rai and G. Waylen (eds) *New Frontiers in Feminist Political Economy* (pp. 43–61). London and New York: Routledge.

Barrientos, S., Kothari, U. and Phillips, N. (2013) Dynamics of Unfree Labour in the Contemporary Global Economy. *Journal of Development Studies* 49: 1037–1041.

Barrientos, S., Mayer, F., Pickles, J., et al. (2011) Decent Work in Global Production Networks: Framing the Policy Debate. *International Labour Review* 150: 299–317.

Beneria, L. and Floro, M. (2005) Distribution, Gender and Labor Market Informalization: A Conceptual Framework and a Focus on Homebased Workers, forthcoming in, Cornell e-Publishing. In N. Kudva and L. Beneria (eds), *Rethinking Informalization: Precarious Jobs, Poverty and Social Protection*. Ithaca: Cornell University.

Benería, L., Berik, G. and Floro, M. (2016) *Gender, Development and Globalization: Economics as if People Mattered*. New York: Routledge.

Bieler, A. and Morton, A.D. (2014) Uneven and Combined Development and Unequal Exchange: The Second Wind of Neoliberal 'Free Trade'? *Globalizations* 11: 35–45.

Bieler, A., Hilary, J. and Lindberg, I. (2014) Trade Unions, 'Free Trade', and the Problem of Transnational Solidarity: An Introduction. *Globalizations* 11: 1–9.

Boeri, N. (2016) *Boundaries of Home and Work: Social Reproduction and Home-Based Workers in Ahmedabad, India*. CUNY Academic Works. New York: City University of New York.

Boeri, N. (2018) Challenging the Gendered Entrepreneurial Subject: Gender, Development, and the Informal Economy in India. *Gender & Society* 32: 157–179.

Bowles, P. and Harriss, J. (2010) *Globalization and Labour in China and India: Impacts and Responses*. Houndmills, Basingstoke, Hampshire: Palgrave Macmillan.

Burchielli, R., Buttigieg, D. and Delaney, A. (2008) Organizing Homeworkers: The Use of Mapping as an Organizing Tool. *Work, Employment & Society* 22: 167–180.

Burchielli, R., Delaney, A., Tate, J. and Coventry, K. (2009) The FairWear Campaign: An Ethical Network in the Australian Garment Industry. *Journal of Business Ethics* 90: 575–588.

Burchielli, R., Delaney, A. and Coventry, K. (2014) Campaign Strategies to Develop Regulatory Mechanisms: Protecting Australian Garment Homeworkers. *Journal of Industrial Relations* 56: 81–102.

Burchielli, R. and Delaney, A. (2016) The Invisibilization and Denial of Work in Argentinian Garment Homework. *Relations Industrielles/Industrial Relations* 71: 468–493.

Carswell, G. and De Neve, G. (2013) Labouring for Global Markets: Conceptualising Labour Agency in Global Production Networks. *Geoforum* 44: 62–70.

Chun, J. (2012) The Power of the Powerless: New Schemas and Resources for Organizing Workers in Neoliberal Times. In A. Suzuki (ed.), *Cross-National Perspectives on Social Movement Unionism: Diversities of Labour Movement Revitalization in Japan, Korea and the United States* (pp. 37–60). Oxford: Peter Lang.

Chun, J. and Williams, M. (2013) Labour as a Democratizing Force? Lessons from South Africa. *Rethinking Development and Inequality* 2: 2–9.

Delaney, A. (2016) Barriers to Redress: Leather Footwear Workers in Tamil Nadu, South India. *Non-Judicial Redress Mechanism Report Series 12*. Melbourne: Corporate Accountability Research.

Delaney, A. and Connor, T. (2016) *Forced Labour in the Textile and Garment Sector in Tamil Nadu, South India: Strategies for Redress*. Melbourne: Corporate Accountability Research.

Delaney, A. and Tate, J. (2015) Forced Labour and Ethical Trade in the Indian Textile Industry. In L. Waite, G. Craig, H. Lewis, et al. (eds), *Vulnerability, Exploitation and Migrants: Insecure Work in a Globalised Economy*. (pp. 244–255). Basingstoke: Palgrave.

Delaney, A., Tate, J. and Burchielli, R. (2016) Homeworkers Organizing for Recognition and Rights: Can International Standards Assist Them? In J. Jensen and N. Lichtenstein (eds), *The ILO From Geneva to the Pacific Rim*. (pp. 159–179). Houndmills, Basingstoke: Palgrave Macmillan and the International Labour Office.

Delaney, A., Burchielli, R. and Connor, T. (2015) Positioning Women Homeworkers in a Global Footwear Production Network: How Can Homeworkers Improve Agency, Influence and Claim Rights? *Journal of Industrial Relations* 57: 641–659.

Delaney, A., Burchielli, R. and Tate, J. (2017) Corporate CSR Responses to Homework and Child Labour in the Indian and Pakistan Leather Sector. In K. Grosser, L. McCarthy and M. Kilmore (eds), *Gender Equality and Responsible Business: Expanding CSR Horizons (pp. 170-184)*. London New York: Routledge.

Dunaway, W. (2014) *Gendered Commodity Chains: Seeing Women's Work and Households in Global Production*. Stanford: Stanford University Press.

Elson, D. (2015) *Value: The Representation of Labour in Capitalism*. London and New York: Verso.

Elson, D. and Pearson, R. (1981) 'Nimble Fingers Make Cheap Workers': An Analysis of Women's Employment in Third World Export Manufacturing. *Feminist Review* 7: 87–107.

Fraser, N. (1996) Social Justice in the Age of Identity Politics: Redistribution, Recognition, and Participation. *The Tanner Lectures of Human Values*. Stanford University.

Fraser, N. (2008) Mapping the Feminist Imagination: From Redistribution to Recognition and Representation. *Scales of Justice: Reimagining Political Space in a Globalizing World*. New York: Columbia University Press.

Fudge, J. and Owens, R. (eds) (2006) *Precarious Work, Women, and the New Economy: The Challenge to Legal Norms*. Oxford: Hart Publishing.

Gereffi, G. (1994) Capitalism, Development and Global Commodity Chains. In L. Sklair (ed.), *Capitalism and Development* (pp. 211–231). London: Routledge.

HWW. (2004) Organising for Change: Women Homebased Workers in the Global Economy. In J. Tate (ed.), *Final Report on Mapping Homebased Work*. Leeds, UK: Homeworkers Worldwide.

ILO. (2016) Decent Work in Global Supply Chains. *International Labour Conference*. Geneva: International Labour Office.

ITUC. (2016) Scandal Inside the Global Supply Chains of 50 Top Companies. *Frontlines Report*. Brussels: International Trade Union Confederation, 44.

Jenkins, J. (2013) Organizing 'Spaces of Hope': Union Formation by Indian Garment Workers. *British Journal of Industrial Relations* 51: 623–643.

Jenkins, J. and Blyton, P. (2017) In Debt to the Time-Bank: the Manipulation of Working Time in Indian Garment Factories and 'Working Dead Horse. *Work, Employment and Society* 31(1): 90–105. 10.1177/0950017016664679.

Mezzadri, A. (2016) Class, Gender and the Sweatshop: On the Nexus between Labour Commodification and Exploitation. *Third World Quarterly*37: 1877–1900.

Pearson, R. (2014) Gender, Globalization and the Reproduction of Labour: Bringing the State Back In. *New Frontiers in Feminist Political Economy* (pp. 19–42). London and New York: Routledge.

Phillips, N. (2011) Informality, Global Production Networks and Dynamics of 'Adverse Incorporation'. *Global Networks* 11: 380–397.

Prieto-Carrón, M. (2014) Bringing Resistance to the Conceptual Centre: Threats to Social Reproduction and Feminist Activism in Nicaraguan Commodity Chains. In W. Dunaway (ed.) *Gendered Commodity Chains: Seeing Women's Work and Households in Global Production* (pp. 225–240). Stanford: Stanford University Press.

Posthuma, A. and Nathan, D. (2010) *Labour in Global Production Networks in India*. New Delhi: Oxford University Press.

Powell, B. (2014) *Out of Poverty: Sweatshops in the Global Economy*. New York: Cambridge University Press, 175.

Purkayastha, B. and Subramaniam, M. (2004) *The Power of Women's Informal Networks: Lessons in Social Change from South Asia and West Africa*. Lanham: Lexington Books.

Rai, S.M. and Waylen, G. (eds) (2014) *New Frontiers in Feminist Political Economy*. London and New York: Routledge.

Rainnie, A., Herod, A. and McGrath-Champ, S. (2011) Review and Positions: Global Production Networks and Labour. *Competition & Change* 15: 155–169.

Reinecke, J. and Donaghey, J. (2015) After Rana Plaza: Building Coalitional Power for Labour Rights Between Unions and (Consumption-Based) Social Movement Organisations. *Organization* 22: 720–740.

Rowbotham, S. (1999) New Ways of Organising in the Informal Sector: Four Case Studies of Trade Union Activity. *A HomeNet Study Pack*. Leeds: HomeNet.

Selwyn, B. (2011) The Political Economy of Class Compromise: Trade Unions, Capital-Labour Relations and Development in North East Brazil. *Antipode* 43: 1305–1329.

Selwyn, B. (2013) Social Upgrading and Labour in Global Production Networks: A Critique and an Alternative Conception. *Competition & Change* 17: 75–90.

Selwyn, B. (2014) Commodity Chains, Creative Destruction and Global Inequality: a Class Analysis. *Journal of Economic Geography* 15: 253–274.

SEWA. (2016) *Self-Employed Women's Association Annual Report 2015–2016*.

Silver, B. (2003) *Forces of Labour: Workers Movements and Globalization Since 1870*. Cambridge: Cambridge University Press.

Shamir, H. (2016) Unionizing Subcontracted Labor. *Theoretical Inquiries in Law* 17: 229–255.

Skeggs, B. (2014) Values Beyond Value? Is Anything Beyond the Logic of Capital? *The British Journal of Sociology* 65: 1–20.

Taglioni, D. and Winkler, D. (2014) Making Global Value Chains Work for Development. *Economic Premise*, 143. May, World Bank, Washington. https://openknowledge.worldbank.org/handle/10986/18421

Tsing, A. (2009) Supply Chains and the Human Condition. *Rethinking Marxism* 21: 148–176.

Vosko, L. (2006) Gender, Precarious Work, and the International Labor Code: The Ghost in the ILO Closet. *Precarious Work, Women, and the New Economy: The Challenge to Legal Norms*. Oxford: Hart Publishing.

Webster, E. (2015) The Shifting Boundaries of Industrial Relations: Insights from South Africa. *International Labour Review* 154: 27–36.

Webster, E., Lambert, R. and Bezuidenhout, A. (2008) *Grounding Globalization: Labour in the Age of Insecurity*. Victoria: Wiley-Blackwell.

Williams, M. (2015) Transformative Unionisation and Innovative Campaigns Challenging Inequality. *Global Labor Journal* 6: 253–265.

World Bank. (2018) Making Global Value Chains Work for Development. https://openknowledge.worldbank.org/handle/10986/18421?locale-attribute=en

Wright, E. (2000) Working-Class Power, Capitalist-Class Interests, and Glass Compromise. *American Journal of Sociology* 105: 957–1002.

Xhafa, E. (2014) Trade Unions and Economic Inequality: Perspectives, Policies and Strategies. *International Journal of Labour Research* 6: 35–55.

6

HOMEWORKERS ORGANISING

Transnational to local

Introduction

Women have always been over-represented in informal homework. Perceptions of gender and socially constructed gender norms explain why informal homeworkers have been labelled 'unorganisable' (Rowbotham, 1998). Historically, many union and civil society groups have considered homeworkers to be outside of the working class. Although women's organisations made some attempts to organise homeworkers in Britain and Europe in the early 1900s (Rowbotham and Mitter, 1994; Prügl, 1999), male dominated unions argued that the promotion of the rights of homeworkers would undermine the hard-won entitlements of workers in factories. They were driven by a fear that recognition of homework as work would undermine the status of men's work and weaken the collective strength of the working class. This view came to dominate, and unions supported the banning of homework instead of the organisation and mobilisation of homeworkers as workers (Boris, 1994; Rowbotham, 1998). Early attempts to organise homeworkers in India show unions rarely moved beyond the perception of homeworkers as housewives being supported by their husbands, therefore questioning why they might need higher wages. Such attitudes were reinforced by colonial, class and caste constructs of gender to keep women in the private sphere of the home and preserve the public sphere – where collective organising has traditionally occurred – for men (Lindberg, 2001; Priyadarshini, 2016).

The high incidence of homework in many supply chains around the world is a testament to the fact that the banning of homework was not a successful strategy. Today, following those of the early 1900s, additional regulatory factors are at play in structuring the gendered nature of homework and creating barriers to collective organising. As we explored in Chapter 5, the widespread adoption of neoliberal policies has produced institutional configurations that have promoted the autonomy

and wealth of financial institutions and undermined the authority of national structures of accountability for transnational business. Other regulatory changes at the
national level have also undermined freedom of association and the power of the
union movement. Homework is shaped by the dynamics of both supply chains and
domestic economies; employers, subcontractors and those with governance power in
supply chains have manipulated and exploited gender divisions of labour to their
advantage (Mies, 2014). Women homeworkers are forced to balance the role of
worker and housewife, bearing the burdens of both roles (Boris and Prügl, 1996;
Mies, 2014). When work is undertaken within the home, this contributes to
women's isolation, and in turn, their invisibility in the public eye. These changes in
institutional configurations make it more difficult for homeworkers to make collective claims to redistribute risk and profit along supply chains.

Yet, various empirical studies show that women are not unorganisable; it is rather
the case that different forms of organising and mobilisation are required than for
male, factory-based workers, taking into account these institutional challenges. In the
20th century, the experiences of the Working Women's Forum in Chennai South
India, and Self-Employed Women's Association (SEWA) in Ahmedabad North India
in organising the informal sector and home-based women workers, have demonstrated that new forms of mobilisation and struggle as part of the working class are
possible (Rose, 1992; Nachiappan and Rajan, 2008). No doubt, organising homeworkers has unique challenges compared to organising factory-based workers. Given
that non-standard – informal – workers now form the majority worldwide in both
the economic South and North, viewing these workers as less than 'real workers' or
unorganisable (Gallin, 2001; Burchielli, Buttigieg and Delaney, 2008; Burchielli,
Buttigieg and Delaney, 1999) is not simply supportable based on the evidence.
Worse, such views have dire consequences for solidarity amongst the working class
and the strength and influence of unions.

This chapter discusses various transnational, grassroots and labour initiatives that
directly facilitate the organising of homeworkers and seeks to understand what has
made some strategies more successful than others. We find that successful collective
organising depends on taking into account the specific needs of women in
designing organisational structures and representation strategies. The gendered
nature of homework has implications for how collective organising occurs, what
form it takes, and how homeworkers are able to navigate their way from the private to the public sphere – the space outside the home.

The evidence that we present in this chapter shows that homeworkers need a
collective organisation to gain visibility, be heard and recognised by governments,
unions and corporations. Their position as workers is linked in many different ways
to their identities and situations as women in the family or society at large, or as
members of particular communities, such as indigenous women or minorities.
Building new homeworker organisations can promote self-identification and self-
recognition as workers. Collective organising promotes both self and broader
societal recognition of the economic contribution of homeworkers to household,
national and global economies.

Our discussion concentrates on the needs of homeworkers to develop collective strategies underpinned by the notion of rights. The concept of 'rights' in the gender justice framework is linked to fundamental rights of freedom of association and collective bargaining. Collective organisation and representation are central to improving homeworkers' identification as workers, recognition by government, corporations, employers and society to enable participation in the broader social dialogue (Fraser, 2005). In order to access rights, homeworkers need to take the necessary steps to address their collective needs, that go beyond survival, toward accessing rights and redistribution. We argue that organising impacts across all four dimensions of the gender justice framework outlined in the introduction to this book; recognition, representation, rights and redistribution. We take up the discussion of the gender justice dimensions through the chapter and in the concluding comments.

Explanations for participation in collective action

In this chapter, we build on the extant literature that provides explanations for participation in collective action and the conditions that enable organising. Traditional theories of industrial relations provide an explanation for individual participation in collective action and organisations. Worker mobilisation identifies collective interests; it is achieved by a promotion of injustice frames – largely generated by leaders (Tilly, 1978; Kelly, 1998). Mobilisation theory explains the conditions and processes that can enable organising. It is consistent with the organising model approach that has been adopted by some unions in global North economies to increase and promote active membership (Frege and Kelly, 2004). A critical component of mobilisation theory is the construction of social identity that promotes positive in-group behaviour and negative out-group behaviour. This is necessary to attribute the injustice to the government or employer and for agency to be determined. For home-based workers in the informal economy, mobilisation requires some preliminary steps prior to the establishment of the 'injustice frames' and the formation of social identity: considerable attention must first be given to acknowledging the individual's isolation and to facilitating the recognition of their identity as worker (Burchielli et al., 2008).

Traditional theories of institutional change contend that change occurs when powerful actors have the will and ability to change institutions in favour of new ideas (Steinmo, 2008). But what about when the agents of social change – homeworkers and their allies – are not powerful? Here, the idea of networked power is useful. This chapter is framed around this idea, as we observe that homeworker organisations, internationally and locally, have generally operated as networks. Networks can be understood as providing channels for transmission of both material and ideational resources, knowledge sharing, influence, alternative forms of power, i.e. associational and social power, and solidarity (Wright 2000; Silver, 2003). Social movement literature describes transnational advocacy networks (Keck and Sikkink, 1998) and transnational feminist networks (Moghadam, 2005) functioning through a common agenda and links across national boundaries. Women homeworkers often join together to develop collective responses to their situation, more often the types of networks they establish are informal and often difficult to sustain (Purkayastha and Subramaniam, 2004; Delaney, Tate and Burchielli, 2016). Homeworker organisations may take various forms, for example, as informal networks, as a combination of a formerly registered organisation or union, an informal group, association, cooperative or self-help group. These various forms of organisation are less likely to be acknowledged, nor are they just a substitute for formal collective organisations (unions), since in many countries informal workers face obstacles to belonging to a union (Burchielli et al., 2008).

Braithwaite (2006) has proposed that such networks are particularly useful in settings with significant governance deficits, which is often the case in developing economies, and where agents are relatively weak. Network structures and processes enable participating actors to contribute to processes of social influence over targeted decisions and outcomes through a number of mechanisms. Social movement literature suggests the potential for marginalised workers outside of traditional union structures lacking associational power, to build broader linkages through which to establish forms of social power (Silver, 2003). Feminist scholars have noted the need to highlight the strategies and lived experience of women as network actors (Kuumba, 2001; Purkayastha and Subramaniam, 2004). Frequently women may form informal networks, that offer new modes for capacity building, and organising potential, but these networks may not be formally constituted or recognised (Moghadam, 1999; Kuumba, 2001; Purkayastha and Subramaniam, 2004; Moghadam, 2005). Rowbotham (1998), draws on experience of European homework networks to conceptualise a homeworker network as the 'weapon of the weak' and to promote the positive role of homeworker transnational and local collective strategies. Kabeer, Milward and Sudarshan (2013) extend the idea of informal women workers organising in networks as the weapon of the organised.

A number of network functions seem to play particularly important roles in helping to achieve institutional change and create opportunities for resistance as discussed in the examples of homeworker organising in this chapter. In the next section, we build on the industrial relations literature by drawing on the transnational organising and network theories. We use these frameworks to analyse how the homeworkers' network at the transnational level has functioned to support homeworker advocacy and organising around the globe – the formation of which has been important in developing new homeworker informal associations and unions and homework representation at the local and transnational level. We show how the transnational homework network consists of informal and formal group members and participants that do not neatly fit within the traditional social movement literature definition of a movement or within concepts of a labour union drawn from the industrial relations literature.

The international homeworkers' network: transnational organising and solidarity

The international homework movement can be understood as a network. This network, the International Homeworkers Network (IHN) began with local groups working to address the needs of some of the poorest women workers (Rose, 1992; HomeNet, 1995). In the 1970s, new unions emerged with the objective to represent primarily women, informal workers, including homeworkers. Two women's unions were established in India, the Self-Employed Women's Association (SEWA), a breakaway group from a textile labour association in Ahmedabad, and the Working Women's Forum (WWF), based in Chennai. Existing unions such as STIBTTA[1] in Madeira, Portugal, a traditional textile union, shifted its focus from textile workers to the needs of homeworkers, since they had come to out-number union members (Martens and Mitter, 1994). Homework groups in the United Kingdom had begun to form with the assistance of local councils to address the needs of homeworkers. The West Yorkshire Homeworking Group is one such example. The West Yorkshire Homeworking Group in Leicester revealed a shift in attitude, where advocates changed from doing for, to engagement with, home-workers (Tate, 1994a). The homework group sought homeworkers' views about their needs and priorities, what they want and what kind of organisation they could form. Homeworkers, rather than being 'helped', were encouraged to develop their leadership skills (Tate, 1994a). In the late 1970s and early 1980s, homeworkers from the UK participated in homeworker exchanges that encour-aged the hope that the situation of homeworkers would improve. These exchanges led to increased activism around homework in the UK, the establishment of a UK national group on homework (NGH), and further to the extension of links with homework groups emerging around the globe (Tate, 1996b).

By the late 1980s and early 1990s, homework groups were coming to under-stand how important international mobilising was to the local work of organising. The growing number of homework groups and unions working around home-work related activities through the 1980s and into the 1990s enabled a new level of cooperation. The importance of this international cooperation was understood not only to lie in the importance of influencing international fora like the ILO, but also in order to intervene in supply chain governance.

> It is vital to complement the work through international organisations by establishing links between the grassroots organisations. The companies which employ homeworkers, or sell the goods produced by homeworkers, in an area like West Yorkshire often themselves operate on a world scale and we have to respond likewise.
>
> *(Tate, 1994b: 215)*

In 1990 an international meeting was held in the Netherlands, attended by a number of homework groups from the United Kingdom, Europe, South East Asia,

India and the Middle East. The exchange of experiences, ideas and solidarity by homeworkers, and homeworker groups assisted in identifying homeworker needs. These included the need for improved visibility of the work and the workers. That the work is underpaid, undervalued and that workers lacked recognition were found to be common features of homework across the globe (Tate, 1996b; Prügl, 1999a). A critical mass of homework and union organisations focused on homework had developed by this point in time, to sufficiently identify the strength of the exchange and solidarity (Boris and Prügl, 1996). The European group on homework had begun to meet and contribute to the lobbying process for homeworker recognition through the campaign for an ILO convention on homework. Further, they formed a coalition of homework groups, unions and researchers including women trade unionist to improve homework visibility and protection (Tate, 1996a).

Around this time the union and development agency, SEWA, despite not being recognised by Indian union federations, sought and gained recognition through joining international trade unions. SEWA grew quickly to establish itself as a union that organised women in informal employment (Jhabvala, 1994), using its union status to lobby at the ILO for informal workers to be placed on the agenda, then being invited to participate in a homework expert panel. In 1990 SEWA, along with unions from Britain, Canada, Portugal and the Netherlands, attended the ILO expert panel meeting on homework. The experience of SEWA and other homework groups at this time impressed on unions and governments that international recognition could contribute to having greater influence and place poor and marginalised women workers on the agenda (Tate, 1994a; Tate, 1996b). The coming together of homeworking groups across Europe, SEWA in India and groups from South East Asia, and the newly formed Self-Employed Women's Union (SEWU) in South Africa solidified transnational links and the focus on homework issues. At this time, many feminist scholars were also engaged through their research and activism in supporting homeworker groups. Research and several key texts on homework emerged over the 1990s which contributed to increased recognition of the gender dimensions of homework, provided important analyses of the tensions of homework under capitalism and exchange of ideas amongst activists and scholars (see Allen and Wolkowitz, 1987; Boris and Daniels, 1989; Martens and Mitter, 1994; Rowbotham and Mitter, 1994; Boris and Prügl, 1996).

At an international level, lobbying efforts coalesced around the effort to have an ILO Convention on Homework passed. International forums conducted by the ILO created the opportunity for groups to meet and further develop policy, strategies, and ways of working collaboratively (HomeNet, 1995). A spin off benefit of participation in these forums and discussions at the ILO on the possible Convention in the early 1990s was the opportunity for many groups to meet and discuss mobilisation strategies. One of the conclusions drawn from such meetings was that unions alone could not successfully organise homeworkers (Tate, 1996b). Similarly, the homeworker groups realised that to secure improved working conditions for homeworkers would involve building alliances at the local, national and international level, alongside work to organise, gain legislation and campaign on broader issues affecting homeworkers.

The emergence of the international homeworkers network (IHN) HomeNet International (HNI) in 1994 as a registered organisation is consistent with a number of conditions highlighted by Keck and Sikkink (1998) as favourable for Transnational Advocacy Networks (TANs) to operate under. Framing the politics of homeworking as 'poor, invisible and unrecognised women workers' within the informal employment workforce, the IHN effectively used international forums such as the ILO to secure the convention and put homework on the agenda (HomeNet, 1995). The campaign for the ILO homework convention on behalf of homeworkers, a traditionally industrially weak group, had an influence on nation-state behaviour, policy and institutional procedures; this is evident in how governments and unions voted to support the ILO convention on homework, and the inclusion of homework in broader policy initiatives. In addition, homework groups at the national level gained legitimisation through participation in the International Homeworkers Network (IHN), which gave them some credibility in dealing with government authorities.

Under the influence of the work of HNI, two new networks emerged – Women in Informal Employment: Globalizing and Organizing (WIEGO) in 1997, and Homeworkers Worldwide (HWW) in 1999. WIEGO grew out of the collaboration between three individuals, a representative of Unifem, one from Harvard University and a representative from Self-Employed Women's Association (SEWA). These three individuals formed an executive committee in 1997. HomeNet and StreetNet, a newly formed international street vendors' network, were both members of the steering committee (HomeNet, 1999a). SEWA has been the mainstay and a strong proponent of WIEGO (Jhabvala, 1999; Jhabvala, 2001). WIEGO is a transnational network working to improve the voice, visibility and validity of the working poor, especially women (WIEGO 2018). SEWA has held a key position in WIEGO and strongly influenced the platform and strategy, which was to advocate and represent the informal workers at international forums, in particular, the ILO (Tate 2000a; Jhabvala, 1999; Jhabvala, 2001; Tate, 2001).

Two years after the formation of WIEGO, the entire HNI board supported the formation of a UK based group in 1999, HWW, that sought funding to support new organising work in regions where organising had not previously been established (Tate, 2001). Differences within the HNI board and membership had surfaced and tensions continued over HNI involvement in WIEGO, the nature of HNI representation in WIEGO, and concerns around the WIEGO top down approach (Tate, 2000a). The HNI board worked to develop a new international structure but could not agree on a number of key points. A critical point of difference emerged around the nature of which groups could vote under the proposed new structure. HNI links with new groups had expanded rapidly due to the emergence of support groups (HomeNet, 1999c). The support groups defined their role as being to identify homeworkers in their regions and encourage and support them to form their own organisations (HomeNet, 1999b). Ana Clara in Chile, the

Turkish Homeworkers Group and in India, Agriculture, Dairying, Industries, Tree Plantation, Handicrafts/Home-based work and the integration of Women (ADHITI), are all examples of support groups (HomeNet, 1999b). The homework support groups played a critical role in the process to facilitate new homeworker organising (HomeNet, 1999b; ADITHI, 2003). Evidence available indicated that there was an increase in new homework group formation through the work of the support groups (HomeNet, 1999d).

A point of difference amongst HNI board members around the new HNI structure focused on whether support groups would have a direct vote alongside membership organisations. A number of issues and tensions existed within the HNI board, which can be summarised as the relationship and role of HNI with WIEGO and SEWA's prioritising of policy work at the international level, specifically at the ILO, over international organising work, support for the new HNI representative structure, and grassroots representation within WIEGO (Jhabvala, 1999; HomeNet, 1999d; Tate, 2000a; 2001; 2002a). These differences in priorities are some of the issues that contributed to the divisions amongst HNI, and the departure of a few homework groups altogether. Many groups had noted that the strength of international network was based on the social and political nature of the network and solidarity between homework groups, rather than the makeup or existence of the HNI board (Tate, 2002b). Such diversions in agenda, strategy and objectives are not uncommon in organisations, particularly, when a movement expands, or the focus moves beyond its original reason for coming together (Tate, 2001; 2002a; 2002b). The HNI under the auspice of HWW grew significantly between 1996 and 2001 and extended its reach to new groups and unions. The network had increased support for homeworker organising and engagement with homeworkers through the mapping activities described later in this chapter and continued to extend this work beyond HNI (HWW, 2002a).

The funds for the mapping program had been secured and an initial pilot year had been trialed in 2000. Following the dissolving of the HomeNet board, the previous HNI coordinator was employed by HWW as the international program director, therefore enabling continuity of the network's activities. HNI funding had expired and HWW continued to produce the HNI newsletter and communicate the mapping program strategies and events. The HWW International mapping program (IMP) coordinated by HWW and discussed later in this chapter, has been substantial in supporting grassroots organising. As the mapping program evolved, the majority of HNI network members, either as direct or indirect participants of the mapping, continued to be involved to facilitate new organising and to expand the network. Without the UK organisation HWW, and funding for the mapping program, homeworker organising would not have progressed to the extent it has since 2000 (Tate, 2002a; 2002b). HWW's main focus has been in supporting homework organisations and new homeworker organisations; subsequently, this evolved into a new transnational network registered in 2005 under the name Federation of Homeworkers Worldwide. WIEGO has continued to support informal workers, assisting an international network of street vendors,

Street Net, and worked with the domestic workers' network to secure the ILO Convention on domestic work. WIEGO has successfully raised funds to produce research and publications on a broad range of informal economy and informal women workers' issues with a development focus.

It is our view that participation in a transnational network appears to be enabling to national groups to engage in social dialogue processes, reinforced by campaigning and grassroots membership building and empowerment in the localities where homework is concentrated. This, in turn, strengthens the work at the international level, since developments that advance homework recognition in one country can be documented and used as an example for others to adapt to their own national context. While local homework group achievements are largely driven by local conditions, groups can benefit from participation in the transnational organisation through solidarity and support established with other nationally based groups and others in their region, facilitating *representation* – one of our four dimensions of gender justice. In this way, the international homework network displays some of the characteristics of a transnational feminist network (Moghadam, 2005).

The lessons learnt from the early network HomeNet International indicates there is a degree of fragility, which challenges homeworker networks' sustainability due to lack of resources, political differences and tensions over directions and priorities of the work. The nature of homework groups at the national and local level structure and membership is often fluid, displaying similarities to the informal work arrangements of homework.

The next section discusses one of the key activities of Homeworkers World-wide: the international mapping program. This mapping is discussed in later sections where we analyse how the IHN functions.

Case study: the HWW International mapping program

Building on the past success of HomeNet International, the mapping program promoted organising and new regional and international networks as an integral part of organisation building. Organising within the mapping program went beyond the establishment of local homeworkers' groups. Many rural and city-based groups organised into national groups and international links were forged between various national groups. Mapping in Chile led to mapping in other Latin American countries and to the emergence of a strong regional network of homeworker organisations in Brazil, Bolivia and Mexico. The program strength in sharing country experiences resulted in an internationalising of homeworkers' experiences and validated women's experiences as being part of an international movement.

> … (Homeworkers participated) in the Regional Meeting in Bolivia. It was of great importance to meet other homeworkers, other forms of production, the culture of a beautiful country and the regional projects. The result was very positive, and the experience renewed the energy to keep working,
>
> *(Homeworker, Bolivia)*

In recognition of the importance of global advocacy, the new international homeworkers' organisation (Federation of Homeworkers Worldwide – FHWW) was registered. Thus, organising – at every level – was an integral component of mapping.

> For us, a priority was, the international Federation of home-based workers because then we can go to the Government with a 'voice'. Improving literacy through the REFLECT centres, lobbying around tree plantation, girl child-labour and putting pressure on the Government to do a large media campaign on home-based workers, is critical, so is the national action for the informal sector.
>
> *(Srinivasan, 2003: 1)*

The mapping process developed a 'mapping pack', which included guidelines on how to conduct mapping; how to organise homeworkers, and forms for data collection (HWW, 2002a) in both horizontal and vertical mapping contexts. Horizontal mapping (HM) refers to the method used to document the identifying characteristics of the homeworker, their location and industry sector, by contacting individuals in their homes or communities. HM focuses on discussions and data gathering on demographic characteristics of homeworkers, their home situation, their work processes, their employment relationships, payment amounts and processes and the problems and issues that they face (HWW, 2004). In contrast, vertical mapping (VM) refers to a process that identifies the chain of production linking homeworkers, subcontractors, intermediaries, buyers and brand owners.

As well as data collection, another crucial activity in the mapping process relates to training. During the mapping project, it was common practice to train a number of the newly identified homeworkers as part of the action research team, which assisted in organisation building. Action research teams were established, and training was conducted in key areas. Researchers and grassroots leaders received training in the research method and in organising strategies, with the clear objective of building an organisation through their ongoing contact with homeworkers as they conducted the interviews and collected the relevant data (HWW, 2004). In homeworker mapping, research, training and organising are simultaneous and inter-related processes, rather than parts of a sequence. The mapping included various difficulties, such as defining who was a homeworker, and various organising outcomes including self-help savings groups, worker collectives, cooperatives as well as some new unions. Moreover, the mapping program indicated that homeworkers participated most successfully when they were able to benefit from advocacy and services, including training to enable participation. The mapping as organising approach provides organising models and approaches for unions and other labour rights groups to support new homeworker organising and can encourage new groups to get started.

Successful organising has often begun with training members of the organising groups, who have little experience with homeworkers and the international network. This training is based on the general concept of homework and examines questions such as, 'what is homework?', and 'who are homeworkers?' The second level of training involves leadership training for women homeworkers. This training can assist in identifying potential leaders, who can then receive additional training, and build their own capacity to train other homeworkers. Training is a fundamental step in the organising process, as is the coming together of homeworkers to define their own needs and demands, and to plan for the type of organisation that can best represent them.

It was proposed to work in focus groups because they open the possibility of reducing the psychological and social isolation which immobilises women workers in the poorest areas.

> Activities were prepared which allowed them to express their personal situation and the team had to work on self-knowledge as a tool for change. Knowing themselves they will be able to know their peers and then analyse critically the social context.
>
> *(Organiser, Chile)*

This kind of training was developed most intensively by the organisations undertaking the mapping projects, particularly CECAM in Chile using a popular education process. CECAM developed a two-year program of leadership training for leaders of their local groups and trade unions, covering topics such as women's role in the economy and society, the history of women and the labour movement, personal development and group work, and international organising of home-based workers (CECAM, 2003).

A critical factor in the HWW mapping model is that while it encouraged some consistency of data collection from each group, it also encouraged organising strategies and types of organisation that reflected the needs and circumstances of the homeworkers contacted and the involvement of homeworkers in the process. The mapping demonstrates a bottom-up approach ensuring staff and homeworkers led the research and combined organising strategies and that the focus remained on building their own organisations, facilitating *representation* – one of our four dimensions of gender justice.

In India, organising resulted in forming savings-groups which provided access to finance for loans to pay off debts, and to pay for schooling and health. Belonging to savings groups increased women's annual incomes twofold; their financial independence enabled their involvement in collective activities (ADITHI, 2003). Another new collective formed in India involved leaf plate-makers, who had previously sold the leaves on to a middle person who made the plates. Through vertical mapping, workers discovered their place in the supply chain, and realised that if they worked together by pooling the leaves and producing a higher quality plate, they could sell directly rather than through an intermediary. Workers collectivised and purchased a leaf plate machine and began to produce plates for local markets, and other distribution points. The mapping process enabled the women to develop new skills and knowledge and gave them the confidence and understanding to produce and market their own plates. In addition, they were able to more than double their annual incomes.

Organising within the mapping program went beyond the establishment of local homeworkers' groups. Rural and city-based groups organised into national groups and international links were forged between various national groups. Mapping in Chile led to mapping in other Latin American countries and to the emergence of a strong regional network of homeworker organisations in Brazil, Bolivia and Mexico. The program strength in sharing country experiences resulted in an internationalizing of homeworkers' experiences, validating women's experiences as being part of an international movement. In recognition of the importance of global advocacy, the new international homeworkers' network developed from the mapping, the Federation of Homeworkers Worldwide (HWW, 2003a). Thus, organising – at every level – was an integral component of mapping.

Sustainability of homework groups to organise

The mapping approach demonstrates that when support mechanisms are in place, homeworkers are more likely to form new organisations and develop the skills to sustain ongoing organising. Existing organisations, such as unions or NGOs, with experience in training and organising workers can provide critical support to the emergence of new homeworker groups. These organisations and their resources can provide homeworkers with training to build their worker identification; they can help homeworkers to identify their group needs, to define how to go about improving their lives, and to identify the structure or type of organisation that will best meet homeworker needs or that is best suited to the national context.

CECAM in Chile developed a variation on this way of organising, based on geographical areas (CECAM, 2003). In the course of the mapping program, CECAM supported the development of a number of groups of homeworkers in different localities in Santiago, the southern city of Concepcion, on the coast and in the mountains. Most of these groups registered as trade unions, which was legally possible in Chile with a minimum of 25 members. Membership was only for homeworkers, including both dependent and own-account. In some cases, as with the seaweed workers on the coast, all members were involved in the same work. In others, the work done by the homeworkers was in different sectors, depending on the economy in the local area. The local unions gained strength by setting up a regional and national organisation and eventually affiliating to the national trade union federation (CECAM, 2003). The mapping experience shows that new organising initiatives led to successful forms of representation of homeworkers – one of our four dimensions of gender justice.

Another common pattern of organising has been small local groups, initially informal, later exploring some form of legal registration. In Nepal, for example, the mapping process focused on those in certain sectors, *pote* (jewellery), garments, *dhaka* (weaving) and knitting and small savings groups were set up, based on the self-help group (SHG) model. As the organisation has grown, they have formed both a cooperative and a women's trade union for homeworkers (HWW, 2004). In Brazil, local associations of homeworkers were formed. In Turkey, informal groups have been established which in some cases have registered as cooperatives (HWW, 2003a). In Bulgaria, an association of homeworkers has been formed, whose membership is mainly dependent homeworkers making shoes, and in Serbia, an association whose membership is mainly own-account (HWW, 2003b).

In Turkey, a support group has been operating for some years to encourage homeworker organising. In 2006, the homeworker groups formed a new group called the Partners Committee, which led to the homeworkers taking over all the responsibilities from the working group.

> 'From now on, responsibilities for all tasks, public meetings, national con-
> ferences, planning meetings, membership of the international federation – are
> all our own. We have now made the decision to take charge of all this our-
> selves and to represent ourselves on all platforms. We do not want decisions
> made against our wishes when they are supposed to support us...We have had
> a lot of discussions amongst ourselves...We shall reach out to all the people
> who are homebased workers like us. We will have discussions about our
> demands and policies at national level, we all want to unionise ourselves.'
> Homeworker representative, Turkey.
>
> *(HWW, 2008)*

Organiser training was developed most intensively by the organisations under-taking the mapping projects, particularly CECAM in Chile using a popular education process. CECAM developed a two-year program of leadership training for leaders of their local groups and trade unions, covering topics such as women's role in the economy and society, the history of women and the labour movement, personal development and group work, and international organising of home-based workers (CECAM, 2003).

An organiser from Chile described some of the training of homeworkers in the following terms:

> After talking about their needs, we started basic workshops on the history
> of organising in Chile, self-development, the position of homework in
> the economy. Workshops on different techniques such as analysing the
> market, how to present the product and how to calculate the price. We
> find that home-based workers usually forget to include the cost of their
> time, the economic workshop covers this. Another one is on gender
> needs identifying where the men and women have different issues; 40% of
> the families have female heads. Male chauvinism is very strong in Latin
> America so the issue of domestic violence is regularly raised at weekly
> meetings.
>
> *(Organiser, Chile, 2005)*

This process is similar to traditional grassroots organising carried out historically where groups of workers join together to improve their work conditions and income and otherwise to defend their rights while advancing their interests. What distinguishes the organising process for many homeworker groups is that, given the absence of trade union support in initial stages, the steps to move to the stage of forming their own groups may require others to provide some initial training, leadership development and support to locate other homeworkers. An organiser described the leadership development undertaken in Chile.

> In the second year, we developed leader training. A school for workers with the first level being basic literacy; the second level economics, political rights and the drawing up of policies. The third level covers methodologies, representation, advocacy and campaigning, organisational sustainability (autonomy). This doesn't mean they're on their own but that they can exist independently gaining support from other sources, which is important.
>
> (Organiser, Chile, 2005)

Forms of homeworker organisations and obstacles to organising

The process of organising homeworkers is not usually easy or straightforward. In contrast to street-vendors for example, it is not always obvious what homeworkers have to gain from organising, especially in the case of dependent workers. Many homeworkers work in isolation in their homes, do not perceive themselves as workers and are very busy, having multiple tasks apart from their paid work, usually household and childcare responsibilities. In rural areas, they often work in agriculture, even sometimes migrating to other areas to work, as in the case of *Santhali* women from Jharkhand who migrate to West Bengal for months, twice a year. In urban areas, women sometimes combine homework with other ways of earning an income, such as street selling.

In general, there is now much greater visibility for homeworkers, often disguised wage workers working for supply chains, nationally or internationally. For these women, the struggle is for recognition as workers, and equal treatment with other workers. There is still a long way to go to find ways to make this equal treatment a reality, but the issues remain clear.

> Now the situation is very different from before, as a result of our organisation. We have made sure that the problems faced by homeworkers are seen as an important issue. We have to make sure that our campaign continues. We cannot relax. As soon as we relax, we get walked over.
>
> (Homeworker, Madeira, Portugal)

Own-account workers still enjoy far less recognition as workers. One of the key issues facing most own-account workers, and many piece-rate workers, is the lack of regular work. This forces women to accept bad conditions and low rates of pay, and to switch to different kinds of work when necessary. Hence for organisers, a major issue is not only recognition and defence of rights at work, but the creation of employment, which in the case of own-account workers means helping them gain access to markets. In many developing countries, many schemes exist to help women producers – for example for credit, technical training and marketing, sometimes with grants to help them get started. Own-account workers can access these schemes when they are organised and benefit from them. A tension remains however between attempting to solve the immediate economic issues of marketing, and the longer-term struggle for recognition as workers and for rights to employment and social protection.

> What is important is that we want to reclaim the concept of worker, whether piece-rate or own-account, instead of the idea of the micro-entrepreneur.
>
> *(Homeworker, Chile)*

The reframing of women self-employed as a source of untapped entrepreneurial potential, or microcredit being presented as the solution to a range of women's work issues – such as the need to secure a flexible work-life balance, or preference for being their own boss – is common (Boeri, 2018). More often the women lack basic forms of enterprise development support, such as information, marketing opportunities, regulatory and social supports. Furthermore, many of these women are located at the intersections of different kinds of inequality: class, race, caste, occupation, and worker legal status. As such, building shared identity, and individual and collective agency represents an even greater challenge (Kabeer et al., 2013)

A constant tension exists between the day-to-day demands of everyday life and work and the longer-term struggle to improve rights. In Turkey, for example, small cooperatives were initially developed, but could not expand, mobilise and encourage increased membership since the cooperative could only provide work for a limited number of workers. At this point, they realised that they were not viable. This led to an extensive discussion amongst homeworkers about what type of organisation they wanted and what would suit their collective needs. Later they decided to shift their focus to the struggle for recognition and rights as a trade union, particularly at the national level (HWW, 2007). They have now moved towards the longer-term aim of establishing the national union, so that they can focus on the broader political and representative issues, rather than purely on economic sustainability (HWW, 2007).

The challenge they faced in registering the union was significant. The Union of Home-based Workers (Ev-Ek-Sen) was launched in November 2009; as Ev-Ek-Sen focused on organising homeworkers, they also sought to build alliances with other unions and labour groups. However, many Ev-Ek-Sen members reported that they were treated as 'poor women without awareness of their class or of their work context' (Hattatoglu and Tate, 2016: 109). In a declaration by the Union in 2010, they highlighted the confusion that occurred surrounding workers' status, how homeworkers are often confused with micro entrepreneurs. Many of the homeworkers are members of cooperatives, as well as union members.

> We, home-based workers, are among the most invisible sections of precarious workers, so there are times when even we find it difficult to explain that we also work, that we are also workers like all other workers. It is not unusual for our own-account work to be confused with micro-entrepreneurship. We are, however, workers. For, in most cases, our own-account work is carried out side-by-side with work on order or piece-rate work (depending upon factories) ....
>
> *(extract from translation of declaration by Ev-Ek-Sen, 2010, cited in Hattatoglu and Tate, 2016)*

The struggle by Ev-Ek-Sen to be recognised under the Turkish constitution highlights how powerful institutions can prevent recognition of a homeworkers' union. Ev-Ek-Sen equated the challenge to have the union recognised by the state with the right of homeworkers to organise (Hattatoglu and Tate, 2016).

Given the insecurity of work for dependent workers, organisers have found that they can sometimes bring women together around issues other than those directly arising from their work. In Toronto, for example, the union organised English classes and family activity days for homeworkers who were mainly from migrant communities. Similarly, in Australia, the mainly migrant women workers were offered English classes as a way to link them to union activities. In Chile and Bolivia, literacy training was identified as a key issue. SEWA in India brings thousands of women together through the provision of services through the SEWA Bank, health and childcare programs. In some cases, particularly in the global North countries, such programs are important for overcoming the isolation of homeworkers and building trust and confidence. Women become more confident and aware that they are part of a larger workforce.

> When we work as homeworkers, we always think that we are the only ones doing it. But now we have realised that it is not only us. There are many others like us, doing the same things. We have seen that there is another reality.
>
> *(Homeworker, Chile)*

Although we have outlined various benefits which may flow on to women from organising, we note that the possibilities for organising to transform the working lives of homeworkers are limited in the short-term. Firstly, a need exists to work together with homeworkers in advocacy work. The need for recognition as workers, and for new initiatives to support a basic level of social and economic security in their lives, can be an important interim step toward organisation building. A change in the women workers' perceptions of themselves is often necessary to developing organising strategies.

Empowerment through organising

Through organising, there can be a change in women's perception of themselves as doing something to earn some money to help their family and realising that they are not alone in this – that other women are doing similar work, sometimes even for the same employer and industry. Through the process of education and information, homeworkers begin to see how their own home-based work is linked with wider economic trends and patterns of production, both at the national and international level.

> In the neo-liberal system, workers are treated as things, instruments of work, not human beings. We have to create collective spaces where workers are valued as human beings and where they can achieve their humanity. This may not be money, but it is as important as bread for living.
>
> *(Homeworker and organiser, Chile)*

As their self-confidence and knowledge grows, they see themselves as workers who are entitled to make certain demands of society: for recognition of their work, and their contribution to the national economy, and for certain rights. They begin to demand the right to a basic level of economic and social security in return for the long hours of work that they do.

> I love to work with women. All the responsibility for the family lies with women. Women have to manage everything: house, education and family. If we make women more aware, it is easier for us to organise and fight for our rights.
>
> *(Homeworker, India)*

Through working with others at the local, national and international level, they also begin to see how their combined efforts can bring about change. As one homeworker described her motivation to form a homeworkers' organisation.

> We have to form an organisation to get rid of poverty from the world, and we should think not only of ourselves but of others as well, we are all women.
>
> *(Homeworker, India)*

The development gender empowerment/entrepreneurial discourse focuses on economic empowerment, for women engaged in informal employment, to gain a wage, or some income assumes women will make a change for the positive in their lives (Boeri, 2018). Homework groups that have focused on establishing a mix of organising, advocacy and services have established more sustainable and representative organisations. ADITHI in India, has worked to build self-help groups and through extensive training and literacy support established ongoing homeworker groups that are self-managed. The training and support enabled the women to identify their demands and present them to local authorities. An organiser in India describes homeworkers coming together to collectively present their demands.

> At the meeting of home-based workers on March 8, more than 5,000 home-based workers came together. They presented their demands to the elected president of the nagar panchayat (local village body) and the Deputy Development Commissioner. The women had walked long distances in the sun, yet their enthusiasm was undaunted.
>
> *(Organiser, India)*

Kaloian in Bulgaria has organised dependent workers in footwear and bag-making to improve piece rates across local and international supply chains. A homeworker and an organiser shared their relative perspectives on building a homeworkers' organisation:

> We say that we are all homeworkers. We have some power and some rights. We would like to build up our organisation and find ways to protect ourselves. Starting this work was like entering a tunnel, where you could not see any light at the end. Going to the meeting was like seeing the light at the end.
>
> *(Homeworker, Bulgaria)*

> Bulgaria has recently ratified the International Labour Organisation Convention on Home Work and is planning to pass a law for homeworkers. This is a major step forward for the homeworker organisations in Bulgaria who have over the last few years made homeworkers visible by developing organisation among them. It seems likely that substantial numbers of dependent homeworkers, working in the garment and footwear sectors, will be able to take advantage of this new law to improve their conditions. The government has also agreed to look at ways of regulating other groups of homebased workers, not dependent on specific companies or employers, but working on their own account.
>
> *(Organiser, Bulgaria)*

CECAM in Chile supported homeworkers to improve wages through mapping the seaweed supply chain and negotiating directly with buyers to improve home-workers' income. In Bolivia, training and research into production costs and the supply chains led homeworker producer groups of cheese, flowers and *maca* to negotiate improved prices. This approach focuses on the collective needs of workers and less on the economic sustainability or income of individuals. The comments below from an organiser in Serbia highlight an awareness that there is no quick fix to the problems they face, but organising offers a means to address their issues.

> Through their own example of associating and organising, women pointed out that despite all problems and troubles it is easier if women are organised. It

does not mean that problems will be solved 'now' and 'immediately', but it certainly means support and opportunity to find gradual solutions.

(Organiser, Serbia)

More recent examples – SAVE in Tirupur, Tamil Nadu India, and CIVIDEP based in Bangalore India – have begun activities with homeworkers, in part in collaboration with HWW. In Tirupur, SAVE has worked with garment home-workers to form self-help groups, developed training materials and built alliances with trade unions to advocate for more effective government schemes and ben-efits. In the Ambur area of Tamil Nadu, the focus has been on reaching thou-sands of footwear homeworkers. CIVIDEP anticipates that the process to build organisation amongst footwear homeworkers is a medium to a long-term project that may lead to the establishment of their own union. CIVIDEP's experience as a support organisation for garment women workers in Bangalore to establish the Garment Labour Union (GLU) was achieved with ongoing support from Oxfam UK over a ten-year period. An important lesson here is that organising is possi-ble, though it may vary in the type of organisation structure it takes, but that considerable time is necessary to establish a sustainable, homeworker-led home-worker organisation.

The fragility of homeworker organisations and ongoing sustainability

Examples from the mapping program highlight homeworker collective organising and organisation building are achievable. Various types of organisations formed by homeworkers over this period include unions, community-based member organi-sations, self-help groups, non-government organisations NGOs, cooperatives, and networks, networks usually national taking the form of an umbrella organisation or federation. SEWA in India is frequently cited as a successful model since it incor-porates development work alongside union organising activities, and incorporates many sectors of informal women's work. We note that, despite the many positive examples, many are less successful, since considerable social, political and economic barriers that challenge successful organising remain.

Some years later, some of the homework organisations involved in the mapping have ceased to exist, for example CECAM in Chile. Elsewhere, Self-employed Workers Union (SEWU) in South Africa and the homeworkers' network in Por-tugal, the National group on homeworking in the UK have all ceased operating for various reasons. Many face internal struggles due to the difficulties in conduct-ing the work, lack of resources and opportunities to secure funding. Others con-tinue with their work but function in a lesser capacity or refocus their work to areas funders are willing to support, such as micro-credit. In Brazil, groups have always been clear that they needed to build strong collective associations, but fol-lowing the end of the mapping program, they were in need of funds to continue their organising work. The only funds they have been able to secure have been subject to funding body requirements to focus on micro-credit and micro-enterprise development, rather than collective organising (HWW, 2006).

Lack of capacity for homeworkers to pay dues, the precarious nature of work, and vulnerability of homeworkers in society present numerous challenges to be overcome to maintain organising activities and to sustain a homeworkers' organisation. Homeworker organisations are constantly seeking support to maintain their work and to support organising. In some countries, the support groups retreated to allow the homeworkers to run the organisation; this also created challenges for their ongoing sustainability. This is relevant to homework organisations that are established as trade union structures and rely on membership from members, but without the scale of large numbers of members, they will always rely on external funding to survive. The potential to have established the direct representation of homeworker members is challenging when workers are poor and cannot afford to maintain membership fees. NGOs may be criticised for claiming to represent workers without a direct membership constituency to inform policy and actions. The fluidity of the type of homeworker group established in different country contexts may not fit neatly with the traditional trade union representation structure.

The ongoing sustainability of homework groups, unions, cooperatives or whatever form of organisation workers develop is always a challenge. We discuss the mapping approach in this chapter as a framework for developing sustainable groups. However, we acknowledge that this approach has its limitations since there is no one-size-fits-all solution. The benefit of this approach is that it enables and requires workers to be involved to achieve the best outcomes. While the mapping program did not aim to promote a best-practice organising model, *each group* made an important contribution to further understanding key aspects that can contribute to successful organising. It should be noted that many of the groups achieved a lot in a relatively short time period of one to three years. Encouraging homeworkers to develop organising capacity through the mapping process can lead to workers becoming the major actors in broader political, economic and social outcomes with numerous beneficial consequences for them.

We also note that the role of the IHN was a critical factor in bringing groups of newly formed homeworker organisations together, to share experiences and knowledge. The role of HWW in the mapping project was to facilitate new organising at the local, national, regional and transnational level. Homeworker groups were given small amounts of funding to conduct the action research, and document their work, but the aim was not to make groups dependent upon funding from the IHN. Fragility is a concern for homeworker networks; the Federation of Homeworkers Worldwide (FHWW) which was founded by homeworker organisations in 2005 has struggled to raise funds, therefore the work of the IHN has been supported by HWW.

Homeworkers groups that are organising homeworkers may fit some of the characteristics of a union–community coalitions, though many working directly with homeworkers have attempted to engage unions in the work of organising and policy activities but have been unsuccessful. An exception to this is the TCFUA in

Australia, detailed in earlier chapters, that demonstrates how the union sought out community partners to establish a community campaign or organising strategies around homeworker issues. There are many examples of homeworker groups that have established working relationships with unions including CECAM, Chile; Central de Mujeres, Bolivia; CEMUJ-B, Bolivia; the Homeworkers' Working Group, Turkey; and the National Group on Homeworking, UK. In many instances the homeworker groups are leading organising efforts, but engaging with unions in broader campaigns around rights, policy, legislation and social protection.

Another aspect of the organising approaches described above indicates that groups have attempted to mobilise around the multiple identities the women traverse, as many women did not see themselves primarily as workers. The organising incorporated the needs of women as mothers, workers, carers of children and others, as community members organising clean water or childcare, as women coming together to discuss family violence or community problems. This is consistent with broader examples of organising informal women workers (Kabeer et al., 2013). The development of a longer-term strategy for policy change involves working with a range of other organisations that can support their demands and who in many cases have a common interest in working with organisations of homeworkers. Participatory organising processes that include training, skills development with attention to the needs and involvement of women as leaders have proven to be successful. So too have gender inclusiveness strategies that provide women with the skills and capacity to participate in the broader political and social change agendas at national, regional and transnational levels. Future opportunities may arise for global and regional cooperation between union and homeworker groups with the aim to exchange, cooperate and support campaigns, increase corporation accountability and facilitate new organising activities.

Network mechanisms and processes to support homeworker organisation

How do IHNs support local homeworker organisations? In this section, we examine in more detail how the transnational network has supported homeworker organising at the local level. The international homework network (IHN) has emerged as a movement of homework organisations focused on labour rights and organising of workers. Consistent with the concept of a transnational feminist network (Moghadam, 2005), the activities of the IHN focused on influencing political change and improving homeworker conditions. In this section, we bring together concepts from the literature on mobilisation, transnational feminist networks and the transnational advocacy social movement literature to summarise our findings of the role of the IHN in this chapter.

1. Support for the creation of organisations and representation

Networks of homeworkers are often formed as substitutes for more formal collective organisations. In most countries, there are signifying barriers to homeworkers forming trade unions, either because they are unable to meet the threshold number of members to register, or because they are not perceived to be 'employees' under the labour laws of that country. Without the capacity to form a more formal workers' organisation, homeworkers either form associations or collectives, or rely on entirely informal structures. Rather than being structured as formal national and international union confederations, local homeworker groups have formed looser alliances with homeworker groups in other areas of the same country, homeworker groups in other countries, and international homeworker bodies.

Because homeworkers' wage work is disguised and frequently a clear employment relationship is not evident, homeworkers are often not considered to be employees able to join unions. In Turkey, for example, only those workers with a formal employment contract can join or form a trade union (Hattatoglu and Tate, 2016). Where existing unions have not taken up the challenge of organising homeworkers, homeworkers might start up a new union, but often new unions are precluded from being formed. In Bulgaria, to set up a new trade union involves a signed up membership of 10,000, an impossibility for a group in the early stages of organising (HWW, 2007).

In many countries the obstacles, bureaucratic, legal and attitudinal, to forming new homework organisations and unions are many. Support organisations, often NGOs and women's organisations, have played a critical role in establishing new homeworker groups that may, over the long-term, build into more formal or semi-formal organisations. The role of groups such as ADITHI in India, CECAM in Chile has brought together individuals via existing networks to create new homeworker organisations. For example, CECAM[2] conducted training for trade union women, and drew on this network to create new contacts to locate homeworkers in Chile and to build a national homeworkers' network. Therefore, networks can function as substitutes for a formal organisation in a temporary capacity or ongoing, depending on the local circumstances. Consistent with social movement literature, informal networks can function as networks of resistance (Kuumba, 2001; Purkayastha and Subramaniam, 2004).

The IHN provides support for new homework organising and new homework organisations through meetings and exchanges and network building. Organising here implies an articulation of consciousness, a mobilisation and politicisation amongst women workers around collective strategies, based on women workers' needs, demands and priorities (Kelly 1998; Frege and Kelly, 2004; Burchielli et al., 2008).

Organising is encouraged since it is considered the substantial and crucial process for homeworkers to improve their visibility, recognition, representation and rights (HWW 2004). Documenting successful organising strategies, knowledge sharing, for example, interviewing homeworkers and organisers about their successful strategies has been an important way to facilitate and share lessons on what organising strategies work. Worker-to-worker exchanges have been an additional important way to bring homeworker groups together, to discuss and share organising experiences, on issues specific to certain sectors, for example, garments or embroidery. In an embroidery workshop held in Leeds, UK, in 2002, workers and organisations from several countries shared experiences around marketing, design, social protection and organising strategies. They discovered that the organisation structures that represent these homeworkers varied. Some are large regional or national organisations; others are local village organisations. These have unique starting points and paths of development and place a different emphasis on advocacy, training, social services, business development and marketing. Groups more advanced in some of these areas shared their knowledge and importantly inspired those beginning their organising journey that change is possible (HWW 2002a).

The IHN enhances the *representation* of homeworkers and their representatives through advocacy, policy development, and supporting the creation of new homeworker groups and lending them recognition and legitimacy (Keck and Sikkink, 1998). Representation of the IHN at transnational and national forums, for example, the International Labour Organisation (ILO), and the Ethical Trading Initiative (ETI) has boosted homeworker rights in various ways. It has led to the ILO Convention on Homework and influenced the ETI to develop a comprehensive homework policy to guide corporate members to implement their own policy. Additionally, information sharing to assist newly formed homework groups to facilitate knowledge sharing, documenting success stories, and conducting research that prioritises the lived experience of homeworkers, through academic and public publications has been vital for efforts to enhance homework visibility and amplify the effects of advocacy. These activities have, in turn, influenced global institutions, government and policy makers, corporations, trade unions, women's organisations and NGO labour groups in many countries to improve collective bargaining opportunities and improve the material and political position of homeworkers in society.

2. Conduits for normative or material resources

Networks can help to address the problem of *weak actors influencing strong targets* through their role in enabling the transfer of power resources between actors. This possibility has been acknowledged clearly in some existing work on regulatory networks, such as Drahos and Braithwaite's notion of 'networking around capacity deficits' (Braithwaite and Drahos, 1999; 2000). International homeworker organisations have played a crucial role as conduits of both funds and also ideas about how to organise. The collaboration between transnational and local NGOs in the example of HWW and CIVIDEP has developed to support organising amongst footwear homeworkers in Tamil Nadu and led to a new homeworker association being formed. This local network of homeworkers has little associational power since they function outside traditional labour structures, but through linkages; with HWW and CIVIDEP the homeworkers are establishing associational and social power, in that they have increased leverage in the supply chain (Wright, 2000; Silver 2003). This is illustrated through their capacity to meet and discuss issues affecting their lives with brands and employers through meetings aimed to focus attention on homeworkers' rights and improving their work conditions. The transnational to local links have a longer-term goal to assist homeworkers to establish a representative organisation or union (Delaney, Tate and Burchielli, 2016).

We observe that the effects of such support are often cumulative, as a number of networks involving relatively weak actors contribute to snowballing pressure on structurally more powerful institutions. Even where they are not clearly coordinated, the exercise of pressure within multiple networks and coalitions can generate 'webs of influence' (Braithwaite and Drahos, 1999; 2000) which chip away in multiple, albeit marginal ways at different nodes of influence within a contested and pluralist domestic political arena (Cerny, 2006; 2007). Importantly, however, such dynamics can cut both ways. 'Countervailing networks' resist network building efforts of worker groups, as has emerged in a variety of forms across the case studies discussed in earlier chapters. For example, HWWs collaboration with global brand Pentland, and CIVIDEP in India, (see Chapter 4) created a countervailing network. Pentland is a corporate member of the Ethical Trading Initiative and can be a powerful collaborator to assert influence in other forums that NGO network members cannot access.

3. Infrastructures that build solidarity

The IHN supports the building of *solidarity* between homeworkers as individuals and between homeworker organisations. Solidarity describes activities to strengthen homeworker networks and campaign activities, for example supporting local homeworkers' rights through campaigns and activities with global brands; conducting research and documenting. Homework organisations have recognised the benefits of having an international organisation. The existence of an international organisation has been critical in the improvement in visibility and representation of homeworkers. It has assisted groups to be taken seriously by policy makers and to participate in national and international forums. Further, it has linked the homeworker organisations with broad alliances that share similar views around being part of a transnational homeworkers' movement. The importance of support from other homework groups is illustrated by the experience of the homework organisation Kaloian in Bulgaria, established during the international mapping program:

> We say that we are all homeworkers and we have some power and some rights. We would like to build up the organisation and find ways in which we can protect ourselves. At the moment, the most important thing for us in Bulgaria is to get the same price for all homeworkers doing the same work. I hope that we will be able to build a big organisation of homeworkers in Bulgaria. I would like our organisation of homeworkers to be connected with similar organisations around the world. We need to have meetings of different organisations at the international level. The most important thing for us is to make these connections.
>
> *(Tate, 2002b: 4)*

The homework groups access and provide solidarity through participation in the network, based on opportunities to share experiences, peer learning, exposure to new ideas, and discussion in relation to international policy. The linking of local activism and collective organising with support from the transnational homework network demonstrates that the application of a variety of resources can maintain organising efforts and supports work at the local and national level. Therefore, the activities of the IHN can be best described as *transnationalism from below*.

One way that the IHN builds solidarity is by serving as a communicative infrastructure in which processes of deliberation and socialisation of values and norms occur. Some networks structure and facilitate these more normative patterns of influence more directly than others. The process of bringing workers together, in worker to worker exchanges and communicating through an international newsletter and website is an example of how transnational networks can address the lack of visibility of homeworkers and their organisations and establish patterns of influence that highlight initiatives around organising, success in legal reform and struggles that require solidarity action. These solidarity activities are formed around 'protest frames' consistent with the purpose derived from local homeworker networks' demands and needs (Kelly, 1998; Burchielli et al., 2008).

International networks are not necessarily stable. As we discussed in the previous section where we discussed changes in Homenet International, WIEGO, Homeworkers Worldwide, and the Federation of Homeworkers Worldwide are coalitions of actors often reconstituted, with new actors being recruited to networks through various means. Sometimes this entails recruitment of obvious allies. Global union bodies and women in unions have sometimes been called on for solidarity, for example, particularly in negotiations around the ILO Convention on Homework. Feminist networks amongst unions and scholars have been an important resource to the IHN, in securing the ILO Convention on Homework and more recently by conducting shared research projects around footwear homework in global supply chains in India and Bulgaria (Moghadam 2005). The success of homeworker networks described here can be seen as part of the broader effect of the feminist networks subversion of the gender divisions of labour. This creates an opportunity for more equal division of unpaid domestic and paid labour, and, with it, recognition and rights for homeworkers who were previously invisible; this fits within the redistribution dimension of gender justice.

4. Bridges to access multiple and diverse targets

Networks can also act as bridges to access multiple and diverse targets, thereby helping to overcome the challenge of dispersed authority and distant targets. The dynamics of the interactions between multiple networks and coalitions are constituted at different scales, are relatively autonomous from one another, and can involve distinct yet sometimes overlapping groupings of actors.

There is perhaps a kind of 'strength of weak ties' (Granovetter, 1985) logic to this dynamic. This speaks to the value of multi-layered networks, and the fact that networks do not always need strong coordination and likeness of participants. Moreover, it highlights the dynamism of networks. Once targets are identified, the network structures and resources can be moved around to be directed at appropriate targets and new relationships and connections can be built cumulatively over time to generate new capacities. One outcome from the activities of the mapping program was the identification of multiple sources to address the needs of footwear homeworkers in different global geographic locations. The networked approach was able to analyse the global footwear supply chain to identify common strategies toward brands. This was followed by agreement on campaign activities HWW would initiate to focus on certain brands in the United Kingdom and Europe. The overall aim was to enable groups to utilise this information to lobby for improvements for homeworkers at the local level. The networked approach was able to bring awareness and improve homeworkers' rights – linking the rights dimension of gender justice.

5. Conduits across political environments

The IHN case shows that networks acting as conduits at a more macro scale are able to import established norms and material incentive structures between differently configured political environments. The transfer of norms between companies linked within transnational supply chains, in response to market pressures associated with campaigns targeting consumers and investors, is an example of this, and indicates how such leakage of societal norms and associated material leverage can be transferred between political contexts. Such dynamics have been particularly important in consumer-based campaigns. The IHN has effectively used information sharing, meetings and case studies to establish successful strategies. Important gains in one country were documented and celebrated globally, countries that faced similar challenges – for example, working to secure national legislation on homework were encouraged to conduct exchange visits to learn from what others have achieved. Additionally, recent activities by HWW to highlight the conditions amongst the UK and European based footwear brands of homeworkers' working conditions led to commitments from some brands to follow Pentland's example, to discuss improved methods to map their supply chain beyond the first-tier supplier. In so doing, they facilitated norms transfer between corporations. Earlier we identified the IHN as transnationalism from below, which fits within a broader social movement literature that acknowledges women's informal networks can function as networks of resistance (Kuumba, 2001). Networks of resistance impact in the redistributive gender justice dimension since this enables worker actions to challenge preconceived notions of gender roles, and capacity of homeworkers to participate in social dialogue previously closed to them. Homeworker networks create solidarity and resistance opportunities and have the potential to create broader change. Therefore, solidarity and resistance contribute to the redistribution dimension of the gender justice framework.

Conclusion

In this chapter we described the importance of network functions in helping to achieve institutional change and create opportunities for resistance as discussed in the examples of homeworker organising cited. We built on the industrial relations literature by drawing on the transnational organising and network theories. We used these frameworks to analyse how the International Homeworkers Network (IHN) at the transnational level has functioned to support homeworker advocacy and organising around the globe, exploring the importance of the IHN in developing new homeworker informal associations and unions and homework representation at the local and transnational level. We have shown how the international homework network consists of informal and formal group members and participants that do not neatly fit within the traditional social movement literature definition of a movement or within concepts of a labour union drawn from the industrial relations literature. Because women homeworkers' experience does not fit existing theoretical constructs it can easily be overlooked.

Therefore, our discussion of the IHN and organising case studies challenge historical perception that homeworkers are 'unorganisable', and visibilised the homeworker transnational activism. The examples from the mapping program discussed indicate that successful organisation building is based on collectively exploring themes about women and their work, and engaging with women's multiple identities as workers, mothers, wives, caregivers and community members. The case study examples inform our understanding of the structure and form a local homework network may take, for example, a union, self-help groups, network, or cooperative. Organising examples show that the form of organisation structure adopted by the local homework network is based on the women workers needs, and reflects the political, social and cultural realities of their location.

We argue that organising impacts positively across all four dimensions of the gender justice framework: recognition, representation, rights and redistribution. Collective organising and mobilisation of the most invisibilised workers construct a means to empower and visibilise homeworkers. Organising is a necessary response for homeworkers, to challenge institutional and structural inequalities toward a means to redistributive justice. There are important lessons to be learned from the historical and more recent success of organising homeworkers; we discuss this in relation to the homework gender justice framework in the following chapter.

Notes

1 Sindicato do Trabalhadores da Industria de Bordadas, Tapecarias, Texteis e Artisanato da RAM (the Embroider Union in Madeira, Portugal).
2 CECAM was previously Anna Clara that conducted training for women trade unionists in Chile.

References

ADITHI. (2003) Bihar and Jharkhand. *Homeworkers Worldwide Policy Workshop 8–12 September*. Zlatibor, Serbia: HWW.

Allen, S. and Wolkowitz, C. (1987) *Homeworking: Myths and Realities*. London: Macmillan.

Boeri, N. (2018) Challenging the Gendered Entrepreneurial Subject: Gender, Development, and the Informal Economy in India. *Gender & Society* 32: 157–179.

Boris, E. (1994) *Home to Work: Motherhood and the Politics of Industrial Homework in the United States*. New York: Cambridge University Press.

Boris, E. and Daniels, C. (1989) *Homework: Historical and Contemporary Perspectives on Paid Labor at Home*. Urbana and Chicago: University of Illinois Press.

Boris, E. and Prügl, E. (eds) (1996) *Homeworkers in Global Perspective: Invisible No More*. New York: Routledge.

Braithwaite, J. (2006) Responsive Regulation and Developing Economies. *World Development* 34: 884–898.

Braithwaite, J. and Drahos, P. (1999) Ratcheting Up and Driving Down Global Regulatory Standards. *Development* 42: 109–114.

Braithwaite, J. and Drahos, P. (2000) *Global Business Regulation*. Cambridge: Cambridge University Press.

Burchielli, R., Buttigieg, D. and Delaney, A. (2008) Organising Homeworkers: the Use of Mapping as an Organising Tool. *Work, Employment & Society* 22(1): 167–180.

CECAM. (2003) *Systematisation: The Process of Building Homebased Workers' Organisation in Chile*. Santiago: CECAM – The Training Centre for Working Women.

Cerny, P. (2006) Plurality, Pluralism, and Power: Elements of Pluralist Analysis in an Age of Globalization. In R. Eisfeld (ed.) *Pluralism: Developments in the Theory and Practice of Democracy* (pp. 81–111). Opladen: Barbara Budrich.

Cerny, P.G. (2007) Multi-Nodal Politics: Toward a Political Process Theory of Globalization. *Annual Conference of the International Political Economy Society*. Stanford University.

Delaney, A., Tate, J. and Burchielli, R. (2016) Homeworkers Organizing for Recognition and Rights: Can International Standards Assist Them? In J. Jensen and N. Lichtenstein (eds) *The ILO From Geneva to the Pacific Rim* (pp. 159–179). Houndmills, Basingstoke: Palgrave Macmillan and the International Labour Office.

Fraser, N. (2005) Mapping the Feminist Imagination: From Redistribution to Recognition to Representation. *Constellations* 12: 295–307.

Frege, C. and Kelly, J. (2004) *Varieties of Unionism: Strategies for Union Revitalization in a Globalizing Economy*. Oxford: Oxford University Press.

Gallin, D. (2001) Propositions on Trade Unions and Informal Employment in Times of Globalisation. *Antipode* 33: 531–549.

Granovetter, M. (1985) Economic Action and Social Structure: The Problem of Embeddedness. *The American Journal of Sociology* 91.

Hattatoglu, D. and Tate, J. (2016) Home-Based Work and New Ways of Organizing in the Era of Globalization. In *Neoliberal Capitalism and Precarious Work: Ethnographies of Accommodation and Resistance*. Cheltenham: Edward Elgar 96–124.

HomeNet. (1995) Rights for Homeworkers. *The Newsletter of the International Network for Homebased Workers*, 1 (Summer), 15.

HomeNet. (1999a) HomeNet-International Organising. Unpublished strategy document. HomeNet International.

HomeNet. (1999b) Circular April 1999. Unpublished memo. HomeNet.

HomeNet. (1999c) Organising for Change: Building the Network: Chile & Turkey. *The Newsletter of the International Network for Homebased Workers*, 12 (December), 15.

HomeNet. (1999d) *International Organising Component*. Leeds: HomeNet.

HWW. (2002a) Initial Summary Evaluation of Pilot Year of Program of Mapping Homebased Work. Unpublished evaluation summary. Homeworkers Worldwide.

HWW. (2002b) *Mapping Homebased Workers: Lessons from the Pilot Year of the Homeworkers Worldwide Mapping Program 2001–2002*. Unpublished evaluation report. Homeworkers Worldwide.

HWW. (2003a) HWW Vertical Mapping Meeting, Instanbul, May 2003. Istanbul, Turkey.

HWW. (2003b) On The Edge Of Survival: Summary Report of Bulgaria Mapping Meeting: 15–17 March. *Bulgarian Mapping Meeting*. HWW, 6.

HWW. (2004) Organising for Change: Women Homebased Workers in the Global Economy. *Final Report on Mapping Homebased Work*. In J. Tate (ed.) Leeds, UK: Homeworkers Worldwide.

HWW. (2006) Homeworkers Worldwide International Meeting, 25–30 March. Homeworkers Worldwide International meeting. Lake Ohrid, Macedonia.

HWW. (2007) European Homeworking Group meeting. European Homeworking Group meeting, November. Instanbul, Turkey: HWW.

HWW. (2008) European meeting in Istanbul. *We Work At Home.*

Jhabvala, R. (1994) Self-Employed Women's Association: Organising Women by Struggle and Development. In S. Rowbotham and S. Mitter (eds), *Dignity and Daily Bread* (pp. 114–138). London.

Jhabvala, R. (1999) SEWA and HomeNet. Unpublished letter. SEWA.

Jhabvala, R. (2001) WIEGO Org and Rep Group Meeting, Geneva 8 to 12 June, 2001. Unpublished meeting report. SEWA.

Kabeer, N., Milward, K. and Sudarshan, R. (2013) Organising Women Workers in the Informal Economy. *Gender & Development* 21: 249–263.

Keck, M. and Sikkink, K. (1998) *Activists Beyond Borders: Advocacy Networks in International Politics*. Ithaca and London: Cornell University Press.

Kelly, J. (1998) *Rethinking Industrial Relations: Mobilization, Collectivism and Long Waves*. London.

Kuumba, B. (2001) *Gender and Social Movements*. Walnut Creek: AltaMira Press.

Lindberg, A. (2001) Class, Caste, and Gender among Cashew Workers in the South Indian State of Kerala 1930–2000. *International Review of Social History* 46: 155–184.

Martens, M. and Mitter, S. (eds) (1994) *Women in Trade Unions: Organising the Unorganised*. Geneva: International Labour Organization.

Mies, M. (2014) *Patriarchy and Accumulation on a World Scale: Women in the International Division of Labour*. London: Zed Books.

Moghadam, V.M. (1999) Gender and Globalisation: Female Labor and Women's Mobilization. *Journal of World-Systems Research* (2): 367–388.

Moghadam, V.M. (2005) *Globalizing Women: Transnational Feminist Networks*. Baltimore MD: The Johns Hopkins University.

Nachiappan, S. and Rajan, S. (2008) The Economic Empowerment of Women: The Case of Working Women's Forum, India. *Journal of International Women's Studies* 10.

Priyadarshini, A. (2016) *Tracing the Invisible Workers: Women Home-Based Workers of Nineteenth Century Bihar*. Department of Transnational Studies. New York: University of Buffalo.

Prugl, E. (1999) *The Global Construction of Gender: Home-Based Work in the Political Economy of the 20th Century*. New York: Columbia University Press.

Purkayastha, B. and Subramaniam, M. (eds) (2004) *The Power of Women's Informal Networks: Lessons in Social Change from South Asia and West Africa*. Lanham: Lexington Books.

Rose, K. (1992) *Where Women are Leaders: The SEWA Movement in India*. New Delhi: Vistaar Publications.

Rowbotham, S. (1998) Weapons of the Weak: Homeworkers' Networking in Europe. *The European Journal of Women's Studies* 5: 453–463.

Rowbotham, S. (1999) *New Ways of Organising in the Informal Sector: Four Case Studies of Trade Union Activity*. Leeds: HomeNet.

Rowbotham, S. and Mitter, S. (1994) *Dignity and Daily Bread: New Forms of Economic Organising Among Poor Women in the Third World and the First*. London: Routledge.

Srinivasan, V. (2003) Notes on Policy Issues. *Homeworkers Worldwide Policy Workshop 8–12 September, 2003*. Zlatibor, Serbia: HWW.

Silver, B. (2003) *Forces of Labour: Workers Movements and Globalization Since 1870*. Cambridge: Cambridge University Press.

Steinmo, S. (2008) What is Historical Institutionalism? In D. Della Porta and M. Keating (eds) *Approaches to the Social Sciences*. Cambridge University Press.

Tate, J. (1994a) Homework in West Yorkshire. In S. Rowbotham and S. Mitter (eds), *Dignity and Daily Bread* (pp. 193–217). London: Routledge.

Tate, J. (1994b) Organising Homeworkers in the Informal Sector: Introduction to Part III. In M.H. Martens and S. Mitter (eds), *Women in Trade Unions: Organising the Unorganised* (pp. 61–93). Geneva: International Labour Office.

Tate, J. (1996a) *Every Pair Tells a Story, Report on a Survey of Homeworking and Subcontracting Chains in Six Countries of the European Union*. Leeds: European Homeworking Group.

Tate, J. (1996b) Making Links: The Growth of Homeworker Networks. In E. Boris and E. Prugl (eds), *Homeworkers in Global Perspective: Invisible No More* (pp. 273–290). New York: Routledge.

Tate, J. (2001) *Relationship Between HNI and HWW, and Mapping Program*. Unpublished discussion paper. HomeNet.

Tate, J. (2002a) HomeNet Future Plans and Current Problems. Unpublished memo. HomeNet.

Tate, J. (2002b) HNI board. Unpublished memo. HomeNet.

Tilly, C. (1978) *From Mobilization to Revolution*, Reading, Massachusetts: Addison-Wesley.

WIEGO. (2018) About WIEGO. Available at: http://www.wiego.org/wiego/about-wiego

Wright, E. (2000) Working-Class Power, Capitalist Class Interests and Class Compromise. *American Journal of Sociology* 105: 957–1002.

7

MAKING CHANGE

A gender justice perspective

One of our principle objectives, stated in the introduction to this book, was to contribute a gender justice approach as a new perspective to analyse and confront the issues and problems of homework. The inequities and injustices inherent in homework conditions constitute a common thread throughout the body of literature on homework because they invisibilise homeworkers, predominantly women, and maintain their weak bargaining position, preventing them from making any improvements to their lives through their work (Boris and Prügl, 1996; Mies, 1982; Allen and Wolkowitz, 1987). Invisibilisation is a powerful device in the diminution of work conditions and protections, part of a political project that serves the dominant interests of capital and patriarchy at the expense of workers. Invisibilisation is socially and politically constructed through social relations ideologically consistent with capitalism and patriarchy (Burchielli and Delaney, 2016), thereby reinforcing the devaluation of women's paid production. Throughout this book we have talked about the social relations of domination such as have devalued women's paid production in the private sphere, and consequently devalued homework that is undertaken in the home location (Federici 2012; Mies, 2014; Bhattacharya, 2017). These unresolved injustices motivated the writing of this book and provided the rationale for our adoption of a gender justice frame.

Borrowing from both feminist and development literatures, we put forward *four gender justice dimensions*, including recognition, representation, rights and redistribution, as organising principles from which to achieve all the main objectives underlying this book: to review and understand the injustices of homework; to guide our proposals for change towards justice; and to structure our work in this book (Fraser, 2008; Utting, 2007).

Across our analysis, we argue that the linkages between capitalist and patriarchal relations explain the inequalities and injustices in homework. In our discussion, we argue that the processes and structures of capitalism and the patriarchy are examples of the economic, social, political and dominant power acts, actors and structures that underlie the relations of domination and that create and determine injustice outcomes in the four dimensions. Together, the *determinants* of injustice (capitalism, patriarchy) and the four *dimensions* of gender justice (recognition, representation, rights and redistribution) make up the early gender justice framework presented in the introduction (see Figure 7.1) and illustrated in the themes discussed in the chapters of this book.

In simple terms, Figure 7.1 indicates that capitalist and patriarchal relations of domination create injustice outcomes in the four areas or dimensions of justice. The arrow between the determinants and outcomes represents the relations of domination that are extensively discussed in Chapter 1 and reiterated in the specific themes of the subsequent chapters.

Features and exemplars of the relations of domination discussed in this volume include: invisibilisation via devaluation of women's work and social reproductive contribution, discourses and acts of violence against women supported by socio-political factors replicated in the workplace and elsewhere; neoliberal patterns of work such as feminisation, informalisation, and neoliberal regulation regimes that contribute to workers being redefined as entrepreneurs, self-employed and non-worker. In addition, global trade, uneven development, and features of supply chain capitalism are some of the manifestations of the relations of domination that affect homeworkers and other workers (see Peterson, 2002; Fraser, 2008; 2017; Tsing, 2009; Federici 2012; Pearson, 2014; Burchielli and Delaney, 2016; Bhatta-charya, 2017)

In this final chapter, we revisit our analysis of the relations and circumstances that have failed homeworkers, in relation to the four gender justice dimensions. We also review the initiatives that have supported homeworkers along the lines of the gender justice dimensions. These include research and various regulatory approaches, social movement approaches and networks of resistance to support

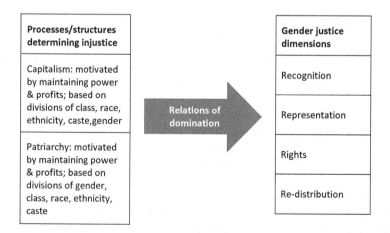

FIGURE 7.1 A gender justice framework for homework

organising and organisation building with homeworkers in specific temporal and geographic locations. In the course of our review, we identify the features that were beneficial for homeworkers and how they addressed the inequities of homework. This discussion generates a subsequent extension of our framework in relation to a strategic approach for bringing about positive change and justice to homework. We subsequently elaborate on an extended gender justice framework for homework later in this chapter (see Figure 7.2).

Given our arguments that injustices in homework are direct outcomes of capitalism and the patriarchy, we frame our proposals for gender justice in homework as a countervailing force directed against capitalism and the patriarchy. Each of the positive initiatives analysed in this book reflects one or other of the dimensions of gender justice. We argue, however, that the organising approach is the only initiative that can achieve positive outcomes in all four dimensions of justice. Organising has a proven track record, historically, as a form of resistance capable of mitigating the effects of capitalism (Tilly, 1978; Kelly, 1998 Rowbotham, 1999; Kabeer, Sudarchan and Milward, 2013). Although we are not naïve enough to think that capitalism and the patriarchy are going to meet their end soon, we are still sufficiently idealistic enough to believe in the power of resistance.

Four dimensions of justice: recognition, representation, rights, redistribution

We define the dimension of *recognition* in terms of the socio-political acts of describing, acknowledging and valuing. We discuss issues in relation to *recognition* in the first two chapters of this book, where we set about to identify and examine the defining conditions of homework through a meta-analysis of key literature, from the 1980s to the present, together with unique data sets collected by the authors and others.

In particular, and in an act of recognition of the realities of homework, we highlight the insecurity of homework, the long working hours, subsistence and inadequate rates of pay, unsafe working conditions, lack of protection from unions and the state, the invisibility of homework, and the predominance of women as

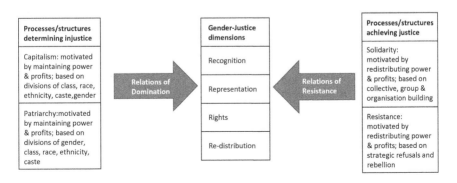

FIGURE 7.2 An expanded gender justice framework for homework

key conditions of homework. We identify these conditions as injustice outcomes in the dimension of recognition, arguing that the labour and contributions of homeworkers are not adequately described, acknowledged nor valued.

In Chapters 1 and 2 we provide various types of evidence of the non-recognition of homework, beginning with the lack of acknowledgement and valuing of homeworkers' social reproductive roles as mothers and carers, which extends to their productive role as workers. Although the combined reproductive and productive tasks of homeworkers ensure they are working around 16 hours per day, remuneration is often below subsistence level and they are barely able to survive.

In our discussion of *invisibilisation* in Chapter 2, we argue that both capitalism and the patriarchy support techniques and strategies in the dimension of recognition to achieve the injustices we perceive in homework, by actively ignoring, not-recognising, describing incorrectly, devalorising, trivialising and delegitimising homework as a form of work (Burchielli and Delaney, 2016). This strongly correlates with patriarchal patterns of domination that utilise gender constructs to attribute a lesser value to women's social reproductive work and so devalue women's paid productive work (Mies, 2014; Federici, 2012; Bhattacharya, 2017). We undertake more specific discussion of the lack of recognition of homework in subsequent chapters where we examine regulatory responses, demonstrating a lack of concern for homeworkers by employers, unions and governments (see Chapters 3, 4 and 5). Moreover, we demonstrate that in supply chains, brands and employers mostly ignore and deny the presence of homeworkers (Delaney, Burchielli and Tate, 2017). And, when firms acknowledge the presence of homeworkers in their supply chains, homeworkers are still inadequately compensated and unprotected.

We conclude that justice outcomes for homeworkers can be achieved in the dimension of recognition by accurately describing, and properly acknowledging and valuing women's unpaid work and paid productive home-based work. We advocate for ongoing research on homework, to accurately describe conditions in distinct geographic and industry locations and for the purpose of informing policy makers and civil society. Recognition, as a type of understanding, is a necessary precondition to the other three justice dimensions.

Our *representation* dimension refers to advocacy on behalf of homeworkers, including both self and collective advocacy, activism and resistance. Themes and issues discussed in relation to representation include: access to and capacity for individual or collective agency; having a voice; being able to influence or make decisions about own working/economic conditions either individually or through collective action/representation, such as a union or labour organisation. In this sense, representation also references freedom of association and collective bargaining. These themes are discussed in Chapter 3, in relation to traditional definitions of the employment relationship that specifically result in the exclusion of homeworkers under many existing employment laws, that lay the foundations for many of the inequitable working conditions characterising homework (Hyde, 2012; Stone and Arthurs, 2013; Fudge, 2014). Chapter 3 also analyses homework laws designed specifically to represent homeworkers, highlighting their potential strengths insofar as they recognise homeworkers as workers, and may be used to seek justice for homeworkers in terms of specific conditions of employment (International Labour Organization, 2003). The limitations of homework laws are analysed in this chapter, in terms of the policy/civil society resources required – but often lacking – to activate or potentiate homework legislation. Alternative models of legislation and policy designed to benefit women informal workers are also discussed here.

Chapter 4 extends the discussion of representation, delivering a critique of corporate social responsibility (CSR), a corporate-centric, voluntary approach that has become the default response to the current regulatory gap. We argue that the vast majority of existing CSR initiatives tend to replicate philanthropic approaches, aiming to do some limited and general 'good works', without actually addressing the harms produced by corporate activities (Jenkins, Pearson and Seyfang, 2002). We further posit that CSR projects rarely address labour rights, let alone homework (Delaney et al., 2017). Examples discussed in Chapter 4 demonstrate the more common approach by brands is to ban homework to avoid any perceived risks to the corporate reputation. CSR approaches frequently fail then to recognise homework.

We describe CSR approaches to homework that compartmentalise responsibility and shield corporations from taking responsibility for the realities of homeworkers' work conditions, thus enabling the corporation to continue to do business-as-usual – to continue to prioritise profit over people and continue to produce various harms to workers and the environment, with little consequence in terms of accountability. Given the voluntary and corporate centred approach of CSR, we argue that CSR approaches do not contribute to improve representation of homeworkers, since they are failing to address the fundamental rights' issue associated with representation: freedom of association (Pearson, 2004; 2014). Few brands have engaged with homeworkers in a substantial way to treat them equal to other workers. One fledgling project with global brand Pentland, currently underway in the UK and India, involves addressing ways to make the supply chain more transparent beyond the first-tier supplier and to develop ways to improve homework piece-rates to reflect a living wage. It is as yet too early, however, to report on outcomes of this project. Additionally, engagement via CSR appears to be responsive to homeworkers' circumstances when embedded with complementary legal obligations, demonstrated in the co-regulation model developed in Australia. These positive initiatives are too few and far between; the evidence points overwhelmingly to the failure of CSR to contribute to representative justice outcomes for homeworkers.

The dimension of *rights* relates to access to basic labour and human rights. It refers to homeworkers having a voice, being able to influence decisions about their own working and economic conditions and being adequately remunerated for their work. It also refers to access to other work-related freedoms, such as freedom from discrimination and freedom of association and bargaining.

Chapter 5 examines the lack of rights for homeworkers, brought about by a range of social, political and economic structural forces that increase their invisibility and enable corporations to ignore their rights. The chapter focuses on the structure and activities of the supply chain, globalised in the 20th century, and the business strategy of outsourcing, that, combined, explain the current surge of homework. It argues that homework is embedded in supply chains that make use of historical and geographic inequalities based on gendered constructs of social reproductive labour, class, race, ethnicity and colonisation (Tsing, 2009).

The social relations of production through supply chains maintains cheap and flexible production and locks homeworkers into irregular work on low piece-rates. Fearful of losing their work, these social relations severely limit opportunities for workers to collectively organise. Homeworkers' invisibility at the margins of long supply chains limits their proper representation by unions and constrains home-workers' ability to demand their rights (Delaney, Burchielli and Connor, 2015). This, in conjunction with pre-existing gender inequalities – homeworkers' location in the private sphere of the home, and the related devalorisation of women's reproductive work in particular – further entrench inequalities and constraints to justice. The chapter argues that corporations take advantage of location-based economic, gender, race and ethnicity inequalities, to maximise their profits without concern for the most exploited workers.

Chapter 6 further examines rights by focusing on the basic labour right of free-dom of association (FOA) in respect of homework. In its broadest sense, FOA does not only refer to being able to form or join a labour union but rather, forming or joining any association, movement, union or campaign that advocates for and/or claims work-related rights. This chapter analyses distinct mobilising and organising strategies involving homeworkers claiming rights across various historical times and geographic locations. This is discussed further in the next section.

In our definition of *redistribution*, we refer to access and initiatives that challenge and correct a range of institutional and structural inequalities and injustices. Redistribution is frequently understood in financial terms. However, we con-template a broader meaning, whereby redistribution is synonymous with gender justice. Throughout our discussion of homework, we provide evidence that homeworkers are discriminated via a range of social, political and economic injus-tices that are related and interdependent. Although we devote considerable space to highlighting the unjust working conditions of homework, we view these as *symptomatic* of broader injustices arising from the relations of domination that is the *modus operandi* of capitalism and the patriarchy. A sustainable solution requires mitigating the power and forces of domination. This, in turn, requires engaging the forces of resistance, which is predicated on greater homeworker participation.

Redistribution then is about correcting various imbalances together, such as increasing homeworker voice, homeworkers' capacity to participate in civil society and capacity to renegotiate their social, political and economic conditions, sup-ported by sympathetic groups and organisations. It is clear that, as a dimension of gender justice, redistribution relates to each of the other three dimensions: recog-nition, representation and rights. Equally, achieving gender justice or redistribution relates to achieving justice measures in all of the dimensions.

Chapter 6 is also about redistribution. It argues that social movement and organising initiatives, framed around transnational and feminist networks have the greatest potential to achieve justice benefits for homeworkers precisely because these efforts are based on achieving gains in all four dimensions of gender justice. Such are exemplified by the International Homeworkers Network (IHN), Homenet International (HNI), Homeworkers Worldwide (HWW) and the mapping program case study. In the next section we summarise a range of activities, and their characteristics, that have had positive outcomes for homeworkers, highlighting which of the dimensions they reference.

Approaches in activism to achieve outcomes for homeworkers

In this section we discuss activist strategies and approaches that have worked for homeworkers, highlighting why they worked and the features that were beneficial for homeworkers. We discuss these important and positive initiatives as examples of what works to create avenues of countervailing forces of resistance for and by homeworkers. We draw out the following four examples, participatory research methodology, regulatory approaches, community unionism approach, and organising and mobilisation through networks, to identify some promising practices for homeworkers.

1. Participatory research methodology

We identified and documented various approaches that have contributed a positive change for homeworkers. The first of these were research participatory methodologies. In Chapter 2 we discussed the West Yorkshire studies, 1978–1986, and the human geography studies in Greece in the 1990s. These studies share similar features in that they make contact with homeworkers and represent their voices, revealing the realities through the lived experience of homeworking women. They describe, for example, the gender divisions of labour that discriminate against women and devalorise their work, and also encourage homeworkers to be participants – not just by providing information and sharing their lived experience of homeworking, but by being active contributors to shape the outcomes to their benefit. Both of these studies also focused on aspects of the supply chain that demonstrated that the persistence of homework is less rooted in women's needs and more on the needs of capital. Further, these studies show that women homeworkers were present although hidden in supply chains, consequently, the research had a positive impact on the recognition of homeworkers. They have also underpinned subsequent strategies to represent, to seek rights and redistribution for homeworkers.

Additionally, feminist researchers from the 1980s to early 2000s published extensively on homework and related issues; many of these books invited key activists from the International Homeworkers Network to co-publish, bringing together the knowledge and expertise of academics and activists to explore the issues relevant to homeworkers. The seminal works on homework provided critical feminist analysis of class, gender and race, and the interactions between capitalism and patriarchy. Many of these works influenced or created ongoing collaborations between activists and scholars (for example, Allen and Wolkowitz 1987; Boris and Daniels 1989; Martens and Mitter, 1994; Rowbotham and Mitter, 1994; Boris and Prugl, 1996, amongst others). The skills and experience of sympathetic researchers have proved to be an important source of power to homeworker activists, offering support to homeworkers to improve their recognition both at the transnational and the local levels. As researchers have co-assisted activists and workers to document, analyse and evaluate trends and reveal new circumstances of global and local social relations of globalised homework, homeworkers gained access to international standards at the ILO and achieved national laws. These outcomes are not insignificant for invisibilised and marginalised women workers.

2. Homework regulation and standards

A second approach to activism relates to the development of regulatory approaches. In Chapters 2 and 3 of this book, we discussed certain key events and organisations, whose activism led to the adoption of Home Work Convention (No. 177), 1996, (the Convention). Despite any of the shortcomings we have previously highlighted around the implementation of the Convention, there were numerous positive impacts for homeworkers, including its subsequent use as a tool for organising homeworkers.

Prior to the passing of the Convention, various related activities were beneficial for homework. This included excellent research, discussed in Chapter 2, conducted with homeworkers, that outlined the conditions of homework, and a number of organising efforts. In India, the Self-Employed Women's Association (SEWA) struggled for recognition of informal women workers as workers, including homeworkers. Concurrently, in Europe, the women's movement and trade unions had begun organising homeworkers. Examples include STIBTTA, the union of workers of embroidery, tapestry and craftwork, in Madeira, Portugal; the West Yorkshire Homeworking Group; and the National Group on Homework, United Kingdom. These grassroots initiatives inspired others to begin work with homeworkers.

Importantly, these efforts provided the impetus for creating regional and transnational networks, such as alliances between homeworker organisations. HomeNet International and Homeworkers Worldwide (HWW) are two such organisations and HWW is still currently active. Homework organisations also allied with trade unions, particularly global union federations, International Union of Food Workers (IUF) and the International Textile, Garment and Leather Workers Federation (ITGLWF) now IndustriALL. These led to recognition of homeworkers as workers with the trade union movement, and in turn to demands on the ILO to put the drafting of a convention on the agenda of its annual conference.

Since its adoption, the Convention has provided leverage to homework advocacy groups for beginning discussions in a policy context with governments. The text of the Convention brought together much of the knowledge about how traditional employment law could be adapted for homeworkers. Its greatest strength lies in recognising and representing homeworkers as workers and acknowledging that, under current arrangements, they work under inequitable and unjust conditions. Further, it has been used as a springboard to initiate new instances of homework organising, such as in Turkey, where it was used by a range of local women's organisations and supported by HWW to organise homeworkers in the early 2000s, as discussed in Chapter 6. As a recognised international standard, the Convention may be used as a tool by homework organisations, or alongside homework national legislation, where it exists to recognise, represent and seek rights and redistribution for homeworkers.

3. Social movement – unions and community approach

The case studies discussed in the book emphasise the capacity of homeworkers working in supply chains to join together with more powerful groups to achieve change. Through forming alliances or collaborating in networks, homeworkers have been able to access and use forms of social power (see Chapter 5).

The few examples of unions working with homeworkers demonstrate that there remain significant barriers to unions developing the capacity to be more inclusive of informal and marginalised women workers (see Chapter 6).

In Chapter 5 we highlight social movement approaches by the Textile, Clothing and Footwear Union of Australia (TCFUA) to improve homeworker representation. The social movement approach in the Australian case highlighted the importance of the Union working closely with community campaign, FairWear. A key driver of FairWear, the NGO Asian Women at Work (AWATW), had established an extensive membership base of homeworkers, who worked closely to support the union campaign. Union and AWATW representatives founded the FairWear campaign which attracted a broad range of activist supporters from student groups, faith groups, women's groups and unionists. This enabled the union to orchestrate a number of wide ranging strategies to improve homeworker recognition to achieve key outcomes. The priorities included: equity for homeworkers in labour regulation, supply chain transparency and corporate accountability, and, improvements to homeworkers' wages and social benefits. Subsequent developments included: various governance mechanisms, including garment industry regulation (Awards); the homeworkers code of practice – a voluntary code; state and national labour legislation deeming homeworkers to be employees; and joint liability between lead firms and suppliers for homeworkers work conditions, underpayments, or failure to be paid for work. These factors combined indicate a significant range of positive benefits.

The TCFUA established itself as the representative of garment homeworkers, even though very few were union members. This was an effective way to develop collective bargaining strategies with the industry. Importantly, homeworkers participated via some sections of the union and AWATW. During the campaign, homeworkers were often portrayed as disadvantaged and exploited women in society. This overarching narrative or frame was used effectively to gain sympathy with media, consumers and government authorities. It was difficult for fashion brands to counter this narrative, since the widespread disregard for compliance to existing laws meant it was easy for the Union and FairWear to demonstrate poor labour practices. Brands that agreed to be part of the homeworker initiatives could join the homeworkers' code and publicly support legislative initiatives. The actions of the FairWear campaign created countervailing forces to shift corporate norms and influence other corporate and government actors. The social movement approach used by the Union and FairWear demonstrates how important to the campaign was homeworkers' increased participation. Furthermore, despite the grand narrative of exploited women, they evolved into leaders who spoke to government enquiries and media and contributed to campaign strategies.

The community–union social movement approach to improving recognition, representation and rights through legislation and industry-wide collective bargaining around implementation of the legislation gave homeworkers access to both associational and social power, reinforcing homeworkers' potential to claim rights through legislation, and from their position in the supply chain to access improved wages and other benefits previously denied to them. Without links to civil society groups and the union, homeworkers would not have been able to gain this level of recognition nor have been able to engage in collective bargaining with government and industry to access rights.

The mobilisation strategies in this example indicate the necessity for unions to join with other civil society groups linked to homeworkers. This approach is an effectual way for homeworkers to develop recognition, representation and rights. Maturing such connections enables homeworkers to become a countervailing force against the social relations in the supply chain. This potentially can enable them to participate through networks of resistance and link to sources of social power that otherwise they could not establish on their own. Consequently, this is an effective method for homeworkers to engage in initiatives that challenge institutional inequalities, such as those created by features of capitalism, used in supply chains, as discussed in Chapter 5. Networks of resistance can activate redistribution measures and support homeworkers to be able to encroach on the economic, social and political forces associated with the powerful under capitalism and patriarchy that usually exclude homeworkers from participation. These measures can be argued to fit within the justice dimension of rights if homeworkers as participants can shape, lead and influence the initiatives. However, we caution that without genuine collective organising there is limited scope for this to occur. We expand on this in the next section.

4. Mobilising and organising through networks

The fourth area of activism demonstrating positive outcomes for homeworkers is a mobilising approach, discussed in Chapter 6. We highlight here the example of organising and mobilising through the international homeworker network. We also discuss the international mapping program (mapping program) coordinated by Homeworkers Worldwide (HWW) as a positive example of homeworker organising and networked resistance. Previously, we discussed some of the limits of mapping, specifically the difficulties of sustaining the organising work. This section focuses on the positive impacts.

The mapping program was coordinated by Homeworkers Worldwide (HWW) and highlights the positive role that transnational organising can play to facilitate local organising, representation and solidarity. The strength of the mapping program was demonstrated through the knowledge sharing that occurred; documenting the successful achievements of homeworker groups, and, publishing case studies of positive organising experiences. HWW provided support for direct exchanges between homeworkers and across organisations that inspired newly formed homeworker organisations to continue their organising activities, despite the many obstacles to overcome.

New homework organisations were established, often enabled by women's organisations taking on a support role to facilitate contact with homeworkers and creating opportunities for homeworkers to participate in the action research process. Training then led them to become leaders and contact more homeworkers. Action research, training and networked support, built homeworker solidarity and recognition at the local level and, as national homeworker groups and networks grew, it contributed to recognition and representation at the transnational level.

Positive effects for individual women included developing new skills, increasing personal confidence, beginning to identify as workers, and developing a political consciousness. These effects for individuals facilitated participation in collective processes and enabled the establishment of new homeworker organisations. This part was necessary, since homeworkers on their own have limited capacity to organise together without some initial steps, such as building common identities with other women around common experiences. Research shows that for informal workers, groundwork such as that described in the early stages of mapping is a necessary precondition for building identities as workers, improving self-advocacy, building leadership and collective advocacy. It also helps create ways for them to improve their economic and social status without losing their work and livelihood (Kabeer et al., 2013).

The expansion of the International Homeworkers Network was a positive outcome from the mapping program. The network expanded as homeworker organising grew across new global regions, for example, Latin America, South Asia, East Asia, and Eastern Europe. Many new homeworker organisations were formed, including unions; self-help groups, cooperatives, national federations and local associations, some of these were registered organisations, but many were not. What became evident is that the structure and form of organisations established was specific to the social and political circumstances at the local level.

The organising cases discussed in Chapter 6 demonstrate how organising contributes to women developing solidarity and leadership capacity, to participate and express their demands, and therefore to gain a seat at the table. This is an important process in shifting perceptions of homeworkers from being at the margins, to being engaged in processes as participants in society – and so linking to the redistribution dimension, discussed further in the next section.

A strength of the mapping approach also emerged around the solidarity features within and between homeworker groups. The formation of local groups demonstrated solidarity between the individual constituents of the local groups. As local groups became part of the transnational network, solidarity grew between different groups across national boundaries. Solidarity then foregrounded activities of resistance, discussed further in the next section. The mapping program approach contributed to the formation of various types of homeworker organisation, and, as homeworker organisation formed either formally or informally, they could take up an advocacy role with government, industry and in international forums, such as the ILO. This form of representation was linked to improving homeworkers' rights, since in many countries lobbying by homeworker groups led to inclusion of homeworkers in legislation. In Bulgaria, for example, the government ratified the ILO convention and followed this by introducing new laws for homework. Such changes are unlikely without the grassroots organisation of homeworkers that enabled representative advocacy, to engage with powerful state institutions to secure such rights.

Solidarity and resistance

The examples of organising discussed in Chapter 6 demonstrate the important role of the International Homeworkers Network (IHN) that emerged as a movement of homework organisations focused on labour rights and organising of workers. The IHN enhanced the representation of homeworkers and their representatives through advocacy, policy development, supporting the creation of new homeworker groups and lending them recognition and legitimacy. The effectiveness of collective action depends on the extent that members share a sense of identity and interests (Kabeer et al., 2013; Tilly, 1978; Kelly, 1998; Burchielli, Buttigieg and Delaney, 2008). The IHN supported the building of *solidarity* between homeworkers as individuals and between homeworker organisations. Solidarity describes activities to unite and strengthen homeworker groupings, and includes the support of fledgling groups. Support is critical to effective organising and the subsequent effectiveness of the group (Tilly, 1978; Kelly, 1998; Burchielli et al., 2008; Kabeer et al., 2013).

The IHN also supported the possibility of, and avenues for *resistance* through network and campaign activities. Resistance describes all manner of activities that refuse and rebel against the effects of domination. For example, supporting local homeworkers' rights through campaigns and activities with global brands; conducting research, and documenting homework conditions and activities. Homework organisations have recognised the benefits of having both local and an international organisation.

The linking of local organising and activism and transnational organising and activism, with support from the transnational homework network demonstrates that the application of solidarity and resistance activities, at local, national and transnational levels, can support and maintain organising efforts at these levels. We described the activities of the IHN as *transnationalism from below* since it is shaped by the homeworker networks at the local level. These solidarity activities were formed around 'identity' and then 'protest frames' consistent with the purpose derived from local homeworker networks demands and needs. This concept fits within a broader social movement literature that acknowledges women's informal networks can function as networks of resistance (Purkayastha and Subramaniam, 2004; Kuumba, 2001; Kabeer et al., 2013).

Building solidarity is fundamental to organising as it creates linkages. In the early stages of organising, linkages are weak. As solidarity grows, however – through shared experiences of small, group acts of resistance – loosely coupled networks grow stronger and can eventually join with others to create networks of resistance. Acts of solidarity and resistance shape and create a countervailing force against power asymmetries associated with the ideologies and socio-political forces of the relations of domination. Resisting the political forces of capitalism and the patriarchy requires such countervailing power as that embodied in groupings of workers.

We suggest that whereas the dominant paradigms of capitalism and patriarchy act to achieve injustice impacts across the four dimensions, the structures and processes of resistance groups are necessary as a countervailing force to achieve justice impacts. This informs revisiting the gender justice framework to explore the relationship between the dominant paradigms and the relations of resistance.

Expanded homework gender justice framework

We have previously discussed the role of the relations of domination in our gender justice framework. In summary, this captures the combined and multiple ideological and socio-political constructs and devices that contribute to the exploitation and oppression that homeworkers experience. However, we now introduce into the framework, the structures and processes that aim to achieve justice outcomes. We describe their weapons, strategies and activities as the relations of resistance.

We further introduce and position the relations of resistance as the countervailing force to the dominant paradigms of capitalism and patriarchy. The relations of resistance include two complementary structures and processes: solidarity and resistance. Combined, solidarity and resistance capture the numerous approaches to address the injustices that homeworkers experience and that are extensively described in this book.

We have given examples, in the cases discussed in this book, of the types of structures/organisations that aim to achieve justice outcomes for homeworkers. They comprise such groups as homework advocacy groups, HWW and HNI; NGOs such as CIVIDEP, the ILO, the FairWear campaign and union federations. Essentially, they are groups that work either directly, or in collaboration, to improve the lives of homeworkers. Although some no longer exist, we have also highlighted new initiatives and organisations, for which we are hopeful.

We have illustrated the processes of the structures aiming to achieve justice for homeworkers through our discussion of the multiple approaches that can be orchestrated across all the gender justice dimensions, of which organising is a fundamental approach, and often preceded by or including activities as research about homework, lobbying, developing legislation, networking, developing leaders, developing policy, developing and activating campaign strategies. Further processes include forms of resistance that are motivated and activated by homeworker networks, in solidarity with other civil society support groups, unions, NGOs, social movements, campaigns, and researchers.

We characterise the relations of resistance as the cluster of initiatives taken in the acts of solidarity and resistance that are developed and implemented by a group or organisation, working with and on behalf of homeworkers at any given time. Whereas capital (and patriarchy) enact the relations of domination to disrupt worker solidarity, curtail union presence and create obstacles to workers collectivising (see Chapter 5), homeworkers, as other workers, may participate in relations of resistance to seek justice and disrupt the forces of capital. *Of course, it's not a level playing field.* Homeworkers lack the unlimited financial resources of capital. Moreover, we have repeatedly stressed the challenges for homeworkers, whose life circumstances limit their opportunities and experiences to engage in solidarity with other workers. Nonetheless, the simple act of homeworkers – not recognised as workers – joining together to be heard, to make demands, to enter dialogue, and to fight for regulated protection is in itself a powerful act of resistance. The notion of women homeworkers being part of, and acknowledged in the public space, and leading change, is powerful.

The solidarity and resistance activities that form the central features of the relations of resistance in the gender justice framework are a way to conceptualise ideological and socio-political regimes that directly oppose the relations of domination and associated asymmetries of power. Being in direct opposition to the relations of domination, relations of resistance create a countervailing force that generates new discourses and constructs new realities – for example, valuing women's work, counting homeworkers' economic and social contribution as important and valued; visibilising women's work in ways that valorise and promote initiatives that have positive outcomes for homeworkers.

The relations of resistance thus interact with the four dimensions – recognition, representation, rights and redistribution – in the gender justice framework. This was illustrated earlier in this chapter, in the positive activism approaches that summarise successful strategies and outcomes for homeworkers. The relations of resistance can obtain justice impacts in the four dimensions of justice; moreover, they can weaken the effects of the relations of domination and challenge and resist the assumptions of capitalism and the patriarchy. The conceptualisation of the relations of resistance in the gender justice framework can be wielded as a weapon of resistance for homeworkers, once considered only as weak and invisible. Notwithstanding the challenges and setbacks experienced along the way in the struggle against the enormously powerful relations of domination, we also acknowledge the many ways that small and large acts of resistance can and do shift and change social relations over time.

Making change: concluding remarks

Until now, we have discussed the many common features of homework around the world, however, in the context of making change we must caution the importance of accounting for local contexts. For those women's organisations, NGO's, unions, activist researchers and others who wish to begin to work with homeworkers to create positive change, we cannot provide a detailed road map. What we offer are the lessons we have learned in our experiences with homeworkers, encapsulated and summarised in the elements of gender justice framework. We intend that this framework be used to guide new initiatives or to refocus existing initiatives that may require inspiration. We hope that it will be reflected upon and debated within and by homeworker networks, unions, NGOs, social movement actors, policy makers, researchers and supporters of homeworkers.

We note that all four examples of activism have had invaluable justice outcomes for homeworkers have all involved homeworkers. Initiatives of the types discussed above will therefore continue to be necessary, and we encourage their development. We further suggest that it is necessary to structure future strategies for change with the objective to achieve success in the four gender justice dimensions.

While each of the gender justice dimensions are important, we do not recommend a focus on any single dimension. Throughout this book, we separated the dimensions for the purpose of our analysis; however, we also pointed out the frequent overlaps between dimensions, and so suggest that separating the dimensions is not useful nor sufficient to address the situation of homeworkers to achieve justice. Justice for homeworkers requires achieving a measure of success in each of the dimensions equally. In so doing, redistribution can be achieved incrementally. Redistribution entails systemic shifts that change institutional and structural disadvantage. To achieve full redistribution would involve homeworkers achieving an increased share of power and profit, the valorisation of unpaid and paid work in the household, community, work and society, to name just a few, therefore, such objectives require strategies that draw on the relations of resistance to achieve fundamental, systemic change. It is an enormously ambitious agenda but one worth pursuing. On this basis, we recommend that local groups should attempt initiatives in the following areas, tailoring them to local conditions.

Homework organising and mobilisation – social movement approaches

Organising homeworkers, using social movement approaches, has shown to be successful when it involves consultation with and participation by homeworkers. Therefore, developing initiatives around legislation, consumer campaigns and engagement with brands all present opportunities to support homeworker organising. In practice, strategies that build and support mobilisation, organisation and networks can offer them more. We further note that each of the examples have depended on the participation of homeworkers. Creating solidarity with and between homeworkers is, for us, the gold standard for helping homeworkers to improve their own lives and conditions. It is also the most challenging because of the multiple disadvantages of homeworkers that create obstacles for their participation. Importantly, solidarity building among homeworkers cannot revolve around a common worker identity that does not exist, therefore workers need to be encouraged to discuss their day to day concerns as women to begin to identify as workers, and through such activities they may begin to identify the commonality of their working lives and the common hopes to determine collective strategies (Burchielli, Buttigieg, Delaney, 2008).

Support, linked to solidarity, is a critical factor in all organising and is particularly important for homework groups. The establishment of alliances between homeworkers and other groupings, be they with academic-activists, NGOs, other civil society groups – unions – or other social movement organisations, must be considered. The solidarity formed through alliances with other unions, NGOs, social movement groups to improve homeworker recognition and rights can build collective representation, to access redistribution via share of profits, participation in society and collective empowerment. Ultimately success in creating redistributive justice in relation to homeworker organising requires civil society actors, in particular unions, to form coalitions and partnerships to create organising models of inclusion for homeworkers and informal workers.

Homework regulation – standards approaches

The development of specific, homework inclusive regulation and standards is valuable for homeworkers. However, we note that in all the instances documented in this book, the development and implementation of regulatory approaches occurred within broader homework social movements, including advocacy, research, and networking. This is because 'organised' groups can achieve a range of outcomes, including research and regulatory ones, therefore instituting improvements in issues relating to recognition, representation and rights.

We note that despite the numerous barriers to suitable regulatory regimes for homeworkers, and the limits to accessing legislation rights even when these exist, there is potential to redefine the rights of informal women workers through the lens of gender justice. We consider it is an aspirational objective to develop new forms of inclusionary national and transnational regulation and standards that challenge neoliberal regimes by challenging the notion of who is a worker. Following this line of reasoning, we propose that regulating responsibility in the supply chain rather than the employment relationship (see Chapter 3) needs to be considered.

The potential to make systemic change in regulatory regimes to challenge the gender contract will only be achieved through networked resistance, therefore drawing on relations of resistance to achieve redistributive justice.

Homework research approach

The case studies discussed in this volume highlight that many successful initiatives reflect the local context and there is no one-size-fits-all approach to any initiative. Our analysis of the historical and contemporary examples of homeworker organising that arose directly out of research methods, such as in the mapping example, indicates that research can have powerful consequences when it is combined with organising and regulatory approaches.

Features such as homeworker participation, used in action-research methods, and partnerships with local and transnational networks, to describe, document and support homeworker initiatives are important. The examples discussed in relation to homework research indicate that if research is used alone, disconnected to the realities and lived experience of homeworkers, it does not contribute to, or support homeworkers in achieving gender justice. Conversely, lessons drawn from earlier feminist scholars emphasise the importance of research being inclusive and supportive of the needs of homeworkers and homeworker networks. It is our view that it is important to expand on and replicate instances of research drawing on the dimensions of justice and the relations of resistance, to challenge gender regimes, and challenge the notion that homeworkers are unorganisable. Such research projects can subsequently be used to stimulate new organising initiatives.

References

Allen, S. and Wolkowitz, C. (1987) *Homeworking: Myths and Realities*. London: Macmillan.
Bhattacharya, T. (2017) *Social Reproduction Theory: Remapping Class, Recentering Oppression*. London: Pluto Press.
Boris, E. and Daniels, C. (1989) *Homework: Historical and Contemporary Perspectives on Paid Labor at Home*. Urbana and Chicago: University of Illinois Press.
Boris, E. and Prügl, E. (eds). (1996) *Homeworkers in Global Perspective: Invisible No More*. New York: Routledge.
Burchielli, R., Buttigieg, D. and Delaney, A. (2008) Organising Homeworkers: The Use of Mapping as an Organising Tool. *Work, Employment & Society*, 22: 167–180.
Burchielli, R. and Delaney, A. (2016) The Invisibilization and Denial of Work in Argentinian Garment Homework. *Relations Industrielles/Industrial Relations* 71: 468–493.
Delaney, A., Burchielli, R. and Connor, T. (2015) Positioning Women Homeworkers in a Global Footwear Production Network: How can Homeworkers Improve Agency, Influence and Claim Rights? *Journal of Industrial Relations*, 57: 641–659.
Delaney, A., Tate, J. and Burchielli, R. (2016) Homeworkers Organizing for Recognition and Rights: Can International Standards Assist Them? In J. Jensen and N. Lichtenstein (eds) *The ILO From Geneva to the Pacific Rim* (pp. 159–179). Houndmills, Basingstoke: Palgrave Macmillan and the International Labour Office.
Delaney, A., Burchielli, R. and Tate, J. (2017) Corporate CSR Responses to Homework and Child Labour in the Indian and Pakistan Leather Sector. In K. Grosser, L. McCarthy and M. Kilmore (eds), *Gender Equality and Responsible Business: Expanding CSR Horizons* (pp. 170-184). London New York: Routledge.
Federici, S. (2012) *Revolution at Point Zero: Housework, Reproduction and Feminist Struggle*. Brooklyn: PM Press.

Fraser, N. (2008) Mapping the Feminist Imagination: From Redistribution to Recognition and Representation. *Scales of Justice: Reimagining Political Space in a Globalizing World*. New York: Columbia University Press.

Fraser, N. (2017) Crisis of Care? On the Social-Reproductive Contradictions of Contemporary Capitalism. In T. Bhattachaya (ed.) *Social Reproduction Theory: Remapping Class, Recentering Oppression*. London: Pluto Press.

Fudge, J. (2014) Feminist Reflections on the Scope of Labour Law: Domestic Work, Social Reproduction, and Jurisdiction. *Feminist Legal Studies* 22: 1–23.

Hyde, A. (2012) Legal Responsibility for Labour Conditions Down the Production Chain. In J. Fudge, S. McCrystal and K. Sankaran (eds) *Challenging the Legal Boundaries of Work Regulation* (pp. 83–99). United Kingdom: Hart Publishing.

International Labour Organization. (2003) The Scope of the Employment Relationship. *International Labour Conference, 91st Session, Report V, fifth item on the agenda.*

Jenkins, R., Pearson, R. and Seyfang, G. (eds) (2002) *Corporate Responsibility and Labour Rights*. London: Earthscan.

Kabeer, N., Sudarshan, R. and MilwardK. (2013) *Organising Women Workers in the Informal Economy: Beyond the Weapons of the Weak*. London: Zed Books.

Kelly, J. (1998) *Rethinking Industrial Relations: Mobilization, Collectivism and Long Waves*. London, New York: Routledge.

Martens, M. and Mitter, S. (eds) (1994) *Women in Trade Unions: Organizing the Unorganized*. Geneva: International Labour Organization.

Mies, M. (2014) *Patriarchy and Accumulation on a World Scale: Women in the International Division of Labour*. London: Zed Books.

Mies, M. (1982) *The Lace Makers of Naraspur: Indian Housewives Produce for the World Market*. London: Zed Books.

Pearson, R. (2004) Organizing Home-Based Workers in the Global Economy: An Action Research Approach. *Development in Action* 14: 136–148.

Pearson, R. (2014) Gender, Globalization and the Reproduction of Labour: Bringing the State Back. In S. Rai and G. Waylen (eds) *New Frontiers in Feminist Political Economy* (pp. 19–42). London New York: Routledge.

Peterson, V.S. (2002) Rewriting (Global) Political Economy as Reproductive, Productive, and Virtual (Foucauldian) Economies. *International Feminist Journal of Politics* 4: 1–30.

Purkayastha, B. and Subramaniam, M. (eds) (2004) *The Power of Women's Informal Networks: Lessons in Social Change from South Asia and West Africa*. Lanham: Lexington Books.

Rowbotham, S. (1999) *New Ways of Organising in the Informal Sector: Four Case Studies of Trade Union Activity*. Leeds: HomeNet.

Rowbotham, S. and Mitter, S. (eds) (1994) *Dignity and Daily Bread: New Forms of Economic Organising among Poor Women in the Third World and the First*. London: Routledge.

Stone, K. and Arthurs, H. (eds) (2013) *Rethinking Workplace Regulation: Beyond the Standard Contract of Employment*. New York: Russell Sage Foundation Press.

Tilly, C. (1978) *From Mobilization to Revolution*. Reading, Massachusetts: Addison-Wesley.

Tsing, A. (2009) Supply Chains and the Human Condition. *Rethinking Marxism* 21: 148–176.

Utting, P. (2007) CSR and Equality. *Third World Quarterly* 28: 697–712.

INDEX

Page numbers in *italics* denote illustrations, **bold**, a box and n, an endnote